With Respect to Old Age:
Long Term Care - Rights and Responsibilities

A Report by
The Royal Commission on Long Term Care

Chairman: Professor Sir Stewart Sutherland

Presented to Parliament by
Command of Her Majesty

March 1999

Cm 4192-I   £18.00

To the Queen's Most Excellent Majesty

MAY IT PLEASE YOUR MAJESTY

We, the undersigned Commissioners, having been appointed by Royal Warrant on 17 December 1997 to examine the short- and long-term options for a sustainable system of funding of long-term care for elderly people, both in their own homes and in other settings, and, within 12 months, to recommend how, and in what circumstances, the cost of such care should be apportioned between public funds and individuals, having regard to:

- the number of people likely to require various kinds of long-term care both in the present and through the first half of the next century, and their likely income and capital over their life-time;

- the expectations of elderly people for dignity and security in the way in which their long-term care needs are met, taking account of the need for this to be secured in the most cost-effective manner;

- the strengths and weaknesses of the current arrangements;

- fair and efficient ways for individuals to make any contribution required of them;

- constraints on public funds; and

- earlier work done by various bodies on this issue.

And whereas Your Majesty deemed it expedient that the Commission should also have regard to:

- the deliberations of the Government's comprehensive spending review, including the review of pensions;

- the implications of its recommendations for younger people who by reason of illness or disability have long-term care needs;

- the cost of its recommendations; and

- the views of all interests likely to be affected by its recommendations, in particular to users and carers.

Humbly submit to Your Majesty the following Report.

Contents

Contents

Chairman's Introduction

THE APPOINTMENT OF THE COMMISSION

1. Our appointment as a Royal Commission was announced on 4 December 1997 by the Secretary of State for Health, the Rt Hon Frank Dobson MP, with the following terms of reference:

   "To examine the short and long term options for a sustainable system of funding of Long Term Care for elderly people, both in their own homes and in other settings, and, within 12 months, to recommend how, and in what circumstances, the cost of such care should be apportioned between public funds and individuals, having regard to:

   - the number of people likely to require various kinds of Long Term Care both in the present and through the first half of the next century, and their likely income and capital over their life-time;

   - the expectations of elderly people for dignity and security in the way in which their Long Term Care needs are met, taking account of the need for this to be secured in the most cost-effective manner;

   - the strengths and weaknesses of the current arrangements;

   - fair and efficient ways for individuals to make any contribution required of them;

   - constraints on public funds; and

   - earlier work done by various bodies on this issue.

   In carrying out its remit, the Royal Commission should also have regard to:

   - the deliberations of the Government's comprehensive spending review, including the review of pensions;

   - the implications of their recommendations for younger people who by reason of illness or disability have Long Term Care needs.

The Commission's recommendations should be costed.

The Commission is asked to give opportunity to all interests likely to be affected by its recommendations to give their views on issues within the terms of reference, and in particular to users and carers."

2.   The Commission held its first meeting on 6 December 1997 to decide the pattern of its operation and received its Royal Warrant on 17 December. It met for the last time on 15 February 1999, having had 15 meetings.

3.   The massive early response from individuals, public service bodies, the private sector, and relevant voluntary organisations to the Commission's wide invitation to comment or to submit evidence, is clear indication of public concerns which need to be resolved and quickly.

4.   The responses were passionate, yet temperate and informed by the realities, sometimes painful, of the situations in which people found themselves. We acknowledge with gratitude those many who gave of their time, expertise and experience to support our work.

WHY A ROYAL COMMISSION?

5.   When Royal Commissions are created, the cynical view is that either a difficult issue is being kicked into the long grass so that someone other than Government can take the blame for problems which are impossible to solve or unpalatable in their solution, or that a seemingly independent body will be told by Government to deliver an unpalatable response it does not want to take responsibility for itself. In the first case we can expect a Royal Commission to take years to reach its conclusions, and in the second the Government of the day will tell it when to report.

6.   Neither of these views apply in our case. I strongly believe that in the case of funding long-term care for older people we have a unique combination of a subject to which there is no obvious answer but one for which, in the UK, something needed to be done quickly. By agreement in advance our timescale was set at around one year. This is because it was quite clear that the present unsatisfactory state of affairs should not be allowed to continue, and that the Government's clear willingness to formulate policy and to act should be informed by the Commission's Report. The Commission is happy to have delivered its Report in just over a year from when it was set up.

7.   I have every belief that the Government will consider the Commission's findings very carefully indeed. We make a number of recommendations which require no legislation and could be implemented quickly. Throughout our work Government Ministers have been scrupulous in not seeking to influence the Commission in any way and Government Departments have been helpful in providing information when it was asked for. We have not sought, nor did we feel pressured, to formulate our proposals by reference to any judgement or prediction as to what might be "acceptable" or otherwise to the Government. That would be to undermine the very purpose for which we were appointed, namely based on wide

consultation to come to an independent but informed judgement on the issues we have been asked to consider.

8.   There is loss as well as gain in reporting so quickly and truncating the period available for consultation and deliberation. Some of the matters which we would wish to have tackled in detail will require further study by others, and the complex issues in question will doubtless benefit from such a fresh perspective. We should, for example, have wished to spend significantly more time tackling that element of our terms of reference which asked us to have regard to "the implications of our recommendations for younger people who by reason of illness or disability have long-term care needs". However, we take the view that further detailed work in this area is required of a kind that was not compatible with meeting the main elements of our remit within the agreed timescale. We have given some indication of where these points lie.

9.   Our remit, as we interpreted it, encompassed a number of key elements. Clearly an assessment had to be made of current funding provision and its adequacy for current and future demography. Thereafter any recommendations must take account of the circumstances and reasonable expectations of those who grow or will grow old. Any proposals should reflect fairness in their impact and should be effective and efficient in their delivery. The dignity of those who have or who may come to have need of long-term care should be recognised, as should their reasonable hope of a just and socially inclusive provision. Finally, and of comparable but distinct importance, the Commission must take account of the economic circumstances of both state and citizen.

10.   Even the remit we set for ourselves defined a task which could expand dramatically, and it did. The range of questions which properly arose seemed to cover at least half of the business of Government. Our deliberations took us to the edge of considerations as wide as housing, the built environment, technological and medical research and development, lifelong learning, the current division of funding responsibility between Health and Social Security, the shape of the tax system, and so on we could go. Matters which have the potential to affect every citizen at some point in their lives. These boundaries and our initial reactions to them will be clearly discernible in our Report.

11.   However, we were disciplined in our approach and for the most part avoided the temptation to follow the paths of intellectual vagrancy or eclecticism. The discipline which we observed was based upon two fundamental principles and their various implications:

■   We set ourselves, for reasons which will be spelt out, to create a fair, just and transparent system for funding and delivering long-term care;

■   We wished to recommend a funding system, which from a variety of perspectives, recognised the importance of shared responsibilities between the individual and the state.

As a consequence we were in search of a series of proposals which would give due weight to fairness, efficiency and effectiveness, human practice as observed, real costs, and the acceptance of responsibility for self and others.

12.   In the light of all of that a central element in our proposals is the agreement of the need to share the risk which is implicit in the statistics, and the way in which they will be interpreted: those who live to the age of 65 have in rounded terms a one in five chance of needing residential care. (This varies between men and women, reflecting the fact that women live longer.)

13.   Our recommendations are grouped around two main themes. The first is to make the distinction between the costs of personal care on the one hand, and living and housing costs on the other. The second is to anticipate the evident need for a series of continuing tasks and functions which we have made the responsibility of our proposed National Care Commission.

14.   Our remit did not explicitly include a requirement to address the quality of care provided. However, the recommendations which we do make will, we believe, have significant implications for the encouragement of high-quality care and care which is more appropriate. It was impossible to avoid the issue in our deliberations.

15.   It was also not our remit to consider the adequency of current levels of funding, although in our proposals for carers we have suggested extra services which will go towards meeting a considerable amount of need which is not currently recognised by the system.

16.   We do not explicitly address the respective merits of care provision by local authorities, voluntary organisations and the private sector, or on the quality of care each provides. At present all three sectors contribute to a mixture of provision which for the purpose of our analysis and recommendation, we assume will continue.

17.   In our report we analyse the context which gave rise to these conclusions, and set out the model we have used to help test out views in the future (Chapter 2). We analyse just what kind of risk the need for long-term care is and compare it, in theoretical terms, to other kinds of risk, especially the risk of serious ill-health that is not related specifically to old age. We conclude that some kind of risk pooling is the most efficient way of making such provision (Chapter 3). We look at the current system and find that it is neither an efficient pooling of risk nor does it deliver the help which is required (Chapter 4). We look at the ability of the private financial sector to help (Chapter 5). We make a series of proposals for making the pooling of risk more efficient and removing the worst faults with the current system – including our main proposal of separating normal living and housing costs from the exceptional costs of personal care (Chapter 6). We propose a new body which will bring together the many strands of long-term care under a single stewardship for the first time (Chapter 7). We look to the kinds of models of care which we want to see existing in the future (Chapter 8). We look at the implications of our proposals for younger disabled people (Chapter 9). In concluding, we urge the Government to implement as many of our proposals as possible without waiting for the legislation which will be required to implement our proposals in full (Chapter 10).

18.   In view of the complexity of these issues and the uncertainties which accompany any attempt to forecast human need and behaviour, two consequences occasion little surprise, although in the first case inevitably a margin of disappointment.

First, there was not total unanimity on all conclusions and two of the Commissioners preferred to sign a note of dissent which sets points of difference on three issues within a much broader context of points of agreement. I am glad that there is more on which we agree than on which we disagree.

19.   The Note of Dissent indicates specific points of difference as follows:

- the authors reject the principle of personal care being exempt from means testing subject to an assessment of need;

- they reject the emphasis given in the Commission Report to providing support for carers by the provision of better services to those they care for. They prefer the provision of respite care as a priority.

Nonetheless, there is common ground on many other matters with regard to the diagnosis of the problem. On specific mechanisms, however, they suggest alternative emphases and make detailed suggestions accordingly. It is clear that the authors share the main assumptions of the Commission's majority report but go on to develop approaches to these in different ways.

20.   Concern was expressed by the majority of Commissioners that the dissenting note might be read as over-emphasising points of difference and repeating matters discussed in the main Report. As Chairman, I was also concerned about this, but must allow free voice to its authors. I hope readers will concentrate on points of agreement rather than points of disagreement and will also note that the costs of the main Report and those of the dissenting note are very similar, even allowing for the very low costings used in the dissenting note on a number of their recommendations.

21.   The second consequence is that it is imperative that the various factors which contribute to what we refer to as "the funnel of doubt" (see Chapter 2) – the unpredictability of the future, particularly as one advances beyond 15 years – must be monitored regularly. The consequent shifts in the impact of factors as variable as medical and technical advance, social and family structures, and the development of the economy, must inform the implementation of the strategy and broad policies which we recommend. This is an important part of what we propose.

22.   Like others before us, we have drawn the best conclusions we can from the data available to us. At times the straw from which we have had to build our conclusions has been very thin indeed. Therefore, if there is to be any effective monitoring of how care is delivered to vulnerable people the scope of available data should be greatly increased, and we make specific recommendations in this regard.

23.   Part II of the Report contains the results of detailed research which has helped inform the Commission's work. Much of the detail behind our thinking will be found there, including lessons learned from other countries, policy options for carers, the needs of ethnic minorities, a detailed analysis of the current system and an investigation of possible models of care, including the views of users and the costs of different forms of home based care.

24.   Many people carried out research on our behalf, and many broke all records to ensure research was completed within a very tight timetable. We are very grateful.

25.   We must also thank the Reference Group, consisting of the most representative bodies in the field (see page 163), who were unstinting in their efforts to provide us with information when it was asked for, and who were very influential in shaping the work of the Commission early on in its life.

26.   I have already mentioned the many people who wrote in with their personal experiences. Many, often simply told, were powerful in their testimony and moving in their impact. We should also thank all the members of the public who attended our regional hearings in Swansea, Newcastle, Dundee, Worthing, Ipswich and Belfast. Your messages were very clear.

27.   We thank the more than 400 organisations who gave us evidence – much of it complex, well argued and well-thought through. It would have been useful to publish it all, but practicality prevented that. Rather than be selective in our publication, we have asked the Public Record Office to make the evidence to the Royal Commission which is not confidential to be made available as quickly as possible. Those who submitted evidence are listed in full at the end of this volume.

28.   Very many thanks are due to the Secretariat, led by Alan Davey, who patiently guided the Commission through the labyrinth of issues with which we were presented and ensured we had the material to come to a proper conclusion. We are grateful for the dedication, patience, cheerfulness and efficiency with which they handled a very disparate and strong-willed group of Commissioners and a mass of material. For them, Whitehall will surely seem a quieter place after the Commission.

29.   There are many others to thank, including FAS Holdings plc who organised our public meetings, Jonathan Street who handled our public relations, to our proof reader John Button and to the Stationery Office for producing our Report so quickly and efficiently.

30.   And so to my fellow Commissioners. They have given of themselves unstintingly to the task they have been set, and have applied themselves with dedication to reaching a conclusion within the almost impossible timescale we set ourselves.

31.   They have worked hard. There have been 15 meetings of the Commission, including one conference of our Reference Group, four research seminars, six public hearings at Swansea, Dundee, Belfast, Gateshead, Ipswich and Worthing, and one oral evidence day in public in London. Between them the Commissioners have made 100 visits, oral evidence was taken from 66 individuals, and 2,040 written submissions were received from organisations. Much work was undertaken in sub-groups of Commissioners who between them held 30 meetings. In addition we have met and spoken informally to about 1,000 individuals during the course of our work and had 140 meetings. In visits to the UK and abroad, Commissioners visited Germany, Australia, New Zealand and Denmark. Much evidence was received from other countries, particularly the United States of America.

32.   We urge the Government to consider all of our proposals very carefully, as we ourselves have done. We want there to be informed debate on our proposals. These proposals target help on people in need of care, a proper objective for a modern welfare state. They also represent a new approach to inclusiveness for older people, one which will reap many rewards for society as a whole. They represent a new secure choice for the care of our older citizens. The choice regarding our future is now for Government: the will for them to make that choice is with the people.

33.   We have looked at a very large problem indeed, and have given it our best effort. In passing on our findings for others to take forward, we would leave you with the words of Hubert Humphrey:

> *"The moral test of Government is how that Government treats those who are in the dawn of life, the children; those who are in the twilight of life, the elderly; and those who are in the shadows of life – the sick, the needy, and the handicapped."*

It is this spirit which has informed our task, and it is in this spirit we hope our Report will be received.

Sir Stewart Sutherland
February 1999
Edinburgh

Executive Summary and Summary of Recommendations

The Commission have begun from the point of view that old age should not be seen as a problem, but a time of life with fulfilments of its own. To provide security in old age and proper care for those that need it our main recommendations are that:

- *The costs of long-term care should be split between living costs, housing costs and personal care. Personal care should be available after assessment, according to need and paid for from general taxation: the rest should be subject to a co-payment according to means.* **(Chapter 6)**

- *The Government should establish a National Care Commission to monitor trends, including demography and spending, ensure transparency and accountability in the system, represent the interests of consumers, and set national benchmarks, now and in the future.* **(Chapter 7)**

The Commission have sought to recommend a way of paying for long-term care which brings improvements in the short term and which is affordable and sustainable. It is a complex issue and none of the options are easy. Three key principles informed the approach we have taken:

- Responsibility for provision now and in the future should be shared between the state and individuals – the aim is to find a division affordable for both and one which people can understand and accept as fair and logical;

- Any new system of state support should be fair and equitable;

- Any new system of state support should be transparent in respect of the resources underpinning it, the entitlement of individuals under it and what it leaves to personal responsibility.

The Commission conclude that doing nothing with respect to the current system is not an option. It is too complex and provides no clarity as to what people can expect. It too often causes people to move into residential care when this might not be the best outcome. Help is available to the poorest but the system leads to the impoverishment of people with moderate assets before they get any help. There is a degree of fear about the system which is of concern in a modern welfare state. It is riddled with inefficiencies. The time has come for it to be properly modernised.

THE COMMISSION'S OVERALL CONCLUSIONS

The broad outline of the Commission's conclusions is as follows:

- For the UK there is no "demographic timebomb" as far as long-term care is concerned and as a result of this, the costs of care will be affordable;

- Long-term care is a risk that is best covered by some kind of risk pooling – to rely on income or savings, as most people effectively have to do now, is not efficient or fair due to the nature of the risk and the size of the sums required;

- Private insurance will not deliver what is required at an acceptable cost, nor does the industry want to provide that degree of coverage;

- The most efficient way of pooling risk, giving the best value to the nation as a whole, across all generations, is through services underwritten by general taxation, based on need rather than wealth. This will ensure that the care needs of those who, for example, suffer from Alzheimer's disease – which might be therapeutic or personal care – are recognised and met just as much as of those who suffer from cancer;

- A hypothecated *unfunded* social insurance fund would not be appropriate for the UK system. A *prefunded* scheme would constitute a significant lifetime burden for young people and could create an uncertain and inappropriate call on future consumption;

- The answer lies in improvement of state provision, but the state cannot meet all the costs of "long-term care" in the broad sense. The elements of care which relate to living costs and housing should be met from people's income and savings, subject to means testing, as now, while the special costs of what we call "personal care" should be met by the state. This would cost between £800 million and £1.2 billion a year (at 1995 prices);

- Currently an estimated 2.2% of taxes from earnings, pensions and investments is spent on long-term care in residential settings and in people's homes. Improving entitlements in the way we propose will add 0.3% to this bill, rising to 0.4% in the middle of the next century;

- Although people will still need to meet their living and housing costs should they need care, it will be clear what they will need to make provision for – and such provision will be affordable by more people;

- Other options are available at lesser cost to make specific improvements to the current system. They include disregarding the value of the house in the means test for 3 months, changing the limits of the means test, and making nursing care wherever it is provided free. Each option would involve increases to current spending each year of between £90 million and £220 million;

- Because of the uncertainty of the data, the lack of trust in the present system among older people, and the cynicism as to Governments' future intentions which exists amongst younger people, a new body, the *National Care Commission*, should be established. Its task would be to look at trends, monitor spending, ensure standards, and visibly represent the voice of the silent majority of consumers now and in the future;

- The system needs more effective pooling of budgets, including bringing the budgets for housing aids and adaptations into a single pot;

- The Commission recommend that more care is given to people in their own homes. Therefore the role of housing will be increasingly important in the provision of long-term care;

- More services should be offered to people who have an informal carer;

- More data should be collected on younger disabled people, to enable better planning of services, and the Government should consider the read-across from the provision of free personal care to the Independent Living Funds.

The Commission's report is intended to lead to a genuine modernisation of a system of financial support about which there is considerable disquiet and concern. We expect it will be given very careful consideration by Government, resulting in full debate within and across the countries of the United Kingdom on how a civilised society should meet the cost of caring for of its older citizens.

The Commission's recommendations represent a unique opportunity for a new contract between Government and people and between all generations of society. This will ensure that the nation's resources which are spent on the care of older people are more effective and will promote increased social cohesion and inclusiveness. If our proposals are accepted, the nation will have demonstrated that it values its older citizens and is prepared to give them freedom from fear and a new security in old age.

SUMMARY OF RECOMMENDATIONS

Our main recommendations:

- *The costs of care for those individuals who need it should be split between living costs, housing costs and personal care. Personal care should be available after an assessment, according to need and paid for from general taxation: the rest should be subject to a co-payment according to means.* **(Chapter 6)**

■ *The Government should establish a National Care Commission which will monitor longitudinal trends, including demography and spending, ensure transparency and accountability in the system, represent the interests of consumers, encourage innovation, keep under review the market for residential care, nursing care, and set national benchmarks, now and in the future.* **(Chapter 7)**

On funding we recommend:

■ *The Government should ascertain precisely how much money, whether from NHS, Local Authority Social Services and Housing budgets, or from Social Security budgets, goes to supporting older people in residential settings and in people's homes.* **(Chapter 4)**

■ *The value of the home should be disregarded for up to three months after admission to care in a residential setting (with appropriate safeguards to prevent abuse) and the opportunity for rehabilitation should be included as an integral and initial part of any care assessment before any irreversible decisions on long-term care are taken.* **(Chapters 6 and 8)**

■ *Measures should be taken to bring about increased efficiency and improved quality in the system, including a more client centred approach, a single point of contact for the client with devolved budgeting, budgets shared between health, social services and other statutory bodies and greater integration of budgets for aids and adaptations.* **(Chapter 8)**

■ *The Commission set out a number of other changes to the current system, such as changing the limits of the means-test, or making nursing care free, which would be of value in themselves, but which would be subsumed by our main recommendation.* **(Chapter 6)**

■ *The resources which underpin the Residential Allowance in Income Support should be transferred to local authorities.* **(Chapter 4)**

■ *The Government should consider whether "preserved rights" payments in social security should be brought within the post 1993 system of community care funding, or whether some other solution can be found to address the shortfall in funding experienced by this group.* **(Chapter 4)**

■ *The Government's proposals on pooled budgets should be taken further, with pooled budgets being implemented nationally.* **(Chapter 8)**

■ *Budgets for aids and adaptations should be included in and accessible from a single budget pool and a scheme should be developed which would enable Local Authorities to make loans for aids and adaptations for individuals with housing assets.* **(Chapter 8)**

■ *The system for making direct payments should be extended to the over 65s, subject to proper safeguards and monitoring.* **(Chapter 9)**

On the provision of services we recommend:

■ *Further research on the cost effectiveness of rehabilitation should be treated as a priority, but that this should not prevent the development of a national strategy on rehabilitation led by the Government to be emphasised in the performance framework for the NHS and Social Services.* **(Chapter 8)**

■ *Further longitudinal research is required to track the process and outcomes of preventive interventions and to assess their impact both on quality of life and long-term costs.* **(Chapter 8)**

■ *It should be a priority for Government to improve cultural awareness in services offered to black and ethnic minority elders.* **(Chapter 8)**

■ *The role of advocacy should be developed locally, with backing from central Government.* **(Chapter 8)**

■ *There should to be wider consultation on the provision of aids and adaptations and on what should under a new system be free and what should be subject to a charge.* **(Chapter 8)**

On help for carers we recommend:

■ *Better services should be offered to those people who currently have a carer.* **(Chapter 8)**

■ *The Government should consider a national carer support package.* **(Chapter 8)**

On information and projections we recommend:

■ *The National Care Commission should be made responsible for making and publishing projections about the overall cost of long-term care at least every five years.* **(Chapter 2)**

■ *The Government should set up a national survey to provide reliable data to monitor trends in health expectancy.* **(Chapter 2)**

■ *The Government should conduct a scrutiny of the shift in resources between various sectors since the early 1980s, and should consider whether there should be a transfer of resources between the NHS and social service budgets given changes in relative responsibilities.* **(Chapter 4)**

■ *A more transparent grant and expenditure allocation system should be established. This is a task which could be referred to the National Care Commission.* **(Chapter 4)**

■ *Further longitudinal research is required to track the processes and outcomes of preventive interventions and to assess their impact both on quality of life and long-term costs.* **(Chapter 8)**

In relation to younger disabled people we recommend:

■ *In the light of the Commission's main recommendations, the Government should consider how the provision of care according to need would relate to Independent Living Fund provision for the personal care needs of younger disabled people.* **(Chapter 9)**

Implementing the Commission's recommendations:

■ Many of our recommendations can be implemented without the need for primary legislation. Examples include the disregard of housing assets for the first three months, changing the means-test limits, or extending the provision of free nursing care. The National Care Commission could be established as a shadow body within Government. We would urge the Government to implement our proposals as soon as possible. The need for change is pressing.

The full text of the Commission's report is available on the Royal Commission's website at www.open.gov.uk/royal-commission-elderly/

Glossary of Terms

activities of daily living (ADLs) and instrumental activities of daily living (IADLs) –
ADLs and IADLs are measures of dependency. The degree of difficulty people
experience in carrying out ADLs and IADLs denotes their level of dependency.
Information on dependency in the elderly population in Great Britain is recorded
in the General Household Survey. ADLs relate to personal care tasks of bathing
and washing, dressing, feeding, getting in and out of bed, getting to and from the
toilet and continence management. IADLs relate to domestic tasks such as
shopping, laundry, vacuuming, cooking a main meal and handling personal affairs.
Both ADLs and IADLs have traditionally been used by social services in assessing
elderly people's need for long-term care. ADLs are also used by long-term care
insurance companies to assess claims from policy holders. For a successful
insurance claim an individual must be unable to perform a specified number of
ADLs (even using special equipment devices or modified clothing if appropriate)
without the help of another person on every occasion. Benchmark ADL
definitions are as follows:

washing – the ability to wash in the bath or shower (including getting
into or out of the bath or shower) or wash by other means;

dressing – the ability to put on, take off, secure and unfasten all garments
and, as appropriate, any braces, artificial limbs or other
surgical appliances;

feeding – the ability to feed oneself once food has been prepared and
made available;

toileting – the ability to use the lavatory or manage bowel and bladder
function through the use of protective undergarments or
surgical appliances if appropriate;

mobility – the ability to move indoors from room to room on level
surfaces;

transferring – the ability to move from a bed to an upright chair or
wheelchair and vice versa.

attendance allowance (AA) – social security benefit payable to people who become
severely disabled at age 65 or over as a contribution towards the extra costs of
disability. To qualify individuals must establish a need for care from others. The
benefit is payable at two rates depending on extent of this need. There is no
obligation to spend the benefit on meeting care needs. The benefit is non-
contributory, not means tested and not taxable.

disability living allowance care component – the equivalent to AA for people who
become disabled before age 65. The care component has three rates depending on
need for care from others. There is also a mobility component to disability living
allowance. Rights to this allowance carry on beyond age 65. The benefit is non-
contributory, not means tested and not taxable.

domiciliary/home care – personal care or practical help provided to older people in their own homes.

elderly/older people – people over the age of retirement. In the context of those needing long-term care this generally means people over 80 years of age.

housing costs – rent or mortgage and council tax.

income support – social security benefit paid as an income supplement to those with less money coming in than the law says they need to live on. Calculated on a case by case basis, non-contributory, means-tested,

independent living (1993) fund – discretionary trust set up by the Secretary of State for Social Security which pays cash directly to severely disabled people aged 18–65 to enable them to buy personal care and domestic help so that they can continue living in the community. The Fund works in partnership with local authorities in developing suitable packages of care.

invalid care allowance – social security benefit payable to carers who provide 35 hours a week of unpaid care to a severely disabled person. Severely disabled person must be getting AA or the two highest rates of the care component of Disability Living Allowance. Can only be paid for the first time to carers under age 65. Carer must not be in full-time education, nor earning more than £50 per week after the deduction of certain expenses. Non-contributory, not means-tested, taxable.

living costs – the normal expenses of daily life: heat, light, food, laundry, cleaning and other sundry expenses.

means-test for residential care – the statutory means-test operated by local authorities when people enter residential settings to determine what contribution they should make towards their fees. Under the means test, people with assets above £16,000 get no public help with the fees for residential or nursing homes. Assets of between £10 – £16k are assumed to generate a notional income of £1 per week per £250 of capital, and this notional income is taken into account in the means-test. Assets below the lower limit of £10,000 are disregarded for the means-test. Income is also taken into account.

nursing home – an establishment which provides residential and nursing care for sick, disabled or elderly infirm people, including the elderly mentally ill. It may be run (rarely) by the NHS, or (usually) by the private or voluntary sector. Some nursing homes are dually registered as nursing and residential homes.

personal care – the care needs, often intimate, which give rise to the major additional costs of frailty or disability associated with old age. It includes the associated teaching, enabling, psychological support from a knowledgeable and skilled professional, and assistance with cognitive functions (e.g. reminding, for those with dementia) that are needed either to enable a person to do these things for himself/herself or to enable a relative to do them for him/her (see Chapters 6 and 8).

practical help – assistance with everyday living such as meals, cleaning and housework, shopping etc (further defined in Chapter 6).

preserved rights – (people with) continuing rights to higher levels of social security income support benefit to pay residential and nursing home fees.

residential care – care for older people in an institutional setting, that is, either in a residential or a nursing home.

residential (care) home – an establishment which provides residential care, not including nursing, for disabled or elderly infirm people including the elderly mentally ill. It may be run by a local authority or by the private or voluntary sector. Some residential homes are dually registered as residential and nursing homes.

List of tables and Figures

 List of Tables

Chapter 1
Ageing into the new millenium

This chapter looks at the opportunities and challenges offered by ageing, and goes on to establish a set of values which has informed the Royal Commission's work.

1   In one sense, growing old is easy. We start to grow old the day we are born. But many aspects of old age are more difficult. As physical strength begins to fail, the importance of older peoples' wisdom and experience should take its place, as in many societies it still does. However, in some societies, ours included, many people seem to have lost some sense of what the oldest can offer the youngest. We have lost an awareness of old age as a time of life valuable in itself, preferring instead to concentrate on it as a "problem" or a "threat".

1.1   Until the twentieth century in western industrial societies, life for most people could, with justification, have been described as nasty, brutish and short. It could be particularly brutish for people who were unfortunate enough to grow old and be poor. When Beveridge produced his report on the future of state insurance against the contingencies of unemployment, sickness and growing old, poverty and the workhouse were a real worry for many people. Thanks to Beveridge, to the enormous advances made in the science of medicine, and rapid improvements in people's standards of living, nutrition and lifestyles, and the decisions of successive Governments, the prospects for old age have advanced considerably since then.

1.2   Now, many more people may expect to live at least twenty or perhaps thirty years beyond retirement. Most people will have an active old age supported by pensions and other financial provisions, and benefit from a National Health Service which is able to meet their immediate health care needs. While older people are still poorer than other members of society, for the majority there is a greater sense of security in old age.

1.3   But a sizeable minority of older people today are likely to need special care as they grow more frail. How that care should be financed into the next century, is what this Report is about. There is reasonable clarity about trends in the next 10 to 15 years, but much less about trends beyond that.

1.4   Particularly uncertain are trends in incomes. According to Government projections, summarised succinctly in the report by the *Pension Provisions Group* (1998)[1], pensioners **overall** are better off than they once were. They will continue, **as a group** to become better off. However, a large number will still have low incomes in retirement. So while some pensioners will be relatively **well-off**, and others not **badly-off**, a large number may find themselves, for various reasons, living at or close to the poverty line as measured by the Department of Social Security. If they have savings these are likely, partly because of the encouragement to home ownership in the 1980s, to be tied up in bricks and mortar – an unwieldy asset which is not easy to liquidate, but is in any event their home.

1.5   This situation will be compounded by current developments in the National Health Service which appears to be increasingly driven by performance measures which encourage it to treat people and get them out of hospital as quickly as possible – perhaps too quickly in the case of older people. We will examine in later chapters the unintended effects this policy can have on older people.

1.6   In recent years in the UK, for various complex reasons which we look into later on, it has become common for older people often upon discharge from hospital, or from their own homes, often in a crisis, to go into residential or nursing homes. As a result they are forced to sell their homes, sever their links with their local community and end their days in settings which are usually caring and supportive, but which in some senses remove older people from our sight and from society at large. Individuals then suffer social exclusion; society colludes in this by too often regarding older people in these settings as being not only out of sight but also out of mind.

TECHNOLOGY IN THE FUTURE

1.7   People constantly look to modern technology to improve their lifestyles. This includes for example, personal computers, the use of the Internet, technology used in hospitals, the telephone and the television and devices such as washing machines and vacuum cleaners. One of the ways in which life could improve for older people is in the harnessing of new technology in new, imaginative and profitable ways.

1.8   Such use of technology will enable older people to be cared for more easily so that they feel secure in their communities without the need for other, more expensive interventions. In the second part of our Report, we set out some research commissioned from the Age Concern Institute of Gerontology at King's College London. One part of this looks at the prospects for technological aids which will enable people to live safely in their homes. The Commission has seen many examples of these aids and while some of them are not yet ready to be marketed, their time will come. It is important that in designing new houses, account is taken of the ability of technology to help people live everyday lives. Current technology can help through, for example, devices for opening windows, turning taps on and off, raising and lowering work surfaces, setting alarms, turning off lights, and indeed, monitoring whether people are moving and may or may not need help. This, together with the possibility of swift communication with those who can provide help, are all possible within current technology. Such technology need to become widely available, so that it can help people. Getting such products to market will help shape the future[i].

1.9 Technology has also unleashed in recent years unparalleled possibilities for access to information and for intellectual fulfilment in the broader sense of the word for everyone who has access to a computer. There are now new possibilities for bringing the world directly into people's lives via a computer screen, or interactive digital television. Television, radio and the Internet are not the sole domain of the young – they can enrich the lives of all of us. Older minds need stimulation as much as their bodies may come to need care. The role of depression and social exclusion in diminishing the overall well-being of older people is an important issue. Technology can and will help.

THE VALUES OF THE COMMISSION

1.10 The purpose of this brief introduction has been to stress the Commission's strong belief that old age should be seen as the opportunity that it really is. This can already be seen at work in society through older people acting as carers, supporting families, providing wisdom and advice and playing an active part in society at large. But these positive realities are often overshadowed by negative images. We have set out some of the opportunities which old age offers. We wholly repudiate any remaining negative images and urge society as it approaches the new millennium to take a different and more positive view of ageing. We came to this view very early on in the consideration of our task, and this approach underpins all of our proposals.

1.11 Inherent in much of the political language used in respect of old age are a number of underlying assumptions which lead to the notion that old age – and the care of those who have finished their working lives and who may have changing needs as their health changes – is somehow a "problem". People see it as a "problem" that society is somehow managing to contain at the moment. Given the likely increases in numbers of older people (as a result of demographic factors, advances in medicine, and overall improvements in levels of income and of lifestyles), people go on to assert that the "problem" will increase in intensity over time, and may be regarded by some as increasingly "insoluble". This approach to older people treats them as a homogeneous group when such is far from the case. It also fails to recognise the perceptions that older people themselves may have of their own needs and aspirations.

1.12 Seeing old age as a "problem" is of relevance not just to the provision of long-term care. It applies to the provision of incomes in old age, health care, housing, transport, the facilities for daily life which everyone takes for granted in their youth and middle years. To some extent it may even be reflected in the rhetoric of politics – the "new" Britain is portrayed as "young" and "modern" and this might (unintentionally) seem to exclude older people. However, this would not be to give proper recognition to a central plank of the Government's election manifesto which is to address the fundamental issues of insecurity in old age – hence the creation of this Royal Commission and other initiatives, such as "Better Government for Older People".

1.13   A similar debate has been taking place for some time in the field of disability. Organisations in that field have argued that the needs of disabled people should not be seen as a "problem" for society but something society readily accepts and deals with in a normal way. For example, regulations on the design of new buses and building regulations governing the design of new houses and offices will in future ensure that they are accessible to disabled people. Houses built under the new regulations are also houses which are good for children to grow up in and are better for families. Taking account of the needs of disabled people in this way also directly and indirectly benefits society as a whole.

1.14   There is now a clear opportunity to see old age for what it is, a stage of life where we have the gift of time to be able to acquire knowledge and experiences for which there may not have been time during working lives. In this age of opportunity, while physical capabilities or mental faculties may change, people should not necessarily be assumed to be passive recipients of the goodwill of others or inevitably incapacitated, befuddled or redundant. Society should recognise the value inherent in older people, and the value to society in using its ingenuity to help older people to continue to realise their potential more effectively.

1.15   The Commission have noted the Department for Education and Employment's commitment to lifelong learning. We wholly approve of this concept, but in our view it should be expanded into learning not just for employment but for a better life. That means learning for a life that expands beyond the working age and into retirement. There is a tremendous opportunity here to enrich the lives of older people by encouraging them to seek, and make available more opportunities for, lifelong learning. We believe that this should be part of an holistic approach to the health and well-being of older people which should begin by refusing to condemn them to a life of isolation or to assume they do not want to be part of wider developments in learning.

1.16   The figures we set out in Chapter 2 show that in future society will be ageing. Unless adequate provision is made with costs spread across society in a fair and progressive way, the chances are that poverty and, a lack of dignity and choice will be the reality for many. This is a scandalous waste and is unacceptable.

1.17   Older people are already avid consumers of third age educational opportunities. They volunteer, they use and transfer their skills to the younger generation in schools and in business. Many benefit from travel at home and abroad. They are a generation on the move, a sleeping giant that Governments will ignore at their peril. In future older people will not tolerate the privations and insults suffered by earlier generations.

1.18   In the light of the foregoing, the Commission have established the following set of values which have informed all its work and recommendations:

- Older people are a *valuable* part of society and should be *valued as such*.

- Old age will come to increasing numbers of the population and this should be seen as a natural part of life and not as a burden.

- Old age represents an opportunity – for intellectual fulfilment and for the achievement of ambitions put on hold during working lives. Those who are involved in Government, or who provide and develop products and services should work to make available to old people the tools to enjoy education, leisure and their day to day lives.

- To compartmentalise old age and to describe old people as a problem is intolerable – morally and practically.

- A more positive and inclusive climate should be created and nurtured, so ensuring the development of more opportunities which can be taken up by older people.

- The whole approach to long-term care should be to view the management of older peoples' needs as a set of positive actions over time which help people to lead the kind of fulfilling lives they want to lead – and to be able to continue to contribute to society in a positive way – both economically and intellectually – and not as a management of decline.

- The funding system for long-term care should provide the widest possible opportunity for older people to lead the lives they want, whether it be in their own homes or in other settings.

- In improving the recognition of the importance of old age, the funding system must also strengthen the links between generations and spread the financial responsibility.

1.19   We are satisfied that the recommendations we make in succeeding chapters are fully consistent with these values, which we expand into a practical framework in Chapter 4. We now set out the quantitative background to our work, before considering specific issues relating to long-term care and its financing.

Footnotes

(i)   The Commission therefore welcome attempts by Government to link those who develop technology to business, such as the Foresight programme. Further joined up thinking will be needed if the full potential of technology is to be realised.

WITH RESPECT TO OLD AGE

Chapter 2
The costs of Long-Term Care Now and in the Future

This chapter looks at the current expenditure on long-term care services for elderly people, the numbers using such services, their sources of income and their assets. A baseline is established for the Commission's projections on the future demand and costs of long-term care. The chapter concludes by looking at what might happen within the range of doubt around these projections.

INTRODUCTION

2   In considering how care can be afforded in the future, we first need to examine the current demand for and the costs of long-term care for older people in the United Kingdom. This can mean either long-term care services which individuals currently pay for themselves privately, contributions towards the cost of state services or the money which the state pays on their behalf. We do not include in this calculation anything for the costs of unpaid care provided by family, relatives and friends. We explain why later on in this chapter. Having set out the costs of long term care now we go on to:

■   develop a platform from which to make projections about the future costs of long term care, by looking at factors such as increases in the numbers of older people in the future, how healthy they will be and the level of unpaid care – these are largely factors over which there is little control; and

■   looking at what would happen to future costs if we speculate as to possible changes over the factors over which there is little or no control.

2.1   It is important to be clear that we are making projections to use as yardsticks for comparisons. They are not predictions or forecasts about the future. This would require forecasting both the future policies of current and future Governments and changes over the coming decade in public expectations and preferences. A projection takes the best information known about a subject, makes plausible assumptions, often based on past experience, about how different the future might be from the present and then takes the figures forward to show what the future might hold. Because the future is unpredictable one single projection is not enough. A number of projections are made on different assumptions to give a range in which the future might be found. This gives us a baseline from which we can cost the effect of policy changes.

2.2   We have used a model for future costings developed for the Department of Health by the Personal Social Services Research Unit of the London School of Economics at the University of Kent.[2] This uses the best information available for the United Kingdom in respect of the underlying factors which will influence future demand and costs.

2.3   Our terms of reference asked us to look at the numbers of people requiring various forms of long-term care through the first half of the next century up to 2051. However, any such projections become ever more uncertain the further away we move from the present. In looking at pensions, for example, the Government used a model that projected pensioner's income to the early part of the next century. The differences in the possible effects of small changes each year soon mount up because of compounding. Projections made for 10 years ahead suffer less from this than projections made for 20 or 30 years ahead; projections for 50 years' time are therefore very uncertain indeed. They suffer from a lack of reliable and consistent data which has dogged our work from the very beginning. While in this chapter we illustrate some projections to 2051 as best we can, we consider that they are not reliable beyond about 20 years. Our recommendations as to how long term care should be paid for are intended to apply within this timescale.

2.4   Later in this Report we make a specific recommendation about a National Care Commission for older people. We want to say straightaway that one of the most important functions of this body must be to keep the projections up to date, where possible improving them, and recommending changes to Government if these seem necessary in the light of future developments. This is important to the future dignity and financial security of older people in generations to come. *The National Care Commission we propose should be made responsible for making and publishing projections about the overall cost of long-term care at least every five years* **[Recommendation 2.1]**.

CURRENT NUMBERS OF PEOPLE AND EXPENDITURE ON LONG-TERM CARE

2.5   Table 2.1 summarises information about the numbers people receiving long-term care services by type of service. About 600,000 people over the age of 65 are getting home care from a local authority. About 480,000 older people are in care homes – that is about 1 in 20 of all elderly people. More detail is available in Research Volume 1.

Table 2.1: Number of people in the UK receiving long term care services by type of service and funding.

Domiciliary care	Number of recipients		
Home care	610,000		
Community Nursing	530,000		
Day care	260,000		
Private Help	670,000		
Meals	240,000		
Institutional care			
Residential care	publicly financed	205,000	Total 288,750
	privately financed	83,750	
Nursing home care	publicly financed	115,000	Total 157,500
	privately financed	42,500	
Hospital		34,000	34,000
All institutional residents			482,250

Source: PSSRU estimates.

2.6   We have had to build from scratch a picture of the current total expenditure on long term care as there is no one central source of for the figures. Government figures on health expenditure for people with long-term care needs are included among the figures for all health service expenditure. We have also had to find a way of estimating what people spend on long-term care from their own resources. Our starting point has been the use of a range of long-term care services for older people with disabilities that prevent them from looking after themselves or from doing household tasks like cooking or shopping. These services include home helps, day care, meals on wheels, NHS community nursing services, NHS long-stay beds, residential care and nursing homes. This information can be found from Government statistics and sample surveys of the population like the General Household Surveys for Great Britain. Information on the costs of these services comes from work done by the Personal Social Services Unit at the University of Kent.[3] Costs and use when multiplied together give the total costs shown in Table 2.2.

2.7   In Table 2.2 we set out our estimate of long-term care costs in the United Kingdom in 1995 (the latest year for which all figures are available) as £11.1bn.

This includes expenditure by the NHS and social services, but not GP services, nor housing or leisure services relevant to community care or unpaid care. It includes the "accommodation" costs of hospitals and care homes but not the living expenditure or rent of people living in ordinary or sheltered housing. It does not include social security expenditure attributable to people with long-term care needs – this is discussed below. About £7.1bn of this £11.1bn figure is paid for by the state directly via the NHS and social services. Older people themselves pay about £4bn. This element of the estimate is subject to considerable uncertainty because there are no reliable statistics collected about private expenditure on long-term care.

Table 2.2: Current expenditure on long-term care services

£ million at 1995/96 prices

Type of expenditure	NHS	PSS net[1]	Private charges[2]	fees[3]	Total
Home care		970	75		1,045
Community Nurse	675				675
Day Care	125	235	20		380
Private domestic				210	210
Meals		95	70	35	200
Chiropody	145			70	215
Residential Care homes		1,910	1,030	1,200	4,140
Nursing Homes	195	1,300	530	750	2,775
Long-stay hospital	1,425				1,425
Total	2,565	4,510	1,725	2,265	11,065

Source: PSSRU estimates for Royal Commission rounded to nearest £5 million.

Notes:
1 *PSS = expenditure on personal social services for elderly people by local authorities, net of charges. The expenditure under PSS also includes people who were in residential care and nursing homes prior to 1 April 1993 and have preserved rights to higher levels of income support as if they were local authority funded.*
2 *Charges are paid by individuals for social services provided by local authorities usually at subsidised rates.*
3 *Fees are paid by individuals directly to private service providers.*

2.8   About £8.3bn of the £11bn total is spent in residential care and nursing homes and the remaining £2.7bn on home care. These figures are broadly in line with those provided independently by industry experts.[4]

SOCIAL SECURITY EXPENDITURE

2.9   The Department of Social Security and the Department of Health and Social Services for Northern Ireland[5] have provided us with figures which show how much social security expenditure in the UK is attributable to people with long term care needs. In 1995/96 (our base year) this was about £6bn. Some of this expenditure – such as the continuing expenditure on higher levels of Income Support for people with preserved rights in residential care and nursing homes is taken account of directly in the £7.1bn of state expenditure referred to above. The remaining expenditure is taken into account in our figures as private expenditure and appears to the extent that it represents spending from Social Security benefits or other income by individuals on items, such as charges for local authority home helps, or the purchase of private domestic help or payment of fees to care homes.

THE INCOME AND ASSETS OF OLDER PEOPLE

2.10   In our terms of reference we were asked to have regard to the income and assets of older people. These indicate the extent to which older people are capable of making contributions now and in the future to the costs of their long-term care from their income and assets

2.11   An analysis of inequality in the UK[6] places the income of older people in perspective with other age groups. It found that nearly two thirds of those over 70 are among the poorest 40% of the population, and only half as likely as the average of other age groups to be among the richest 40% of the population. In its analysis of older people's income and wealth, Swiss Re[7] concentrated on looking at income patterns in those over 55 years of age and acknowledged the difficulties faced by many in funding long-term care from income and savings. It reported average weekly income of those between the ages of 55–69 to be £92.37, with only 3% of that age group having a net weekly income of £275.00 or over. Excluding the value of their home, 57% of those aged 55–69 have savings/investments less than £3000.00 with only 8% having savings/investments over £30,000.

2.12   For the Commission, the DSS analysed income and asset data of single older people aged 75 and over from the 1995–96 Family Resources Survey[8] linking it with council tax banding as a proxy for housing equity. Table 2.3 is illustrative of the proportion of the levels of assets held by the population of single people aged 75 and over in private households and their incomes. It also gives a broad indication of the proportion of this age group that may, depending on income, benefit from the current state financed residential or nursing home care, and possible changes in the upper asset limit of present means test rules (see Chapters 4 and 6). It should be stressed, these figures are estimates.

Table 2.3: Assets and Incomes of older people: Distribution of assets, and approximate mean and median incomes of single people aged 75 or over in private households by asset band

Asset band	Distribution (%)	Mean Income (£ pw)	Median Income (£ pw)
Under £16,000	44	85	70
£16,000 - 20,000	1	90	80
£20,000 - 30,000	3	95	80
£30,000 - 40,000	3	95	80
£40,000 - 50,000	3	95	80
£50,000 - 60,000	6	105	80
£60,000 - 70,000	6	105	80
£70,000 - 80,000	5	120	90
£80,000 - 90,000	5	120	90
£90,000 - £100,000	4	125	95
£100,000 upwards	21	165	110

Source: DSS analysis based on 1995/96 Family Resources Survey[8] data on Council Tax bands, assets and incomes by source. Income relates to individual gross income minus housing benefit, council tax benefit, and disability benefits (attendance allowance or disability living allowance.

2.13   The figures in the Government's recent pension review[9] emphasise these disparities and indicate that since 1981 the gap between the richest and poorest pensioners has grown; the poorest 20% of single pensioners having an average weekly income of £68.00 with the richest 20% having £205. Over the next 25 years the review expects that, on average, the value of pensions paid on retirement will increase in real terms, and for the upper quartile by as much as the rise in earnings. However, it notes that this growth in pensioners' income will not be shared equally.

PROJECTING THE FUTURE

2.14   Our first projection – the "base case" – contains a set of reasonable and plausible assumptions about what might happen in the future to factors for example, the number of older people, over which there is little or no influence or control – even if the Government could make policy changes to influence the future. After that we change those assumptions to test the range of possibilities with a "sensitivity analysis". The future will lie somewhere in the range of our projections. This range of uncertainty is known as the "funnel of doubt".

2.15 We know that a population with more older people would be likely to need a greater volume of long-term care. In the light of increased demand we have projected what the overall health and social care costs would be, the cost to the state and to individuals. Projected costs are shown as a percentage of national income (gross domestic product – GDP). In Research Volume 1 we set out the projections in much greater detail.

THE PROJECTIONS

2.16 The PSSRU model which forms the basis of our work looks at the receipt of long-term care and incorporates measures of all the factors affecting the demand for, use of and costs of long-term care that we describe below. Details of the model have been published by PSSRU.[2] All the results we describe here are the Royal Commission's own projections using underlying data from published sources which are incorporated in the PSSRU model. This model differs from those developed by the Institute of Actuaries and London Economics [10][11] in that it does not attach a financial cost to unpaid care.

WHAT AFFECTS THE DEMAND FOR AND COST OF LONG-TERM CARE?

2.17 This is a complex area discussed in detail in Research Volume 1. Here we outline the five most important factors which affect the future demand for and costs of long-term care.

Demography

2.18 Figures 1 and 2 show what has happened and what is projected to happen to the population of the United Kingdom as a whole since 1901. The population has been growing since the turn of the century. There has been a long-term upward trend in the number of people aged 65 and over as life expectancy has improved considerably. From the turn of the century the number of older people has increased by 400%. Since 1931 the number of older people has doubled. The overall trend established is projected to continue until about 2030 when the population stops growing, as a result of past falls in birthrates. In a sense the UK has already lived through its demographic "time bomb" earlier in this century. The future is much more manageable.

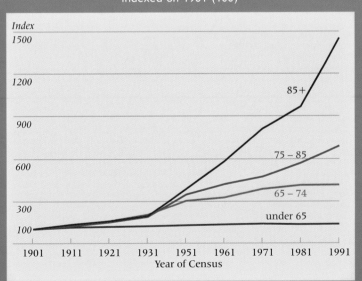

Figure 1: United Kingdom Population
Indexed on 1901 (100)

Notes:
1921 not available for NI, 1926 used, 1931 not available for NI, 1937 used.
The graphs show data as indices to allow consideration of both the individual and relative rates of growth of the different age bands. Each data series are set to a value of 100 in the start year (1901)and changes in later years are measured compared to the start year. An index value for subsequent years are the rates of change over the given time period.

2.19   By 2050 the biggest relative increase in older people is expected in the number of those aged 85 and over – "the oldest old". They will be three times more numerous in 2050 than now. The United Kingdom is not alone among the developed countries in expecting such increases in numbers, but is among the group of countries facing a smaller increase in numbers. Research Volume 1 Chapter 6 gives more information on the international perspective.

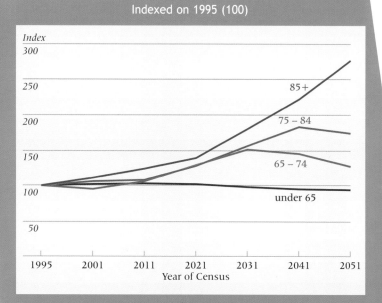

Figure 2: UK Population projections
Indexed on 1995 (100)

Note:
The graphs show data as indices to allow consideration of both the individual and relative rates of growth of the different age bands. Each data series are set to a value of 100 in the start year (1995) and changes in later years are measured compared to the start year. An index value for subsequent years are the rates of change over the given time period.

2.20   In addition to the birth rate, the future size and composition of the population is the result of great strides made in the UK in improving the health of individuals, public health generally and material standards of life. After the post-war and 1960s "baby-booms" the birth rate fell, so the proportion of working to retired people will change substantially after the first quarter of the next century. However, higher productivity from the workforce would make it possible to support a higher ratio of non-working to working people and to do this even if older people's need for help increases.

Health Expectancy

2.21   The health of older people is a key determinant of the need for long-term care. If the larger number of older people are living longer but:

- **experience fewer years of ill health**, the future need for long-term care for each person may reduce and the total may not go up very much from what it is now;

- **experience no longer periods of ill health than the current generation** the need for long-term care for each person will be the same, although the total need will rise;

- **experience more ill health for longer**, the need for long-term care will increase both for each individual and in total.

2.22   Health expectancy measures the numbers of years of life that will be free of chronic illness (which limits a person's ability to carry out tasks like normal housework or shopping) or severe disability (which prevents a person from looking after their personal care needs such as feeding, going to the toilet, bathing or which inhibits their mobility). Any model which projects the future need or costs of long-term care must therefore incorporate a measure of "health expectancy". Our model reflects this by looking at measures of dependency – by using information on activities of daily living; including the ability to carry out domestic tasks and well as personal care tasks.

2.23 A worldwide debate has been taking place about health expectancy trends among older people. The best evidence we can find about the United Kingdom suggests that the factors which are causing us to live longer are also resulting in the extra years of life being free from severe disability. Research from the USA tends to support the view of a general improvement in health expectancy. There is reason for optimism here but we sound a note of caution.

2.24 Our caution concerns the data on which the optimism is based. The data came from the General Household Survey which asks people to report health problems or disabilities. This gives a snapshot of people's health at any one time. While this data can be used to monitor trends in health expectancy, a better way would be by following directly a representative sample of people over time and asking them about their health and how it has changed. But no such longitudinal survey exists for the UK. Had it existed it would have increased our confidence about the trends we assume in health expectancy. Such a survey could also produce other related data, which would be useful at national and local Government levels and in the financial services industry. Getting such data involves committing effort and resources. We have already recommended that our projections should be updated every five years. *We recommend also that to improve the information available to the National Care Commission the Government gives urgent consideration to setting up a national longitudinal survey to provide data to reliably monitor trends in health expectancy* [**Recommendation 2.2**].

The Supply of Unpaid Care from Families, Relatives and Friends

2.25 Any changes to the supply of unpaid care could have important effects on the demand for paid care and thus the cost to individuals or the state. By unpaid care we mean care and support from family, relatives and friends which in terms of hours (and perhaps in terms of monetary value) far exceeds what the state and individuals provide by way of paid for care. It is sometimes assumed that Government can influence the supply of unpaid care by taking certain measures to ensure that families and relatives care for their older people. However, in a free society a Government can do little, short of compulsion or other draconian measures, to influence the way in which families or relatives decide whether to care for their older members. Later on we say what we think will happen to the supply of unpaid care based on changes in society and on past trends.

2.26 There are about 5.7 million people providing some hours of informal care,[12] most of whom will be caring for older people. Most carers spend no more than about 4 hours a week providing unpaid care, but about 800,000 people provide unpaid care for 50 hours a week or more.

2.27 Table 2.4 shows the characteristics of people providing informal care. More women than men provide informal care. People aged between 45 and 64 comprise the single largest group of unpaid carers. The largest group providing unpaid care are those providing help to their parents or their parents-in-law. The General Household Survey shows that of all those providing unpaid care, spouses are the most important source of help with domestic tasks and personal care.

Table 2.4: Characteristics of people providing informal care, GB 1995[12]

	All carers %
Carers:	
Men	40
Women	60
Aged:	
16–24	32
45–64	48
65+	20
Dependent's relationship to care:	
Spouse	19
Parent/parent in-law	43
Child (any age)	9
Other relative or friend	28
Total	100

Source: ONS 1998 based on General Household Survey 1995.

2.28   Whether there will be a reduction in the supply of unpaid care in the future is one
of the most difficult questions we have been asked to consider. This involves
looking very carefully at the different generations and how they have experienced
family and working life, but also looking beyond the supply of long-term care to
looking at evidence about what happens when older people ask their families to
help. There is genuine concern about the effects on the supply of unpaid care
because of changes in family structure brought about by falls in birth rates, higher
divorce rates, re-marriage, greater family mobility and less living together of
families across generations. We have considered evidence from researchers and in
particular from the Carers National Association which contained new research
from London Economics.

2.29   Older women now are less likely to have spouses. The immediate next generation
of older people are more likely to have been married and have children who could
care for them and are also likely to be married when the need for long-term care
arises. However, for subsequent generations a greater number of older people may
have no spouse or partner to care for them because of changes in marriage
patterns, including cohabitation. This has been taken account of in the model.

2.30   An analysis of the 1994 General Household Survey [13] shows a very strong link
between the availability of unpaid care from families, relatives and friends and the
actual receipt of unpaid care. This suggests that the demand for unpaid care
cannot be looked at in isolation from the supply of it and that where older people
need care and have spouses or children in the same household or nearby, they
generally receive care from them.

2.31   We can see no evidence of working women being less willing to provide unpaid care [see Research Volumes 1 and 3], although we are acutely aware of the personal costs to them in both time and money of providing care in this way. We address the needs of carers in Chapter 8.

2.32   Research from London Economics for Carers National Association[14] using a new source of information – the British Household Panel Survey, provides some interesting, but – as the authors themselves acknowledge – far from complete insights into patterns of unpaid care and the tendency of people to care for their elders. The data shows that while about 14–15% of the population are providing unpaid care at any one time, there is a remarkable turnover of people providing such care, but the overall supply of care has not gone down.

2.33   The research looked at the preparedness and likelihood of various groups of people to provide unpaid care, including people who had been unemployed in the previous year but were now working, and also at carers not living with an older person as the carers's wealth and mobility increased. It found that unemployed people were less likely to provide unpaid care, and that carers not living with an older person were more likely to provide care if they were better off. Overall London Economics concluded that the supply of informal care would decrease over time but adduced no evidence to support this conclusion. However, we would expect that as fewer people live with their older relatives, care by "extra-resident" carers will be more important. Of course, the type of care given might change – for example more care at a distance, and less hands on personal care.

2.34   Table 2.5 shows the relationship between levels of dependency and receipt of informal care drawn from an analysis of the 1994 General Household Survey. At first sight it might seem strange that nearly half (46%) of all older people without any level of dependency receive support from an unpaid carer. This is because unpaid carers of older people are more likely to be involved in informal helping than in heavy duty caring, and also because of the way the General Household Survey records help given to all older people whether they are disabled in any way or not. Such help is generally the product of a two way relationship within the family but it is a very different kind of help from intensive support given on account of disability.

Table 2.5: Dependency and receipt of informal care: England 1994

Level of Dependency	% with informal support (for domestic tasks)
No dependency	46
Inability to perform one or more domestic tasks	85
Difficulty performing one personal care task	76
Difficulty performing two or more personal care tasks	83

Source: PSSRU analysis of the General Household Survey England 1994/1995 data[15].

2.35   There is a measure of uncertainty which surrounds any projections about the availability of informal care. The model takes account of a decline in the number of older people who are likely to be married (except that for very elderly men who are more likely to be married). Apart from these changes (the effect of which is minimal – see Research Volume 1), changes in household type and basic demographic changes make it difficult to make assumptions about the future availability of informal care from other members of the family apart from partners. Therefore, in our base case we conclude that after allowing for the factors described in this paragraph there will be no real change in the future availability of informal care.

Use of Services

2.36   The use of services is clearly important in our model. Our projections are largely based on the volume of care services currently used, and assume that the volume of services provided to each older person will be broadly the same in the future as in the past for any level of disability. However, use of services is and has been determined by political decisions and is influenced every day by personal preferences, and we simply do not know how services will respond to demand in 20, 30 or 50 years time. We have however, modelled changes which assume that fewer older people go into care homes or that paid for care services will be provided by local authorities to older people who presently rely on help from unpaid carers.

Care Costs

2.37   For the foreseeable future long term care will be a "people industry". It needs people to wash, dress and provide for the intimate needs of older people who can no longer do these things for themselves. The costs of care in the future will therefore be largely influenced by the earnings of people providing personal care which make up about 70% of the total costs of such services[16]. These will need to be enough to attract the right quality of worker to this kind of work, at the right level of productivity and, of course, to comply with what ever minimum wage level is in force at the time.

2.38   As purchasers of long-term care, Local Authorities have a clear interest in ensuring that there is sufficient such care is available now and in the future at prices they can afford. So they must have regard to the future economic viability of organisations who supply and provide care. On the other side care providers, whether in the public or private sector, have to control costs and purchasers have an interest in this as well.

2.39   Other factors at work include expectations about what care is provided, in what surroundings and the quality of that care – although improved quality may not necessarily cost more and there may be better ways of doing things at the same or less cost. As far as expectations are concerned the example cited most frequently is that people will increasingly expect better standards of accommodation, such as single rooms and en-suite facilities. About a quarter of all people living in nursing homes now share a room[16] and this change from routine sharing of rooms has occurred over a relatively short space of time. The effect on overall costs of changes like this has been negligible. The future is harder to predict. There is an argument that as people become wealthier – as older people will overall – they will consider treating elements of long-term care as a "luxury good" in the economic sense, of which they will consume more as their incomes rise. On the other hand there is a view that most people do not want to spend more than is absolutely necessary on long-term care in residential care or nursing homes, preferring instead to spend money in their homes on aids, adaptations and technologies that would reduce their reliance on help from other people with care tasks. We could make assumptions about what people will want to do with their extra wealth but we are not in a position to do that with any degree of certainty. And in any case while the real incomes of older people will rise overall, the rise will be unequally distributed.

2.40   Unit costs might rise faster than general inflation, perhaps more in line with average earnings increases. The pattern of the past has been that the indices of NHS and Personal Social Services prices (i.e. the price of what it takes to provide care) have risen in real terms by 1.5% and 1% each year since around 1980 respectively. Some commentators have suggested that in the future these costs will increase more in line with average wages (1.5% to 2% per annum on average in the long run) or the general increase in national income (GDP at 2.25% per annum on average in the long run). However, wage costs are only about two-thirds of the costs of long-term care so there is not a simple one-to-one link with earnings.

2.41   In considering our cost projections, the Government will no doubt wish to make a direct comparison with its own calculations. These are done on broadly the same basis, except that we have used a half percentage point higher figure for increases in unit health care costs than used by the Department of Health in its memorandum to the House of Commons Health Select Committee[17]. The impact of the National Minimum Wage has also to be considered. This will be expected to make a step change in wage rates, which will mainly affect the independent care sector. It will add to overall costs only to the extent that it is not paid for by efficiency gains, but the long run rate of growth in social care costs is unlikely to be affected.

2.42   We have had it put to us that instead of using a model built from the factors we have described to project future costs we should simply draw a straight line into the future based on past trends in NHS and social services expenditure of about 3.5% each year (1% more than our projection). This line should also be adjusted upwards by a further percentage point to reflect the fact that incomes will rise and so will the use of long-term care services – the "luxury good" referred to in paragraph 2.39. While this approach has the attractions of simplicity we think it over-simplifies a complex area and could give a very distorted picture of what the future might be like. For example, past expenditure increases take account of an entirely different demographic environment to what is expected in the future, and also takes account of past policy changes, for example the increase in Income Support expenditure for residential care and nursing homes .

THE BASIS OF THE COMMISSION'S COSTINGS

2.43   Our base case makes the following assumptions:

- that the population will grow in the way projected by the Government Actuary's Department and, according to their projections on changes in martial status;

- dependency rates by age remain constant over the next 50 years – this is a conservative assumption given what is known about the likelihood of improvements in health expectancy;

- apart from factors taken into account by the model no change is assumed in the future availability of informal care;

- future levels and patterns of use of care services by dependency will be much the same as now – it is probably unrealistic to make any other assumption;

- we also assume that the unit costs of care increase faster than the increase in general prices (that is in "real terms") by:

  - 1.5% annually for health care; and

  - 1% annually for social services,

  which have been the historical trends in pay and prices.

2.44 Using these assumptions we modelled for the period 1995 (when the model starts) to 2051 to line up with population projections. We have already said that after 2031 the projections are very uncertain. Table 2.6 sets out the current and projected costs of long-term care. These figures are at 1995/96 prices so they are directly comparable across the years. We have also estimated costs as a percentage of future national income (GDP).

2.45 The base case projects that the cost of long-term formal care for older people (paid for by both individuals and the state) could rise from £11.1bn (1.6% of GDP) in 1995 to:

- £14.7 billion in 2010 (1.5% of GDP);

- £19.9 billion in 2021 (1.6% of GDP);

- £28 billion in 2031 (1.8% of GDP); and

- £45.3 billion in 2051 (1.9% of GDP).

2.46 This implies an annual rate of growth in long-term care expenditure of 2.5% each year. During this period national income will have more than trebled. If national income grows more slowly then we would expect slower growth in the future costs of long-term care, but the share of national income would not be affected.

2.47 The model also shows the share of expenditure between the public sector and private individuals assuming no change in the present funding system described in Chapter 4. The increase in contributions from private individuals reflects the use of housing assets (as a result of rising levels of owner-occupation amongst older people) to pay for residential care. To the extent that the funding system is changed, the private and public share will change correspondingly.

Table 2.6: Base case projections of long term care costs for older people, UK at 1995/96 prices

	1995 £ billions	2010 £ billions	2021 £ billions	2031 £ billions	2051 £ billions
NHS Continuing Care[1]	2.6	3.5	4.9	7.0	10.9
PSS net[2]	4.5	5.5	7.2	10.1	16.1
Private expenditure[3]	4.0	5.7	7.8	10.9	18.3
Total[4]	11.1	14.7	19.9	28.0	45.3
% of Gross Domestic Product	1.6	1.5	1.6	1.8	1.9

Source: PSSRU and Royal Commission estimates rounded to nearest £100 million.[18]

Notes:

1. *It is difficult to separate total NHS costs into costs for acute care and costs for long term care. This figure has been arrived at by looking at the costs of 29,000 hospital beds occupied by older people staying more than 55 days and 9,000 nursing home beds in England paid for by the NHS in England (34,000 beds and 11,000 beds for UK). Costs include those for district nursing services, chiropody and day care.*

2. *PSS (Personal Social Services) is expenditure on elderly personal social services by local authorities, net of charges. Includes residential and nursing home care, home help, meals, lunch clubs and day care services. The figure also includes people who were in residential care and nursing homes prior to 1 April 1993 and have preserved rights to higher levels of income support as if they were local authority funded.*

3. *This figure may not be comprehensive because of problems identifying all private expenditure on long term care. It includes expenditure on residential and nursing care, privately arranged home help, privately paid chiropody and lunch clubs.*

4. *We have tried to reconcile the base figures back to those provided to us by the Government, which were of the order of £11 billion. The total above is similar. Social security benefits are not specifically shown in the above table but some of the private expenditure may be funded through monies received from social security benefits. Private expenditure on long-term care is difficult to establish because this expenditure is not systematically recorded.*

5. *Assumes that GDP will grow by 2.25% per annum over this period which is the long run rate of growth in the UK economy.*

SENSITIVITY ANALYSES

2.48   Factors over which there is little or no effective control impact on the base case. We vary assumptions to explore upper and lower limits of uncertainty. The factors which we have varied are listed below. We changed more than one assumption because certain changes appeared to go together. Some scenarios are however less plausible than others (for example it is more likely that health expectancy will improve than decline), particularly those where a number of things go "wrong" all at the same time. The results are shown in Figure 3. The boundaries of the possible future costs of long-term care are defined by two of these sensitivity analyses:

■   the bottom line of the graph showing what would happen if health expectancy improved, i.e. older people were less dependent in future;

- the top line of the graph shows what would happen if there were more people aged 85 and over than expected and if costs grew faster than assumed in the base case, and there were fewer carers.

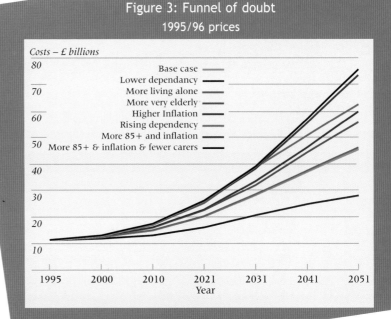

Figure 3: Funnel of doubt
1995/96 prices

2.49 As each year passes the difference between the lowest projection and the highest projection gets bigger. The difference is around £10bn by 2021. The uncertainties from then on are so great that little predictive reliance can be placed on these figures, but it is still useful to compare trends between different scenarios.

SENSITIVITIES TESTED

2.50 We now test six sensitivities designed to establish the range of uncertainty around the base case, without assuming any policy changes. These are:

Care costs

2.51 The results are very sensitive to the real increase in the unit costs of care. This is, in fact, the most sensitive assumption of all in the model. Therefore, we have considered alternative assumptions in the sensitivity analysis. The consequences of increases of 1.5% increase per annum for social services and 2% for health services are shown.

Faster growth in 85+ age group

2.52 Historically projections by the Government Actuary's Department (GAD) for the numbers of people aged 85 and over have proved to be underestimates of actual numbers. This assumption increases the number of elderly people over the age of 85 by 1.26 million in 2051. This is a 30% increase in that age group and an 8% increase in the population overall.

Faster growth in 85+ age group and higher cost

2.53 The cost implications of both faster growth in the 85+ age group and higher price rises occuring together have also been considered. The assumptions for faster growth in the 85+ age group and the higher increase in input prices of pay and other goods are as above.

Health Expectancy

2.54 If dependency levels at each age grow faster in the future than current levels, the implication is that for each age group in the elderly population there will be an increase in the incidence of chronic ill health or severe disability. This is, in fact, a very pessimistic view. To test the sensitivity, age specific disability rates have been assumed to rise by 1% until 2031 and remain constant thereafter[ii]. On the other hand a 1% decrease in age-specific dependency rates (implying a healthier older population) would almost halve the costs between 1995 and 2051 compared with our central assumption.

Informal care

2.55   We have tested the implication of reducing by 1% the number of single people living with others. The model is not sensitive to this change probably because the number of single people living with others is a small proportion (just under 20%) of all single people.

Faster growth in 85+ age group and higher costs and fewer carers

2.56   The assumptions for the 85+ and higher costs are as above. We have taken a more extreme assumption on informal care. We halved the number of single people living with others by 2051 (compared with the base case), and then halved the probability that single people living alone will receive informal help with domestic tasks. The increase in formal services is assumed to be in line with existing users at similar levels of dependency and no informal care support.

2.57   In this chapter we have tried to provide an answer to the question about the future demand for and costs of long term care by making projections based on the number of people receiving them – the future size and structure of the population of older people, their health, the availability of unpaid care, the current costs of these services and how those costs will increase in the future. We recognise that while Government cannot directly control many of these factors it must nonetheless be prepared to respond to them. We are pragmatic about the value of these projections. We cannot forecast the future. The best we can do is project forward a realistic "base case" and accept that the future may lie within it, subject to wide margins of uncertainty. Little reliance can be placed on our projections beyond the first 10–15 years which is why we are recommending that the projections should be revised every five years. If costs do rise more rapidly than projected, society itself will have to take decisions about whether and how they should be met. The need for flexibility to respond to changes in the future is clear. We now go on to look at what we want from a funding system, at the current system and what it delivers and possible alternatives to it.

Footnotes

(ii)   If they had been assumed to continue to rise until 2051, more than 100% of all very elderly women would be dependent.

Chapter 3
Requirements of a Funding System

This chapter considers long-term care as a risk, and what this might mean for the way in which it could be funded, including the balance of responsibility between the state and individuals.

3   The Commission has looked at the issue of the provision of long-term care from first principles, in terms of the kind of risk it comprises both for the individual and the state. This is essential to reaching well-informed conclusions as to the merits of the present system and how it should be changed. In this matter we have been greatly helped by the evidence submitted to us from a number of organisations and individuals, and specifically by the work of a number of expert witnesses.

3.1 In Chapter 2 we made observations on demographic trends and their possible effect on future costs of long-term care. In assessing how long-term care should be paid for, the Commission first considered the kind of risk such care represents to the individual. It is a risk which affects men and women differently. At present, men who live to be over 65 have a 1 in 5 risk of needing residential care, while women over 65 have a 1 in 3 risk[19]. Residential care is not of course the whole story, as many people are looked after at home. The point is that people simply do not know whether they will need long-term care until they get old.

3.2 Making provision for long-term care is thus different from making provision for a pension. Everyone reaching pensionable age expects to start drawing a pension for their later years. The pension is something which people hope they can rely on for an old age which they would like to be comfortable, and for which many have optimistic expectations. Paying for long-term care on the other hand involves making provision in one way or another against catastrophic and, in principle, unforeseeable costs. These costs can be illustrated as follows:

Cost of care at home *	14 hours help per week @ £8.50 an hour = £119/ week=£6,188 per year, £30,940 over 5 years
Cost of residential home *	£247/ week = £12,844 per year= £38,532 for a stay of 3 years
Cost of nursing home *	£337/ week = £17,524 per year = £26,286 for a stay of 18 months

* *The hourly costs of home care is based on Local Authority rates, which include overheads. The cost of residential and nursing homes are averages; lenghts of stay in residential and nursing care are averages.*

3.3   These are considerable sums of money. If a married couple were to save against the risk of long-term care they would need £85,000 to be sure of meeting the average cost of a residential home for each of the couple for three years. Many people live in residential or nursing care for even longer periods and therefore would need a much larger sum of money. Perhaps 10% – 15% of people who enter residential care might require it for more than five years[20], and would become totally impoverished by the time they died.

3.4   One approach to meeting such costs, apart from some means-tested state help for the very poorest, would be to expect people to provide for themselves from their income and savings at the time when costs are incurred. One justification for such an approach would be that meeting the costs of long-term care should be seen as one of many contingencies which may befall people along life's way, and for which they should therefore pay up front themselves (apart from minimalist means-tested help). Such a view has indeed been offered by one or two commentators.

3.5   The Commission do not consider this approach to be a practical one. First, for the pragmatic reason that very few people have, or can expect to acquire, resources on the scale needed , just as very few people could meet medical bills if they became ill through some disease such as cancer or if they had a heart attack. The figures of pensioners' incomes in Chapter 2, Table 2.3, show clearly that now and for the foreseeable future meeting care costs from current income is a sheer impossibility for all but the very rich. By the same token few people will have capital on the scale needed other than by selling their house. These are matters of fact, not of judgement.

3.6   This is not to deny that, at some undefinable point in the distant future, rising real incomes may provide greater practical justification for the approach set out in paragraph 3.4. But for now, and in our judgement for the foreseeable future, this approach does not even begin to be an acceptable answer. The risk of needing long-term care requires provision over and above the private incomes of individuals. As individuals cannot make provision out of their private incomes, some degree of pooling of the risk is necessary.

3.7 Older people need long-term care not simply because they are old, but because their health has been undermined by a disabling disease such as Alzheimer's disease, other forms of dementia or a stroke. As yet these diseases cannot effectively be cured by medical care, but people sufferering from them will require ongoing therapeutic or personal care of different kinds[iii] in order to enable them to live with the disease. In this regard, the only difference between cancer and Alzheimer's disease is the limitation of medical science. The sufferer is in no less need of care because of that limitation. Yet, as we show in Chapter 4, the amount of state help available varies significantly between the two situations.

3.8 Many people who have submitted evidence to us do not understand the supposed difference between these needs for care. This is the basis of the widespread perception of unfairness by those suffering from chronic disabling diseases who thought that they were entitled to free care at the time of need just as they would be if they needed a joint replacement or treatment for cancer. Society cannot wash its hands of what is clearly a sizeable social problem.

BROAD APPROACHES TO FUNDING

3.9 At a very broad level, provision for long-term care could be made in a number of ways:

(1) It could be left to people to decide whether or not to take out private insurance for themselves. Clearly some people could and would do so, but others might not take out insurance, because they could not afford to, or chose not to, or because private insurers refused them cover. They would have to meet the cost of long-term care from income and savings, and the state would probably (but not necessarily) have to make some kind of residual provision for the very poorest.

(2) The state could decide to *compel* as many citizens as possible to insure against the risk themselves through private insurance, thus ensuring a reasonably efficient spread of risk across the whole population. People would be clear what they had been made to provide for. Such compulsion exists, for example, in the case of motor insurance. The state would then have to provide alternative services or insurance premiums for those who could not afford such insurance or who were refused cover.

(3) The state could decide to provide some form of collective provision or insurance against the risk of long-term care, on the grounds of the universality of the risk, the unequal ability of citizens to make provision for themselves, and the inability of the industry to produce universally affordable or effective products (this latter is known technically as "market failure").

3.10 Approach (3) is the way the United Kingdom has chosen to arrange provision for health care, on the grounds of the need for universality of coverage, and to maximise efficiency. The National Health Service ensures that health care is both affordable and available across all social groups, and minimises problems which could arise from the uneven way in which the need, cost and coverage for health care falls to individuals. The costs of ill-health are concentrated on a small number of people – for example out of total NHS spending in England, some

£20bn per annum (out of £40bn in total) is spent on 8 million people in hospital care. Spreading the risk across the whole population and over the lifetime of that population is an efficient way of dealing with both the risk and the cost of providing against it. A point of comparison is with the United States, which for health care operates the first kind of system described above. There a far greater proportion of GDP goes into paying for Health Care, and yet a large proportion of the population below pensionable age are not covered by insurance.

THE APPROACHES CONSIDERED

3.11   In examining in theoretical terms the approaches summarised in paragraph xxx, the Commission considered very carefully how the risk of long-term care compares to the risk of other kinds of ill-health. In evidence to the Commission, a number of experts helped us to make this comparison, and to focus on the question of the extent to which provision for long-term care should be the responsibility of the state, and how much of the individual.

3.12   In relation to approaches (1) and (2) the Commission considered whether the market for long-term care insurance would be likely to work well without any state intervention. For a market to work well, it was put to us (by Nicholas Barr of the London School of Economics), that it requires, among other things, good consumer choice. This depends on good and understandable information, and on the ease and effectiveness with which provision can be improved in response to changes in that choice. It also depends on how catastrophic are the costs of choosing badly as to how to make provision for care[21][22].

3.13   Looking at the "market" for health insurance the insurer is faced with uncertain information about potential customers and with the prospect of excessive claims. The United States experience shows what can go wrong with an over reliance on the market for insurance in health care. There are gaps in coverage and exploding costs. A number of experts strongly put to the Commission that the NHS represented a more efficient means of providing health care than the market could offer if left to itself.

3.14   If we then look at Long Term Care Insurance (LTCI), the problems which arise with health insurance are much greater. For the consumer, the agreement which needs to be entered into with the prospective insurer is complex and relates to a contingency which is by definition a long way ahead. Such insurance is not only offered far in advance, but is based on necessarily also imperfect information as to the benefits that individual may require in the future. Policies for women are more expensive than those for men, because of the greater risk for women of requiring care and because they live longer. There are a large number of uncertainties for both parties, the cost of policies are high and the customer may simply decide not to do anything further. We discuss this in practical terms and in more detail in Chapter 5. Moreover, the current UK market experience, as discussed in detail in Chapter 5 and Research Volume 1, is that people are generally unwilling to take out private insurance for long-term care. The Commission therefore conclude that voluntary private actuarial insurance is unlikely to work on its own.

3.15   Since individual saving is not an efficient way to make provision, some kind of universal provision is clearly necessary under which contributions of whatever kind are sufficient to cover the average cost of care in the light of the probability of requiring it. This would be the most efficient use of people's money, the most efficient spread of cost across the UK and the best guarantee of equity.

3.16   From a theoretical point of view, the Commission are persuaded that universal risk pooling of some kind as in approach (3) represents the most effective way of providing the coverage required. This views the risk of needing long term care as, in practical, moral and social terms the same kind of exceptional risk of having a heart attack or contracting cancer. It requires provision that pools the risks in a similar way. The overall solution here should have regard to what will benefit the majority of citizens at the lowest cost to the nation overall, and remove from as many people as possible fear of the costs of needing to be cared for at the end of their lives. Ideally, also the solution should be one under which people contribute according to their means.

3.17   We favour this approach primarily on the grounds of:

- efficiency – the cost of the risk is spread across as wide a population as possible;

- effectiveness – the whole population is covered in the same way and people are aware of their entitlements; and

- equity – the amount people pay through taxation or a national insurance scheme being largely progressive.

3.18   Having decided that some form of effective risk pooling offers, in theory, the greatest possibility of efficient coverage for the nation overall, the Commission went on to consider:

- how the current funding system fits into such a framework;

- how this system as it stands could be made to work better, including the possible involvement of or partnership with the private sector;

- whether the basis of the current funding system needs to be changed radically;

- what the balance of responsibility should be between the state and the individual.

3.19   The next chapter looks at the current system in terms of the principles we have set out here. We then go on to look at possibilities for changing the current system, so as to alter the responsibilities of state and individual.

Footnotes

(iii)   We examine definitions of different types of care in Chapter 6.

Chapter 4

Analysis of the Current Funding System

This chapter describes the current funding system and analyses it against the theoretical framework which we set out in the previous chapter. It sets out aspects of the system which in our view are unsatisfactory.

4   Having set out a theoretical framework in the previous chapter, and concluding that long-term care was most efficiently covered by some kind of risk pooling, we looked at the current funding system and how it works. In particular, we considered the efficiency of coverage and the value for money offered to individuals and to the nation as a whole. We also had in mind the values we set out at the end of Chapter 1. Out of these values we constructed the following framework for analysis of any funding system (see overleaf):

"Even as an able-bodied person, . . . just trying to obtain information about what services were available, and . . . to convince the people concerned that my mother needed them, was a frustrating and stressful process. Heaven help old people who have no relatives to pester officials on their behalf."

FRAMEWORK FOR EVALUATION

1. Fairness

- *Does the funding system fulfil the reasonable expectations of older people?*

- *Are older people whose health is undermined by chronic disabling illness treated in the same way as those suffering from more acute illnesses?*

- *Does the system penalise those who made their own provision and reward those who did not?*

- *Is the balance of funding between the individual and the taxpayer fair?*

- *Will the burden remain a fair one for future taxpayers given the forecast increase in numbers of the older people?*

- *Does the funding system encourage informal caring?*

2. Maximum choice, dignity and independence

- *Are older people given adequate choice about the care they receive?*

- *Does the system encourage the avoidance of premature or inappropriate admission to residential care?*

- *Does the funding system allow the most appropriate care for the individual?*

- *Is the dignity and independence of individuals compromised by the funding mechanisms?*

- *Does the funding system offer consistent standards of care?*

- *Is the system comprehensible to and navigable by the individual?*

3. Security, sustainability, adaptability

- *Can older people rely on the funding system to provide what they need at a point when they are vulnerable?*

- *If things go wrong, can the individual do anything about it? Who is ultimately responsible and accountable?*

- *Will the funding system remain affordable?*

- *Can the funding system respond to new patterns of care e.g. increased domiciliary care or other different types of care?*

4. Quality and Best Value

- *Is the funding system biased towards particular forms of care, whether or not they are appropriate for the individual?*

- *Does the funding system favour one sort of care provider rather than another, regardless of quality, appropriateness, effectiveness or best value and quality?*

- *Does it offer acceptable and appropriate standards of care?*

- *Does the system provide best value overall?*

Following some general remarks, we apply this framework to the current system and identify what needs to be put right.

THE CURRENT SYSTEM

4.1   The current system is particularly characterised by complexity and unfairness in the way it operates. It has grown up piecemeal and apparently haphazardly over the years. It contains a number of providers and funders of care, each of whom has different management or financial interests which may work against the interests of the individual client.

4.2   Time and time again the letters and representations we have received from the public have expressed bewilderment with the system – how it works, what individuals should expect from it and how they can get anything worthwhile out of it. We have heard countless stories of people feeling trapped and overwhelmed by the system, and being passed from one budget to another, the consequences sometimes being catastrophic for the individuals concerned.

WHAT DO PEOPLE GET NOW?

4.3   The current system of state provision for long-term care, based on the means test as explained below, is financed on a "pay as you go" basis. This means that current taxation pays for the care of those in the system now. The overall cost of current provision is about £7.1bn a year for the NHS and Social Services and £4bn for what people spend themselves. Some of this is underpinned by an estimated £6bn of Social Security benefits – there are no definitive figures which match all elements. The figures on spending, insofar as we can estimate them, are set out in Chapter 2 in Table 2.2.

4.4.   The uncertainty as to the figures is in itself a cause for concern. No-one really knows just how much public or private money goes to support older people in long-term care. Despite our best efforts in the time available, we have been unable to shed definitive light on this matter. In the future this will no longer be acceptable. *We recommend that the Government should ascertain precisely how much money, whether from NHS, Local Authority Social Services and Housing budgets, or from Social Security budgets, goes to supporting older people in residential settings and in people's homes.* **(Recommendation 4.1)**.

4.5   Similar problems are encountered in tracking exactly how benefits are used within long term care, as was illustrated in Chapter 2. The Department of Social Security (DSS) has no operational reason of its own to want to know whether or not benefits such as Attendance Allowance or Disability Living Allowance are used to buy care. It is enough for them to know that benefits are being paid out to people who are entitled to them. However, we have heard of many instances where Local Authorities asked people to claim these benefits and then recovered the money in charges. Clearly some parts of these benefits go towards paying for long-term care. If the Government are determined to see policy develop in a proper way across the boundaries of departmental competence, and that total public money which pays for long-term care is used to good effect, as part of the work in Recommendation 4.1 a proper assessment should be made of the amount of benefits, including Disability Benefits which come back into the system to pay for care.

4.6   Services provided by the National Health Service are generally free at the point of use. They are paid for from NHS budgets financed mostly by general taxation (a small amount being top-sliced from the National Insurance scheme to reflect the "NHS" element in National Insurance contributions). Local Authorities are responsible for assessing the need for "non-health" domiciliary care or residential care. There is a wide variation between authorities in the application of charges for care at home: some charge a small flat rate, some charge full costs, some apply a variety of means tests. This adds to the uncertainty and the sense of injustice felt by individuals. Local Authorities do however, apply a consistent national means test for residential and nursing home care charges, the effect of which we discuss in paragraph 4.15. Some are flat-rate charges which affect the poorer proportionately more, others are means tested.

"Just before Christmas, at a most insensitive time, the social worker arrives at her home and throws down a bill for £1,300 with respect to a payment going back to 1996. Now, she is only a pensioner and has a small pension from her husband because she is a widow . . . they've certainly discovered how to get rid of the elderly here . . . they've discovered that, if you put these kind of bills to them, they almost have a heart attack, and she almost did."

NHS Care

4.7   Although the NHS tries to treat more people by treating them more quickly, older people can take longer to recover from treatment. They may require care which may not be seen as a medically active intervention but is necessary to enable them properly to recover. This could be help from a nurse, convalescence, or rehabilitation. The number of NHS long-stay beds has reduced by 38% since 1983 (a loss of 21,300 beds), and the number of private nursing home places has increased by 900% (an increase of 141,000 beds). Whether this increase in private beds represents a real need will always be difficult to tell, as some of the demand could have been created by the increasing availability of social security payments to pay for places in homes from the early 1980s to 1993. The availability of this money to pay for independent home places has helped to develop the independent care sector.

4.8   Only 8% of these *additional* private nursing home places are paid for by Health Authorities and Health Boards. The rest are paid for by individuals, or by Local Authorities. The total saving to the NHS over this period, also taking into account the cheaper nursing home beds funded by the NHS as a substitute for long-stay hospital beds, was considerable. Some of this cost will have been shifted onto the Social Security system and may be covered by the Social Security transfer payment from 1993 to 1996. It is difficult to tell, but there remains a lingering suspicion that, in order to concentrate its resources on acute care, the NHS has been increasingly reluctant to provide long-term care for older people. The Department of Health have been unable to help us clarify this point. ***We recommend that the Government should conduct a scrutiny of the shift in resources supporting long-term care since the early 1980s, and should consider whether there should be a transfer of resources between the NHS and social service budgets given changes in relative responsibilities*** **(Recommendation 4.2)**.

Care arranged by Local Authorities

4.9   On discharge from hospital, people are entitled to an assessment by the Local Authority, who decide what ongoing care they need. In practice, assessments are based on locally set criteria, so that the type of care a person receives can depend on where he or she lives.

4.10 Care is also charged for in different ways. We have commented on the variety of different mechanisms for charging for care at home. These charges accounted for some £160m in 1995/96 in the United Kingdom (£200m in 1996/97). Some are for what might be defined as "care" such as help setting up in the mornings: some are for what might be termed "living costs", such as meals on wheels. The Audit Commission for England and Wales is undertaking a review of charging for home care, and the Government have commented on the need for consistent charging in the recent English Social Services White Paper[23].

Help from public funds with residential care and nursing home fees

4.11 Where a local authority arranges residential home or nursing home care (includes care in homes owned or managed by a local authority) on the basis of need they are obliged by law to determine what financial contribution the individual concerned should make towards the fees. This is often referred to as the "means test". In practice everybody makes some contribution because everybody has sufficient income to do so. Local authorities work out the contribution by applying a standard set of national rules to the calculation of income and capital. These largely mirror the rules of the Social Security Income Support scheme.[iv] The objective is that after making their contribution towards the fees, people will be left with at least the amount of their personal expenses allowance[v], often called "pocket money".

4.12 Most income is taken into account in full; for example Retirement Pension or payments of Income Support. In some cases, people will be expected to pay the full fees because their income, ignoring any capital, is high enough to enable them to do so and still leave them with their personal expenses allowance.

4.13 Where an individual has capital assets of £16,000[vi] or more the rules are simply that he or she has to pay the fees in full.

remember one lady . . . who was in hospital and all of a sudden received a letter telling her that her house was going to be sold. She immediately discharged herself home . . . it is an iniquitous thing that an elderly person, at their most vulnerable time of life, should have their home sold from under them in order to pay for their care after a lifetime of work and service to the nation."

4.14 In all other cases where people have capital of less than £16,000 they will be expected to make a financial contribution towards the fees. In these cases both capital and income are taken into account. If capital is less than £10,000 this is ignored as is any income it produces. If capital is between £10,000 and £16,000 the actual income is ignored, but for each £250[vii] of capital an income of £1 per week is assumed. This is called the "tariff income" and we refer to it again in Chapter 6. The aim of the tariff income is that a person should spend some of their capital towards the fees. As capital is spent the tariff income falls, rapidly at first and then more slowly. The tariff income is added to the rest of the person's income for the purpose of calculating their contribution to the fees. Total assessed income is then compared with the fees; after deducting the personal expenses allowance, the balance is the contribution which the person must pay. The local authority pays the rest.

4.15 In our view, the effects of this system are anomalous. A person with assets between £10,000 and £16,000 will be asked to pay up to £24 per week, or £1,248 per year from those assets. Someone with assets above £16,000, will need to pay fees of on average £275 per week in residential care or £350 per week in a Nursing

Home, to the provider, (normally nowadays in the private sector), unless or until assets fall below £16,000 when the state may again provide some help. A recent report by the Joseph Rowntree Foundation[24] highlighted that in many cases authorities do not monitor an individual's assets, so that many people may have continued to be charged the full amount when they were in fact entitled to some state help. This demonstrates how complex the system is.

4.16   If a person is in residential care for up to three years, and owns a house worth say £40,000, over those three years the system (by assuming that the house is sold and the proceeds are used to pay for care) will bring him or her to a level where it judges there is sufficient impoverishment to warrant state help. Someone with more assets is less likely to become impoverished in this way. The system at the moment helps people who are poor, demands that people of modest means make themselves poor before it will help, and affects people to a lesser degree the richer they are and better able to afford the sums required. This seems strangely inconsistent, and is at odds with the framework we set out in Chapter 3. The lack of consistency causes much distress to the public, particularly those who have modest assets which can be eaten up very quickly when care is required.

> *". . . those of us who have been [f]*
> *enough in our lives to have our [own]*
> *homes now, we are then faced, if w[e go]*
> *to a nursing home: 'Right. You ha[ve a]*
> *house? Right, we'll have that. You [have]*
> *£50,000 savings, we'll have that', an[d]*
> *all one's life one has paid taxes....,*
> *then suddenly the nest egg one has [built]*
> *up, either for yourself in retiremen[t or]*
> *for your dependants, is taken in ord[er to]*
> *pay for this long-term care."*

4.17   The Government Actuary's Department calculated, based on our estimates of public cost, that in terms of peoples' earnings from employment, from pensions and from investments, the current state funding system of long-term care represents a tax of some 2.2%. This supports a system which provides potential help only to those with assets of less than £16,000. There are no data on the assets held by older people in residential care. As explained in paragraph 2.12 Chapter 2, about 44% of the population of single over-75 owner occupiers are thought to have assets of less than £16,000 (see Table 2.3). This points to the proportion of people who under the current means test would be entitled to receive some help towards the costs of residential care. The rest of the population of single over-75s would have to fund all the costs themselves out of their savings or insurance policies. The savings of many of moderate means will inevitably be tied up in the houses which they have bought during their working lives. They, as Table 2.3 shows, tend to be asset rich, but income poor. A situation where the value of their home effectively dictates whether people are potentially entitled to state help for their care needs does not represent a form of effective pooling of risk of the kind which the Commission thinks is needed.

Expenditure Streams for Long-Term Care

4.18   NHS funds derive mainly from taxation collected and allocated by Central Government, with local decision – making on what is actually spent. The system is relatively straightforward with a clear line of accountability from local health commissioners to the relevant Secretary of State responsible for Health in England, Scotland, Wales and Northern Ireland. Services are commissioned locally from providers primarily in the public sector, with some private sector involvement.

4.19   In Northern Ireland, both Health and Social Services are funded in a similar way from the Northern Ireland Health and Social Services Executive. For both Health and Social Services there is a clear line of responsibility to one Secretary of State, and after devolution to one Minister.

4.20 In England, Scotland and Wales, Social Services are delivered by Local Authorities. Local Authority expenditure is derived from a combination of an allocation of general taxation via a Government grant (which is largely unhypothecated – not earmarked – between services) and money raised locally through council tax and fees and charges. It is important to note that there is far less direct central Government control over the detailed allocation of Local Authority expenditure (as distinct from national totals) than with the NHS, reflecting Local Authority autonomy. Central Government resources used to pay for the long-term care commissioned by Local Authorities consists of a grant covering a number of service blocks, but the individual Local Authority has discretion on how much to spend on each service.

4.21 Following consultation with Local Authority Associations the Government each year determines the amount of grant which goes to Local Authorities overall. This is then divided between authorities according to a formula. Standard Spending Assessments (SSAs) are published which indicate approximately how much the Government expects Local Authorities to spend on Social Services overall – not specifically on older people – to deliver a standard level of service. Most authorities spend at or above the SSA for Social Services as a whole (on average of 9% above). In England in 1996, according to figures supplied by the Department of Health, authorities spent 16% *less* than the SSA on services for older people (a sum of £0.7bn) while spending more on younger disabled people and on children.

4.22 The Commission supports the principle of local autonomy, and understands that the SSA should be seen essentially as an indicative basis for grant distribution. Nonetheless there is some concern that even the figures derived from a formula designed to assess relative need are being squeezed out by other priorities. We do not say that these other priorities are not worthwhile. They self evidently are. But it does suggest that the distribution formula is not right. The Government, in seeking to reassess the formula seem to share this view. *We recommend a more transparent grant and expenditure allocation system, on which the proposed National Care Commission could report regularly. The Commission might in time be asked to recommend a better system of distributing the public money allocated for long-term care* (**Recommendation 4.3**).

4.23 Had the true nature of the current system ever been made explicit between Government and citizens, it would be clear that only the poor are currently meant to receive state support and that a large part of the population is not entitled to any help. Those who could afford to do so could have considered private insurance, while those of moderate means would be aware that whatever savings they had would need to be used up before they were entitled to any help funded by the taxes they had paid. In our view, such lack of understanding has contributed massively to the uncertainty and bitterness felt by large numbers of people at the present time and the lack of preparedness of many. When the Government responds to the Royal Commission's report it must be explicit about what long-term care costs the Government will fund from taxation and what people will have to provide from their own resources. *We recommend that the Government should make a clear statement as to the balance between an individual's personal responsibility for meeting care costs and what support he or she can expect from the state from taxation or any other means* (**Recommendation 4.4**).

I am 80 and for years I and my firm ʌaid our contributions in the belief that I ʌas providing, as Beveridge had stated ʌr all necessary care from cradle to grave . . Only recently have the rules been ʌhanged. I regard this as a blatant ʌreach of contract by the Government ʌho took my money, promising care and ʌhen reneged on the contract after I had ʌaid all my dues. To my mind, this is a ʌaud."

How the Current System has Evolved

4.24   Confusion and uncertainty exist as an intrinsic part of the current system. Looking at its development in its historical context shows how problems have become compounded over the years. In the post-war period, long-term care was provided in residential ("Part III") Local Authority homes ("Part IV" in Scotland), for which there was a waiting list and for which a means test was applied. Particularly ill or frail people might be looked after in the NHS. Two developments changed this:

- The increasing use of social security benefits meant that a public fund, without cap and without a test of care need, and with rules that were eventually uniform throughout the country, was available to fund people in residential and nursing homes in the private sector. Expenditure grew from £350m in 1985 to £2.5bn in 1993/94 and the "market" was shaped in a particular way, driven by what could be paid for rather than what people needed;

- During the 1980s the NHS became aware of its costs for the first time, and was subject to measured performance targets. The perception was that an old person on a ward consumed resources without an easily achievable and identifiable point of recovery. Given the existence of the uncapped social security benefits, residential and nursing home care provided one "exit" from the NHS for many patients.

4.25   These changes induced a new private sector infrastructure of residential and nursing home care and a degree of capital investment that may not otherwise have occurred given restraints on capital investment in the public sector. However, it discouraged domiciliary care (Local Authorities had to provide this out of their own budgets and charges); prevented the NHS and Local Authorities developing joint working and planned commissioning; but gave some old people access to care they could not otherwise have afforded. Whether in all cases it was the most appropriate care will never be known.

4.26   As the 1980s progressed, Social Security expenditure paid to people moving into independent sector residential care and nursing homes spiralled. This caused great concern. An internal Department of Health and Social Security Report – the Firth report – concluded that resources should be transferred to Local Authorities and out of the benefits system. In 1988, Sir Roy Griffiths in a report commissioned by the Government[25] took this further, proposing that Local Authorities should have a care assessment role as well as a budget transfer from Social Security. The intention was to encourage Local Authorities to spend more money on domiciliary care than before.

4.27   Government responded to the Griffiths proposals in the 1989 White Paper *Caring for People*[26]. The aims of Community Care were expressed thus:

- to promote the development of domiciliary, day and respite services to enable people to live in their own homes wherever feasible and sensible;

- to ensure that service providers make practical support for carers a high priority;

- to make a proper assessment of need and good care management the cornerstone of high quality care;

- to promote the development of a flourishing independent sector alongside good quality public services;

- to clarify the responsibilities of agencies and so make it easier to hold them to account for their performance;

- to secure better value for taxpayers' money by introducing a new funding structure for social care.

4.28   One of the departures from Griffiths was the emergence of a Residential Allowance as part of Income Support paid by DSS from central funds, but only if an individual was placed in a independent sector home. This replaced Griffiths' proposal for Housing Benefit to cover accommodation costs. It was introduced for a variety of reasons – primarily to reflect a housing element in independent sector care in residential settings which, if the individual was in their own home, would be paid for out of Housing Benefit. It was not available to those placed in Local Authority homes. The Allowance appeared to make independent sector residential care cheaper for the Local Authority than its own homes. In that respect it may have been intended to provide an additional incentive towards the independent sector. This certainly seems to have been the outcome, as was put to us in numerous submissions and at a seminar the Commission held on the effect of the 1993 Community Care changes (see Research Volume 3 and paragraph 4.47). The Government have proposed transferring the Residential Allowance to Local Authorities in the English Social Services White Paper and using the money in a more carefully targeted way. We agree. In our view the Allowance serves no useful purpose and adds to the arcane nature of the current system. *We recommend that the resources which underpin the Residential Allowance should be reallocated to Local Authorities to use in a way which better meets peoples' needs.* **(Recommendation 4.5)**.

4.29   Griffiths also called for a large degree of ring-fencing of Community Care funds across all client groups, to avoid the danger that other budgets would take money intended to fund Social Services. The amount of ring-fencing suggested by Griffiths never materialised, although there was a smaller degree of ring-fencing in the Special Transitional Grant (STG) which was intended to ease the transition to the new system. As noted in paragraph 4.4 it is difficult to know what level of resources goes into the current system. Ring-fencing would add clarity, but would remove local discretion.

4.30   Another difficulty arises for many people who have "preserved rights" to centrally fixed higher rates of Income Support, because they entered the care system before April 1993. It has been put to us that these rates are becoming increasingly inadequate. Many of the people concerned are in increasingly difficult circumstances. As they survive longer, it seems increasingly difficult to justify treating this group of people differently from those who entered the care system on or after 1 April 1993, for whom local authorities meet fees in full, subject to a contribution based on means. Equity demands that they should be treated in the same way. *We recommend that the Government should consider whether "preserved rights" cases should be brought within the post-April 1993 system or whether some other solution can be found to address the shortfall in funding experienced by this group.* **(Recommendation 4.6)**.

4.31   We have already mentioned the incentive for the NHS to seek savings by passing care responsibilities to Local Authorities without the equivalent savings being passed on as well. More generally the current system, with different budgets held in different places, is perhaps inclined to encourage cost shifting to someone else, without regard for what is best for the individual or indeed for the public purse overall. Proper joint Commissioning, fuelled by better working arrangements without the pointless rivalry dictated by a series of fortresses constructed by budgets, would help to solve this problem. It needs to be encouraged. We discuss this in Chapter 8.

General Comments on the Present System

4.32   Simply describing the current system vividly demonstrates a number of complexities and confusion. No doubt unintentionally, it appears at times to be designed around a series of different bureaucracies, rather than the needs of individual older people.

4.33   The confusion we have described is simply in terms of health and social services. Other services add to the confusion. Housing must also play a part in the future if care is to be delivered properly in people's homes. If people are to stay at home rather than be moved to residential care their accommodation must be part of any assessment, including the need for suitable aids or adaptations. The system is often very slow at responding, with housing priorities being different from those of social services. We comment on this later in paragraph 7.4.

4.34   The Commission is clear about the strong lack of trust in the current system. There are pronounced feelings that Government was meant to underwrite the system in some universal sense through taxation, and it has not done so. People are not clear as to what they should expect. There is a linked feeling that the Health Service is abnegating its responsibility for care and making people rely on their own resources. Delivery at the sharp end is by Local Government, with its less centrally controllable (and more locally variable) system of finance, which produces variations in the implementation of the funding system, which also contributes to unease. The feeling is that a contract with the people has been broken. The reality is that there never really was one and, incrementally, rules were changed without people understanding what this meant. The result is a sense of betrayal, a lack of trust and a genuine sense of helplessness.

4.35   Even describing the current system makes its limitations obvious. Applying the Commission's value framework as set out in paragraph 4 makes that inadequacy more transparent. Informed by evidence received, a study of the literature and our own observations, our analysis of the present system may be summarised as follows:

Fairness

4.36   The current system clearly does not fulfil the reasonable expectations of old people. They feel that they have paid into a system through the National Insurance Scheme which they were led to believe would look after them in later life whatever their needs were. At a key point in peoples' lives they find that they are expected to pay for themselves out of assets they have accumulated over a lifetime for care they had previously expected would be free. We do not say this belief is logical: that it exists is a fact, and the sense of betrayal cannot be denied.

4.37   As the current system relies on the means test, those who have savings or are homeowners believe they are being penalised in that they are expected to put in a large amount of their own resources before they get anything out of it. Even though they pay the bill this often does not feel like a conscious purchase decision. It is often rushed, and by definition made at a time of personal crisis. It also involves using a rather unwieldy asset – their homes – to pay for care.

4.38   The current system does not seek to provide much support to informal caring, although a number of social security benefits for carers have been developed since 1976. Carers' organisations contend that the limit of carers' ability to cope has been reached. The system could do more to offer support for carers.

Maximum choice, dignity and independence

4.39   Under the current system the amount of choice available depends on what is offered locally and the state of the Local Authority budget. In some areas domiciliary care is charged for, in some it is not charged at all. Different levels of service are available in different areas. More consistency is required from the system generally, in relation to both residential and domestic care in respect of both payment and service provision.

4.40   As we have observed earlier in the chapter, in assessing an individual's need for long-term care a local authority can count on the Income Support Residential Allowance to further help support care in an independent residential setting. At the opposite extreme, a domiciliary package would not recover much in fees and might potentially cost the authority more than a residential care place. Securing the most appropriate care of the individual under the current system is precarious. If dignity and independence mean avoiding residential care unless it is absolutely necessary, the current system may be seen to push people into residential care and thereby compromise their dignity and independence at an earlier stage than might be necessary. Even the forms which people have to complete to obtain the various kinds of assistance can be lengthy and complex. This complexity – a complexity which exists at all levels in the care system, militates against choice and dignity. The bias towards residential – based care militates against independence. There must be a re-focusing on the needs of the individual.

Security, sustainability and adaptability

4.41   The present system seems to provide no sense of security for older people. Evidence to the Commission shows widespread anxiety among the older people about what will happen to them. There is a very real possibility that individuals are brought to a point of crisis at which residential or nursing care becomes the only option at the time (for example at hospital discharge). This cannot be

Chapter 4 – Analysis of the Current Funding System

interpreted as a funding system providing what people need. More time needs to be built in to consider the best options for the individual. Where prospects for recovery exist, the system should not drive them out.

4.42   The current funding system provides no incentive for anything other than the residential or nursing homecare option in the private sector in many cases. It can in theory provide greater scope for new types of domiciliary care, but this would mean withdrawing sums from current patterns of provision into which Local Authorities are locked with contracts, their own provision and also from reliance on benefit to underwrite the funding of care. Complaints procedures are complex and are compartmentalised: it is often not clear where complaints should be directed.

Quality and Best Value

4.43   The current system is clearly biased towards residential care irrespective of appropriateness and best value for the individual. For the Local Authority, this can easily represent the option with the least net cost. There are benefit incentives to using private provision, and also incentives to placements in Local Authorities' own homes, which can be more expensive than the private sector equivalent, because of the small marginal cost to the Authority. There can be no confidence that best value is being obtained from the system as a whole. Standards throughout the system are variable. Providers are often small, with commissioning being done on a very local basis. There are examples of both high and low standards and what people get depends very much on where they live and the state of local budgets. There seems to be little definable relationship between quality and cost, as has been pointed out by the Audit Commission in their report *The Coming of Age* (1997)[27].

"I had a sister taken into care. She had just lost an invalid husband and was tricked into a care home. All she needed was a home help. She was fit and talkative but stripped of all she had and I tried to get her out of the bullying, neglectful home. She died after about one and a half years in this horrific place and I think I made it worse by complaints. They lied about everything. I am still haunted . . ."

4.44   The system may or may not be underfunded. Until mechanisms are clearer we will never know. The Local Government Association suggested as part of its spending negotiations with Government an extra £300m was necessary to improve the system. Only when flows of money are clearer will we be able to make a judgement as to the extent to which the system is underfunded.

4.45   As for a level playing field, it clearly does not exist. To a Local Authority, the cheapest form of care is residential or nursing care, which means that domiciliary care is not always considered in isolation from cost. There are a complex number of forces pulling in different directions.

CONCLUSIONS ON THE CURRENT SYSTEM

4.46   On this analysis, the current system is failing. That it is perceived to be failing can also be clearly seen from the letters received by the Commission and by the frank and deeply felt observations made at the Commission's public hearings. There is a sense of bewilderment, a strong sense of loss of control, a sense of actually losing the beloved individual to a system which is beyond understanding and which makes individuals feel beyond help. No amount of statistics or cool analysis can take away the human

". . . A doctor who is prepared to come out, who is prepared to meet needs and who is not prepared to stint on care for, say, an 86 year old. If there is something that needs to be done it is done . . . I have a very good employer who gives me flexibility and gives me support so if the doctors come in, I can take some time, work from home to cover that."

despair which individuals feel when confronted with the system as it is. That is
not to say that the system fails everywhere – there are many examples of good
practice throughout the country and many examples of dedicated staff working
flat out to deliver a great deal of high quality care. The Commission considers that
more should be done to spread good practice nationally. We make
recommendations in this regard later on in the report, and would like to stress our
appreciation that those who work in the care system are often able give care of the
highest quality – despite the unhelpful forces at work in the system itself.

4.47   In addition to the analysis set out in paragraphs 4.36 to 4.46, the Commission held
a seminar to establish the extent to which the Community Care reforms had
achieved their objectives. The following points emerged from a picture of partial
achievement, some of which referred to models of care which are discussed in
Chapter 8:

- There has been more home care, but targeted at the most dependent. It was
felt that prevention was squeezed out;

- Carers had been helped little, and that often services were not being offered
where there was a carer in evidence;

- An over-supply in the residential sector and the effect of Local Authority
purchasing power meant that costs were low and made residential care seem
attractive in cost terms compared to home care. There was also a concern
about quality of services in the residential sector overall;

- There was some change in management culture in social services, but still a
long way to go to ensure more of a client based rather than a service based
approach;

- The division of responsibility between the NHS and Social Services
health/social divide caused a number of problems in terms of responsibility
and accountability, and perverse cost incentives to take a short-term view
based on cost alone remained.

4.48   In professional language, these findings mirror what we have had addressed to us
from the public. The findings are set out in full in Research Volume 3.

4.49   Some of the letters received by the Commission on the system overall make
harrowing reading. We make no apology for extensive quotations throughout the
report. These letters should not be dismissed as being from people whose only
interest is to protect the inheritance of their children or to inherit from their
parents. There is a far deeper sense of injustice and failure to understand what is
going on at a time of crisis.

4.50   Taking all of this evidence together, we have concluded that the current funding
system is in clear need of reform. Within it there are too many flows of funds
which have been designed for different purposes and what the individual does or
does not get out of it depends on a number of complex decisions which are out of
their control. People have no idea what to expect. The tendency of the system to
require impoverishment – and its proof – before it will help leads to despair which
in our judgement is unacceptable. Modestly prudent people risk losing their

dignity, partly as a result of their condition and partly because of how the system deals with it. People have no choice but to receive services for which all but the poorest have no further choice but to pay.

4.51   The aim should be to revise the funding system so as to define a new and clearer relationship between state provision on the one hand and personal responsibility on the other. More specifically:

- The system needs to become simpler, and what the individual is entitled to should be clearer;

- People need to be able to rely on the system – now and in the future;

- What the system delivers must be consistent compared with what the individual needs or wants;

- The system should not encourage residential care (whether private or public) above any other form of care, nor, in requiring the release of assets which might be tied up in property, must it force the premature disposal of that property in such a way that excludes the possibility of a return from residential care;

- If the same kind of care is free from one provider or within one setting, it should be free in all contexts if the state has organised the care, or vice versa. There should be more consistency within the system;

- Whether care is charged for or not – and ideally – the standard of provision should not depend on where people live;

- The first focus of this system should be need rather than services delivered primarily on the basis of means;

- State support in the system should have a greater element of universality than now: services should not be seen as residual services for the poor.

4.52   Having concluded that the current funding system is deficient, we now consider possible changes to it, beginning with the prospects for the further involvement of privately purchased financial products.

"One form we picked up, I know it was not A4 but it was 3 pages. It is not exactly user friendly. These are not designed for people who are older ... they could not, as 85 and 87 year old individuals, wade their way through that. It was a minefield for us."

Footnotes

(iv)   There are differences which relate to the treatment of the value of houses which are up for sale, jointly owned assets and some types of income.

(v)   The allowance is currently £14.45. However in some circumstances local authorities have the discretion to increase this amount. Any increase will reduce the contribution towards fees paid by the person concerned.

(vi)   This will generally include the value of the home, but will not do so if the home is occupied by a spouse or partner or other specified relatives. In some circumstances local authorities have the discretion to disregard the value of the home where it is occupied by someone who is not a spouse, partner or other specified relative.

(vii)   The rule is actually each complete £250 or part thereof.

Chapter 5
Scope for the use of Private Sector Financial Products

This chapter considers the scope for meeting long-term care costs from privately purchased financial products, including insurance.

5   In Chapter 3 we set out the theoretical nature of the risk represented by long-term care and the kind of pooling of provision against that risk which was required. In Chapter 4 we examined the current funding system and found it inadequate in terms of the criteria we have established. This chapter examines the role of the private sector in providing insurance cover or in levering in money in other ways by means of other financial products, including pensions and equity release products[viii]. Research Volume 2 of this Report describes these products and their characteristics in more detail.

LONG TERM CARE INSURANCE

5.1   Given that, in Chapter 3, we suggested that the risk of needing long-term care requires some kind of risk pooling, we considered the extent to which private insurance products could help. Insurance is, after all, a form of risk pooling recognisable to and accepted by many people.

5.2   Commercial Union introduced the first Long-Term Care Insurance (LTCI) product in the UK in 1991. The Association of British Insurers (ABI) estimates that there are now some 23,000 policies in force. Currently 14 companies offer LTCI policies, and others may be considering offering them, but growth of the market has been slow.

5.3   The maximum benefits paid by policies vary between £15,600 and £36,000 per annum. The minimum age of entry varies between 0–45, maximum age between 74–80 for regular premiums, and there is no upper age limit for single premium policies. The average age at which policies are taken out is 67 – it is not until that age that people perceive the risk of needing long-term care. Over 60% of policy holders are women, who cost more to insure as they have more years of severe disability late in life. The risk of Alzheimer's disease or dementia is covered[(ix)], but 10% of applicants are rejected for cover on medical grounds.

INSURANCE ISSUES – POLICIES, CLAIMS CRITERIA AND ASSESSMENT

5.4   LTCI benefits are triggered by the insured person's failure to perform two or three Activities of Daily Living (ADLs) relating to washing, transferring from bed to chair, feeding, toileting and mobility. Mental impairment also triggers benefits. Policies with a trigger of failing three ADLs are much cheaper than those which pay on failure of two ADLs.

5.5   On grounds of consistency, clarity and independent assessment, ADLs perhaps compare well with the wider needs assessments of social services departments, some of which use ADLs among their assessment criteria. For the physically frail, insurers expect failure of three ADLs to correspond to the degree of disability requiring nursing home care, although there is no requirement for the insured to be resident in a home. Failure of three ADLs as a measure would probably therefore exclude many people now receiving residential and domiciliary care through social services. This means that, while insurance with a criterion for claims of failure of three ADLs will cover the end stage of life, for lower levels of dependency a much more expensive policy triggered by two ADLs will be needed to provide cover.

AFFORDABILITY

5.6   Cost is an important barrier to wider take-up of LTCI. A number of factors contribute to the high-cost of premiums. The insurance companies must build up specific funds to meet claims over the long term, so the older people are when they take out contracts the less time there is to build up funds and the higher the premiums. This is a new UK insurance market with little claims experience. The insurance is for a high-cost benefit with a 25% expectation of claim. Health underwriting and claims costs are higher than with other forms of insurance and there is great uncertainty about the future cost of care.

5.7   As an example of cost, a *single premium policy* taken out by a 65-year-old woman with a well-known insurance company for a benefit of £1,000 per month for life for failure of three ADLs, with three months' deferral would cost £9,306 for level benefits. With inflation cover of up to 15% above the retail price index per annum, it would cost £16,408. For a man of 65 the corresponding figures would be £6,430 and £9,228. The inflation indexed is usually general inflation, whereas the pay and prices costs of social care have increased by 1% *above* normal inflation for some years. The pay and prices of the NHS have risen 1.5% *above* normal inflation. Therefore, even with inflation cover benefits may not be enough to cover the rise in the cost of care over time. LTCI is not a mass market product, as it exists at the moment.

5.8   Other options include annuities which are taken out at need and which yield sufficient income to pay for care. These might cost between £40,000 and £50,000. Again, they are a product for the few, not the many.

5.9   There is an additional or conceptual difficulty with private insurance. It is intended to bridge the gap between an individual's income and the cost of care. This means that people with lower incomes have a bigger gap to bridge, so must insure for a higher amount. They are therefore less likely to be able to afford the premiums. People with higher incomes have a smaller gap to bridge, so only need to insure for smaller sums and can more readily afford the premiums. It becomes more affordable the better off you are. The people with the greatest need are the least likely to be able to afford it.

OPTIONS FOR INCREASING TAKE-UP OF PRIVATE INSURANCE

Encouraging take-up of insurance at a younger age

5.10   One way to make LTCI more affordable would be to encourage younger people to take out policies, for a lower premium. Survey evidence suggests that the problem is that they are not willing to do so – they have other more pressing priorities. Both they and the Government consider that saving for a pension has a higher priority. Another problem is that while working women earn less than men on average, premiums for women are more expensive.

Compulsion

5.11   Premiums would be cheaper if the entire population took out private insurance. If there were a common premium structure, regardless of age, sex and health, the premium could, according to one company, be £43 per month for £1,000 per month for life on failure of three ADLs if everyone over age 20 paid for their own benefits. This is a relatively large sum for those on moderate incomes. An alternative might be to make insurance compulsory only for the working population, though this would make for higher per capita contributions and operate as a tax on employment. For example, if insurance was paid for only by those aged between 20 and 64, the monthly premium might be £51.

5.12   Compulsory private provision has not been proposed in evidence to the Commission by either the public or the insurance industry. Professor Gillian Parker's recent public attitude study showed that about 80% of those asked were opposed to the idea of compulsory private insurance and only 15% were supportive. Of the age group 25–54 years only 11% were supportive[29]. In evidence to us, the Association of British Insurers were lukewarm as to the prospect of compulsory private insurance.

Partnership Proposals

5.13   The previous Government proposed alleviating the means test after a period for those who had purchased private insurance. The costs were uncertain and depended on take up, and were identified as being between £160m and £590m. Such schemes have been tried in the United States. Evidence presented to the Commission, and newer evidence presented to a recent Senate hearing in the United States suggest that such schemes have not been a success, with levels of take up being rather low[30]. The scheme as presented by the previous Government

was rather complex, and it was difficult to see where the benefits lay, and to whom.

5.14   Another variation, suggested by a number of those who submitted evidence from the Insurance Industry, most notably by the Norwich Union, suggested a limit of a period of say four years to an individual's potential liability for the cost of their care. This has the merit of establishing a sense of clarity as to what people will need to provide for themselves and, in limiting the amount of liability which the insurance policy would have to cover, might bring down the cost of private insurance policies. We were quoted figures from a number of companies which suggested a decrease in premiums ranging from 10% to 27% – presumably explained by different underwriting or claims criteria. If care costs only were covered (leaving the individual to pay for their own living and housing costs) we estimated costs to the state to be in the region of **£250m**. If the period were three years or two years the costs would be **£360m** and **£510m** respectively. Making all care free under such circumstances would, we estimate, cost **£450m**, **£650m** and **£900m** respectively.

5.15   If there were to be no other major changes to the current system, and the Government were keen to come to a clear position with citizens as to their personal liability, this kind of partnership might have some attractions. It is simple, and clear. People would be in no doubt as to the limit of their potential liability. A couple at 65, seeking a policy with inflation cover, which might cost say 15% (in the mid-range of discounts we were quoted) less than current policies, would need to find around £22,000 to provide cover for themselves. This could come out of an occupational pension lump sum, or it could be bought using equity release. To do the latter, using a shared appreciation mortgage, a house worth £88,000 would be needed. So a large number of people would not be able to insure for the period of their liability, most of whom would be subject to the current means test during that period.

5.16   We have already remarked on people with moderate assets, who seem to suffer disproportionately more under the current system. The great majority of residents die within four years. People with assets between £16,000 and £60,000 would therefore be likely to have died within the period of their own liability and would have used up the value of all of their assets. This group are perhaps unlikely to be able to afford private insurance. In order to have any effect on this group, the four-year proposal would need to be accompanied by changes to the means test. We discuss these later. For people to benefit from this proposal they would need to have assets which could buy insurance for four years AND they would need to survive for more than four years. The numbers who would benefit overall would therefore be small. If the Government were to decide that the private insurance industry required some support this proposal would clearly provide it. Of itself however, it does not appear to do very much to help the Commission achieve its wider aims.

Tax incentives — to take out policies or to use pension lump sum

5.17   It has been suggested that self-provision could be encouraged by giving tax relief on long term care insurance premiums.

5.18   The problem with tax relief and other tax concessions is that normally they are given by Government on money going into or coming out of pensions and insurance schemes, but such concessions are not given at both ends (the tax-free pension lump sum is a rare exception). Currently the proceeds of LTCI policies, with the exception of some immediate needs annuities, are free of income tax for the person needing care. If the tax position were reversed and tax relief were given on premiums in order to boost sales, all those buying policies would gain, but the benefits of the one in five needing care would be taxed. This would be hard to justify. Some Insurers have suggested that a better-targeted way to encourage self-provision might be to increase automatically the tax-free allowances of those receiving benefits from LTC insurance.

5.19   In any event, evidence that tax relief would increase insurance sales is hard to find. To take an analogous example, tax relief was not originally offered on health insurance. When it was subsequently given, sales did not increase vastly. However, when tax relief was recently withdrawn, many people, particularly older people, let their health policies lapse because they could no longer afford them. This may indicate that insurance of this kind is only marginally affordable for older people.

5.20   There are a number of disincentives to taking out private insurance at the moment, in that benefits in cash or in kind count against means tested benefits. Removing these disincentives has been suggested as a way of encouraging the take-up of such policies.

5.21   Were the Treasury to consider a change in the rules regarding the tax free lump sum, they might consider preserving an element solely if it were used to purchase long term care Insurance, although these are matters far beyond the Commission's Terms of Reference. The National Association of Pension Funds (NAPF) said to the Commission that effectively to compel people to use their lump sums in this way would prevent many people being able to pay off their mortgages, and would entail them losing up to a quarter of their pension rights which are currently reflected in lump sums.

Equity Release Schemes

5.22   Equity release schemes are often promoted as a means to enable older people to buy LTCI or for other purposes in old age. The Council of Mortgage Lenders estimates that in 1996, £367bn in unmortgaged equity was available to UK homeowners aged 60+ at an average of around £72,500 per dwelling[31] Around 40% of older homeowners are income poor but equity rich – they have for example, an income of less than £12,000 pa but a house which represents a considerable asset (see Table 2.3). Homeowners in the south eastern regions of England have homes of higher value (the majority of homeowners aged 60+ in northern England have property worth between £25,000 – £50,000 and incomes below £8,000)[32].

5.23   To buy LTC Insurance a couple aged 65 would need about £25,600 to buy single premium LTCI policies with 15% rpi cover, each offering benefits of £1,000 per month for life.

5.24   Current equity release products are of varying complexity and seek to enable householders to release equity without moving (trading down). They form a major potential market for lenders but at present take-up is small. Products currently on the market are described in Research Volume 2. The new shared appreciation mortgages seem the most promising from the borrower's point of view, but these are not available on property worth less than £60,000 (which excludes many homes owned by older people in some parts of the country). They normally allow you to realise a quarter of the value of your house – therefore the couple in paragraph 5.16 would require a house worth around £100,000. Availability of this mortgage source may be limited – it depends on the mortgagees' willingness to commit capital to long-term investment.

5.25 The evidence is that equity release could help better-off older people who are homeowners, particularly those living in areas of high property prices, to fund long-term care, but recent work shows that it will not be an overall solution[33]:

■ two-fifths of all people aged 65 and over have no housing equity – although this may change in the future;

■ the confidence of older people in equity release products was severely dented by defective home income plans in the late 1980s which left buyers worse off. Demand has been slow to recover;

■ older homeowners receiving Income Support or Council Tax Benefit have no incentive to release housing equity. If equity is released to provide an income, or a lump sum which is not spent immediately, it will be taken into account in assessing their entitlement to benefits. If the lump sum from equity release is spent in buying LTCI, the proceeds of the insurance will subsequently be included in local authority means tests. One suggestion is that an amount of annuity income generated by equity release should be disregarded for means tests, as a way of stimulating the market;

■ it is been calculated that only 20% of all those aged over 65 and 40% of all those over 75 could gain an increase in net income of at least £2.50 per week or £130 pa from an equity release annuity. Twenty-five per cent of those who would gain would get less than £500 extra per year. This would not help much with long-term care. Analysis of the distribution of housing equity and income shows that those with least need (the well-off in the south east) are best placed to use equity release schemes;

■ evidence submitted to the Commission by the Joseph Rowntree Foundation[34] suggests that older people are reluctant to put up their home to release equity with commercial lenders.

5.26 If the value of equity continues to rise nationally, in the future there may be more scope for equity release and products may be developed which will release enough money to buy long-term care policies of various kinds. This is a situation which should be monitored, and some of the mechanisms which we suggest later for monitoring developments in long-term care generally could be used to do this. Just because such policies would become affordable does not, of course, mean that people would necessarily want to buy them.

5.27 The Commission have come to the view that the most promising use of equity release to pay for long-term care is where individuals are able to buy into a scheme which has a care element included where it becomes necessary –

exchanging one home for another, but using some of the equity to buy into a form of group insurance. We saw one such scheme run by the Joseph Rowntree Trust near York. We encourage the development of such schemes, and think they should be marketed as a suitable and secure option for the future. However, because of the complexity of the nature of the contract which is being entered into, Government should satisfy itself that there are proper regulatory safeguards in place to give potential purchasers peace of mind.

5.28 Also, given that often one of the best ways of keeping people at home would be to enable them to purchase aids or adaptations, some mechanism for releasing small amounts of equity by loans from Local Authorities may have value. We examine this later in Chapter 8.

Using Pensions

5.29 Financial institutions and members of the public have suggested that pensions offer the potential flexibility needed to provide for long-term care but this is not a universal view:

- The ABI, whose members include many insurance companies providing pensions, suggests that many people would prefer a flexible single package to provide all their financial needs after retirement. Pension providers would like to be able to offer benefits on insurance principles to cover contingencies such as disability, medical insurance and long term care, but at present the tax rules do not allow them to provide these directly as part of an "approved" pension scheme. "Approval" is required for the pension investment to remain tax free. (The different tax treatment of pensions and insurance benefit would also be a complicating factor);

- Legal & General in its evidence to the Commission forecasts that equity linked annuities will be developed which will do more than just protect pensions against inflation – they will provide real growth sufficient for long-term care needs;

- The British Bankers Association suggest that the tax-free status of the occupational pension lump sum could be made conditional on part of it being used to buy LTCI. They also suggest that part of the pension could be deferred in return for a much higher annuity in extreme old age when the pensioner may incur LTC expenses. The Pensions Trust suggest a similar scheme which would allow money to be returned to the estate of the pensioner if no LTC expenses were incurred;

- The National Association of Pension Funds, representing some 800 occupational pension funds, does not support the use of pension funds to finance long-term care. It takes the view that the financing of a good supplementary pension should take priority over funding of long-term care. Many people may not be able to afford to forgo their lump sum for LTCI. Deferring pensions might impoverish younger pensioners, and in the British Bankers proposal pensioners would have to take a gamble on reaching extreme old age before death. It is difficult to tell how many people would take the risk;

■ Using occupational pensions to fund long-term care would result in reduced retirement pensions and make occupational pension schemes less attractive to employers.

Other Suggestions

5.30 Other suggestions made include offering Long-Term Care Insurance as an employee benefit. This would not seem to offer employees a great deal, and the Commission would be reluctant to suggest placing a compulsory burden on employers in this way.

5.31 Opt-outs from state provision have also been suggested, so that an individual will get a rebate for making their own provision. However, we feel that this would potentially leave the state with a disproportionate liability, as the industry will take on the clients who represent the least risk, and we did not think this worth pursuing.

REGULATION

5.32 Although this is not a central part of the Commission's remit, we wish to make some remarks on the regulation of the private insurance industry in relation to the provision of Long-Term Care Insurance. Over time, more people may choose to insure privately, particularly if as the result of the Commission's report, the responsibility of individuals to make their own provision is clarified. People may want to insure against the risk they are left with; they may want to buy higher standards, or even to insure against a change of policy by Government. The market will try to develop products to appeal in different ways.

5.33 We therefore believe very strongly that those who buy such products should be fully informed of the costs and benefits of new products which are devised and of the alternatives available to them. The current regulatory position is that some such products are classed as investment under the 1986 Financial Services Act and are thus fully regulated. The great majority of LTCI products contain no investment element and are therefore not regulated, save for prudential regulation by the Treasury's insurance directorate.

5.34 We regard this position as unsatisfactory. Most LTCI products are sold and are likely to be sold to older people either on retirement (often drawing on their lump-sum pensions entitlement) or, as in the case of so-called "point of use" policies, when they go into residential care. On top of the generally low level of financial understanding amongst the population therefore, risk is magnified as purchasers may be older and indeed at a moment of stress or even of crisis in their lives. Moreover, they require not only information about the products but about the alternatives. Such advice can only be given by someone with a detailed understanding of the State's benefits system. Many financial advisers are likely to be under-equipped in this area, as are many other professionals in the field.

5.35 The Government's reform of financial regulation, announced last year, provides an opportunity to rectify this situation. The draft Financial Services Bill does not itself provide for the regulation of the sale of such products. It does however provide for the Treasury to extend regulation to introduce it.

5.36   The companies that provide the policies have indicated a desire for regulation. Providers have learned from the pensions misselling scandal which has not only cost many billions of pounds in compensation but has also damaged confidence in private pensions provision. Although regulation might add to the costs of providing such policies, they do want a regulatory regime in place to prevent abuse.

5.37.   *The Commission recommends therefore that the Treasury and the FSA urgently begin work designed to bring all private long-term care insurance within the ambit of conduct-of-business regulation at the earliest possible date.* **(Recommendation 5.1)**

CONCLUSION ON PRIVATE SECTOR OPTIONS

5.38   Left to grow without intervention, there seems little reason to think that private insurance will become more important in the UK than it has become over a 14-year period of development in America. At present only 4% – 5% of Americans have taken out LTCI, while 10% – 20% could afford to do so and 80% – 90% could not afford the cost in any event. Marketing through employers and partnership schemes with State Governments have been introduced in America and equity release products are available. According to expert witnesses, and the evidence cited earlier to a Senate committee, private insurance is not now, and is unlikely to become, the major way of funding long-term care in America.

5.39   The industry believe that public education, clarity about what benefits will be available in the future from the public sector and some change in market conditions for the sale of private insurance might increase take-up of policies. For example, some of them said that disregarding insurance benefit for means tests, or a co-payment system, would make insurance more attractive and affordable. Failing this, or compulsion, policies are unlikely to become universally affordable. long-term care is too remote a risk for many people to think of taking out insurance when they are younger – and 10% of applicants will be refused cover anyway on health grounds. The insurance companies consider that regulation of sales of LTCI would promote confidence in their products.

5.40   The Commission conclude that private sector solutions do not and in the forseeable future, will not offer a universal solution. Even schemes for partnership can make only a limited contribution. Inevitably, of course, people may consider one of the many schemes available from the private sector to be worthwhile for them provided they can pay the premiums. Overall however, the funding problem cannot therefore be solved by the private sector.

Footnotes

(viii) In this chapter we have been greatly assisted by the work of a number of researchers, especially Tania Burchardt and John Hills, whose published research for the Joseph Rowntree Foundation, Private Welfare Insurance and Social Security (1997)[28] sets out many of the issues on the role of Private Insurance in Long-Term Care.

(ix)   Genetic tests which may indicate if an individual has a high risk of contracting Alzheimer's disease are now being produced and LTCI companies have an interest in these as a way of minimising adverse selection. The ABI issued a voluntary Code of Practice on genetic testing in January 1998, recently approved by the Government. Under this insurers may not ask people to take a genetic test and existing results will only be taken into account when accepted as reliable. The Government will work with the insurance industry to develop a system to validate them.

WITH RESPECT TO OLD AGE

Chapter 6
Improving Public Provision

This chapter considers the scope for and desirability of increases in the scale of public sector provision towards the costs of long-term care. It describes and evaluates a series of costed options, with the Commission's views on the priority of each.

INTRODUCTION

6   The starting point of this chapter is the key conclusion of Chapter 5, that private financial products whether through the purchase of insurance or annuities are not the basis of a solution to the funding of long-term care. As with the funding of health services, the role of the private sector will in our view essentially be supplementary to public provision for the immediate future. In the options set out below for improving public provision we indicate the role which we would expect private financial provision to play in relation to each of them.

THE CURRENT SYSTEM

6.1   The starting point of our analysis is the present system of state funding of long-term care described in Chapter 4. As noted in paragraph 4.50, this system provides variable amounts of state help to older people who are eligible for it by virtue of their lack of means. It costs some £7.1bn a year, representing taxes of 2.2% of earnings, pensions and investments.

6.2   If the present system were to continue unchanged the contributions required to pay for it in future from an insurance or tax based system would be as in the following Table 6.1[(x)].

Table 6.1: Notional contribution base to pay for public sector costs of existing system of long-term care, UK 1995 prices

Payment basis	Now (1995 prices)	2010	2021	2031	2051
Public Expenditure Costs of Care (£bn)	7.1	9.0	12.1	17.1	27.0
Tax base on earnings +pensions +investments%	2.2	1.8	2.0	2.0	2.1
% age of GDP	1.0	0.9	1.0	1.1	1.1

Source: Projections on contribution rates prepared for the Royal Commission by the Government Actuary's Department; Modelling on expenditure projections by PSSRU/London School of Economics[18].

OPTIONS FOR CHANGING THE CURRENT SYSTEM

We now set out options for building on this system.

Option 1: Disregard the value of the house for up to three months

6.3   Admissions to residential or nursing home care take place at a time of crisis for the people concerned. People are often placed permanently into care away from their own homes when there is a chance of possibly returning. We therefore considered whether any element in the present funding system could be changed to encourage a period of assessment before permanent entry to care in a residential setting. This would allow scope for recuperation and, even more important, rehabilitation. When people with housing assets of more than £16,000 are initially admitted to care at present, they often have to make irrevocable decisions about the disposal of their home, with irreversible consequences for their future. It is true that local authorities have discretion to disregard the home in applying the means test for a short time, but its use depends on the individual authority's financial circumstances. Once the value of the house is taken into account, and it is deemed to be sold, permanent residential care can become virtually inevitable. This issue was clear to us from a number of letters from individuals and submissions from organisations. It was also raised by the Audit Commission at the Commission's seminar on Community Care[35].

"We were absolutely horrified to be advised . . . that should my wife or myself finish our days in a nursing home they would then allow my son six months to sell our home in order to meet the cost of our care . . . our son would then have to find accommodation elsewhere . . . surely this cannot be fair."

6.4   Our proposal is that, for purposes of means-testing, the value of the house should be completely disregarded for up to three months. This would allow time for people to recuperate and regain as much capability for independent living as they could. More expensive hospital beds would be freed up. After the three-month period, a proper assessment could be made as to whether residential care was appropriate. The arrangement should also include people entering long-term care from the community, for whom it would provide a better opportunity to assess whether they needed to leave home permanently. The potential benefits of the proposal are considerable in our view.

6.5   One potential disadvantage of this proposal is the risk of a perverse incentive in that the NHS might seek to accelerate the discharge of patients if some other organisation would pick up the bill. Rules would need to be put in place to ensure that the system was not exploited. Older patients themselves might be more ready to accept early discharge if they knew that their house was secure for the first three months. This suggests that the funding of this arrangement might lie with Health Authorities and Health Boards but on a ringfenced basis. A precedent for this approach is resources which the Government have made available to cope with winter pressures, allowing health authorities to work imaginatively and pragmatically with Local Authorities in helping older people avoid inappropriate hospital admissions.

6.6   The maximum cost of disregarding the value of the house for three months, based on the total annual number of people who enter long-term care each year and who do not qualify for any state support, would be **£90m** per year. It would help between 40,000 and 50,000 over the course of a year. To the extent that the proposal actually kept people out of long-term care altogether, through rehabilitation, there could be compensating savings. The medium to long-term cost implications of adding this proposal to the current system are set out in the following table.

Table 6.2: Estimates of health and social services expenditure with three month disregard for capital assets — UK at 1995 prices projected forward to 2051

Year	1995 prices	2010	2021	2031	2051
Cost: £billion (figures in brackets refer to base case)	7.2 (7.1)	9.1 (9.0)	12.3 (12.1)	17.3 (17.1)	27.5 (27.0)
Tax base on earnings +pensions +investments %	2.2	1.8	1.8	2.0	2.2
% GDP	1.0	0.9	1.0	1.1	1.1

Source: PSSRU model, Government Actuary's Department[18].

6.7   The Commission consider that this proposal, has significant potential benefits for the reasons given above. It is a "stand alone" option, in the sense that it could be introduced separately from or in addition to our other proposals. *We recommend that the Government disregard the value of a person's house for the first three months of entering care in a residential or nursing home.* **[Recommendation 6.1]**.

Option 2: Loans to prevent house sales

6.8   As a possible alternative to option 1 the Commission have considered whether a system of loans, underwritten by the state, might offer relief to people with assets above the means test limit from the pressure of having to sell their homes . This is technically possible now, in that a Local Authority can choose to take a charge on a house which is only realised at death. This approach is clearly convenient for the client. However, it is discretionary and depends on the circumstances of the client and of the individual authority.

6.9   Ultimately, such a scheme would aim to be cost neutral. However, there would need to be an initial outlay of potentially between £1bn and £2.8bn if the aim were to meet from loans all care costs of people with more than £16,000 in capital. The scheme would soon start to bring in receipts from repayments, and as a result costs to the public sector would reduce. But if it were to be fully cost neutral, Local Authorities would need to fund transaction costs and charge interest on loans.

6.10   Government attempts to interest the private banking sector in this sort of scheme have a chequered history. The Commission think it unlikely that renewed interest would emerge in this area. Moreover, the scheme would be complex to establish, and to administer, probably very expensive initially and would leave the state with an uncertain liability. If Local Authorities administered it, they might be left with a complex burden of assets which would differ greatly from one part of the country to another. The Commission consider there little overall benefit to be gained from such a scheme. We do not recommend it.

Option 3: Changing the Means Test

6.11   As noted in paragraph 4.14, if people have assets of less than £10,000 per year these are completely disregarded for the provision of long-term care. People with capital between £10,000 and £16,000 are assumed to have an additional income, based on a **tariff** which assumes a rate of £1 a week for every £250 in assets – or £4 in every £1,000. The tariff is meant to reflect a notional income attributable to the asset. Actual investment income is not taken account of. This notional income is added to other income and is deemed to be paid towards the cost of care. People with assets of more than £16,000 must meet all residential and nursing home fees themselves, and may or may not have to pay for domiciliary care depending on local authority policies.

6.12   As set out in Chapter 4, in our view the arrangements for the means test are too punitive. In particular, people with relatively modest means, for example with property or other capital worth less than £60,000, might lose all of their assets when they go into care and live for an average length of stay of three years. The system seems to impact on them to a far greater extent than those with higher levels of assets. Due to the huge contrast between having assets of £15,999 and £16,001, the system as it stands encourages people to rid themselves of assets whenever they can. "Cheating the system" becomes a strong incentive for worried and vulnerable people, and their families.

6.13   On top of this, and even more important, it is abundantly clear to us that many of the current generation of middle aged and older people feel strongly that to force the means test on them when they are old, when many of them have sought to avoid it during their working lives, is particularly insidious and unfair. We believe these views are genuine and will not necessarily disappear over time. They require a positive response of some kind.

6.14 Clearly there are several ways of changing the means-test system. They include:

- raising the upper capital limit – that is, to widen the band within which people make some contribution to care costs. This is potentially the least-cost way of tackling the means test, especially if current "tariff" levels (see paragraph 4.14) are maintained;

- raising the lower limit, below which assets are not taken into account. This would clearly be considerably more expensive than raising the upper limit as it would benefit those who gain to a greater extent;

- abolishing the assets element of the means test altogether;

- making the income "tariff" more generous.

6.15 Table 6.3 sets out the effect of altering the means test capital limits under a range of scenarios. These are orders of magnitude rather than precise costings. All of these would entitle more people to state help with the costs of long-term care, precise numbers depending on the limits chosen. However, there would always be a dividing line between those who benefit and those who do not.

Table 6.3: Additional annual public cost of varying rates of notional tariff income and asset limits, UK

	Notional tariff income			
	£4 per £1,000 (per week) Current level	£3 per £1,000 (per week)	£2 per £1,000 (per week)	£1 per £1,000 (per week)
No upper limit Lower limit £10k	£160m–£215m	£240m–£330m	£370m–£500m	£575m –£775m
Upper limit £60k Lower limit £10k	£150m–£200m	£200m–£270m	£245m–£330m	£270m–£370m
Upper limit £40k Lower limit £10k	£75m–£120m	£80m–£140m	£100m–£150m	£115m–£175m
Upper limit £30k Lower limit £10k	£55m–£80m	£55m–£85m	£65m–£100m	£70m–£105m
Upper limit £60k Lower limit £40k	£270m–£460m	£270m–£465m	£285m–£485m	£295–£505m
Upper limit £60k Lower limit £30k	£220m–£395m	£245m–£420m	£265m–£445m	£285m–£480m
Upper limit £60k Lower limit £20k	£170m–£310m	£200m–£360m	£240m–£405m	£270m–£460m

Note: The figures are broad UK estimates based on the current population of 100,000 private residents, at current prices. These figures are not net of any potential savings in disability benefits which may accrue.

6.16 Irrespective of the capital limits themselves, there would also be considerable regional variations in the effect of the means test. People living in high property value areas are less likely to be entitled to state help than people in areas where prices are lower. Wider gains of social cohesion and inclusiveness will not be found consistently within this option on its own.

6.17 Reliable figures on the income and assets of people in long-term residential care who meet their own costs are not available. However, DSS analysis of the income and assets of single older people aged 75 and over in private households gives a very broad indication of how altering the upper limit of the means test might bring such people within the state system. It illustrates what proportion of the population of single over 75s would be eligible under the means test for help should they require it as a consequence of going into long-term care at the point which they enter care. The following table illustrates the position. This does **not** show the numbers who would receive care – only a proportion of the percentage would require it. These figures are, we emphasise, rough, and intended to be illustrative:

Table 6.4: Estimated distribution of assets, including housing, of single people in private households aged 75 and over as a proxy for eligibility for state support in residential care at various means test thresholds, UK

Asset threshold (upper limit)	Percentage of single people over 75 theoretically brought within state support system to some degree (%)
Under £16K (as now)	44
Raise to £20K	45
Raise to £30K	48
Raise to £40K	51
Raise to £50K	54
Raise to £60K	60
Raise to £70K	66
Raise to £80K	71
Raise to £90K	76
Raise to £100K	80
£100K +	100

Source: DSS analysis of 1995/96 Family Resources Survey.[18]

6.18   Table 6.4 suggests that the present upper capital limit of £16,000 entitles only about 44% of single old people over 75 to **some** state support towards long-term residential care costs. In our view this is inadequate. In order to bring worthwhile help to people of moderate means who are liable to forfeit all their assets, the current upper limit should be raised to at least £40,000 and desirably to £60,000, thus increasing the present 44% to 60% at a cost of between £75m and £200m. A higher limit could be set at greater cost, but the figures suggest that successive increases above £60,000 would benefit progressively fewer people.

6.19   Alternatively or additionally it would be possible to mitigate the impact of the current income "tariff", for example by reducing the assumed income of £4 a week for each £1,000 of capital to £3. Such changes could cost in the range £100m–£330m a year depending on the option chosen. This would benefit the same number of people, but to a greater extent. In our view the preferable course of action would be to raise the upper capital limit.

6.20   In paragraphs 6.27 to 6.37 we describe and advocate a radical restructuring of means-testing (option (6)). We prefer this option to adjustment of the current means-test limit. If any adjustment were to be made to those limits *we recommend the Government raise the upper capital limit to £60,000 while leaving the lower limit and the income tariff unchanged, subject to review every three years in advance of the Comprehensive Spending Review.* **(Recommendation 6.2)** This option would benefit an estimated additional 40,000 residents at a time who would become entitled to some degree of state help with long-term care costs depending on their means. Private resources would need to meet the remaining costs which could still be substantial in many cases. The additional costs would be between £150m and £200m a year. The medium to long-term cost implications (based on a mid-range cost of £175m) are set out in Table 6.5. We consider the related question of charges for domiciliary care in paragraphs 6.49 to 6.53.

Table 6.5: Estimates of health and social services expenditure with an upper limit of the means test extended to £60,000 at current "tariff" rates — UK at 1995 prices

Year	1995 prices	2010	2021	2031	2051
Cost £billion (figure in brackets refer to base case)	7.2 (7.1)	9.3 (9.0)	12.5 (12.1)	17.7 (17.1)	28.0 (27.0)
Tax base on earnings +pensions +investments %	2.2	1.8	1.8	2.0	2.2
% GDP	1.0	1.0	1.0	1.1	1.1

Source: PSSRU model, Government Actuary's Department[18].

Option 4: Further measures to alleviate the means test

6.21   The Commission have identified other possible ways of alleviating the impact of the means test. They include.

(1) **Limiting liability to pay to four years.** Under this arrangement, the present means-testing system for care costs would remain, but would apply for a maximum of four years after which all care would be provided free. The cost would be up to £250m a year if it only covered personal care costs (see definition of personal care costs in paragraphs 6.43 to 6.48), and £450m if all elements of long-term care were covered. We discussed such schemes under partnership proposals in Chapter 5. We do not support this option because its potential benefits would be limited to people who had higher assets and happened to live longer. People with assets of under say £80,000 would be unlikely to benefit, as they would have spent them down before the period of free care arose. It would only be of use in conjunction with other options, by which time the amount of money required to be spent would involve a more radical change to the means test. The main justification for this scheme would be to help the insurance industry. We believe there are better ways to use this amount of resources to improve funding arrangements.

(2) **Introducing a solely income-based means test.** This is an approach similar to that used in the United States, which has a means test with a low-income limit, but does not take the value of the house into account. Removing the capital element from the means test would cost around £1bn a year. The emotive and practical problems associated with property would be removed, but new perverse incentives would be introduced, encouraging people to convert income into capital. In any case, the amount of wealth expressed as income amongst pensioners is very low, hence the cost to the public purse. There is some evidence in the United States of more mobility between home and different residential settings. This may be a good thing in itself, but equally may reflect pressures from different sources of funding, and might not always be in the best interests of the people concerned. There are better ways of using the resources that would be involved. We do not support this option.

(3) **Abolishing the means test altogether and treating benefits derived in respect of relief of long-term care costs as taxable.** Packages of care would be costed, the value of the care delivered notified to the Inland Revenue, who would tax the individual accordingly. This might appear to be a simple way of operating and replacing an income related means test, which would have similar costs. However, quite apart from the administrative implication the value of the benefits is so high that pensioners would pay more tax. We see little or no merit in such a scheme.

Option 5: Exempting Nursing Care from means-testing wherever it is delivered

6.22   At present, if a person receives nursing care – that is care which involves the knowledge or skills of a qualified nurse, either in a nursing home or a home which is registered to provide both nursing and residential care – he or she has to pay for the nursing care as part of the home's fees (subject to means testing). If however, comparable nursing care is delivered in a hospital or community setting it is completely free to the user. This state of affairs is not justified or defensible. It would hardly be acceptable to begin charging for nursing care in hospital. The right way forward therefore is to abolish charges for nursing provided in nursing homes and dual registration homes. We believe that this should be done.

6.23 Care would however be needed to avoid instituting a new set of perverse incentives. For example, if a home had both nursing and residential places, it might under some circumstances be in the interests of whoever ran the home to fill a nursing place in preference to a residential place. The gateway to more expensive nursing beds would need to be carefully controlled and should be based on a proper assessment of need.

6.24 A possible way of achieving this might be for each publicly assessed place in a nursing or dual registration home to be subject to a subsidy from the Health Authority to meet the part of the fee reflecting this element of care, possibly costing £100 a week, based on the average difference of costs between residential and nursing homes. This would involve a technical transfer to the NHS from Local Authorities. In this way the Local Authority would pay a similar fee whether the client was in a residential or nursing bed. The assessment would decide whether additional NHS money should be brought into play, thus minimising the risk of a perverse incentive and encouraging joint assessment.

6.25 Assuming that the additional nursing costs would be £100 a week, this proposal would cost £220m a year and would potentially benefit 42,500 people who pay for their own care in nursing homes. The medium to long-term cost implications are set out in the following table.

6.26 *The Commission consider that this option has much merit and recommend it should be implemented. It could stand alone, but in practice would be subsumed by the wider restructuring of the means-testing system we propose in option 6.* **(Recommendation 6.3)**

Table 6.6: Estimates of health and social services expenditure where nursing care in residential settings is provided free — UK at 1995 prices projected forward to 2051

Year	1995 Prices	2010	2021	2031	2051
Cost £billion (figures in brackets refer to base case)	7.3 (7.1)	9.4 (9.0)	12.6 (12.1)	17.9 (17.1)	28.5 (27.0)
Tax base on earnings +pensions +investments %	2.2	1.9	2.0	2.0	2.2
% GDP	1.0	1.0	1.0	1.1	1.1

Source: PSSRU model, Government Actuary's Department.[18]

Option 6: A major restructuring of the payment system for residential care

6.27 Some of the options set out above, however meritorious in themselves, would amount to little more than tinkering with the means-testing system. The benefits they would offer, and the numbers who would gain would be relatively small. In our view implementing these options, even as a package, would not do justice to the scale of the problems with the present system as we have identified them or to the strength of the views expressed by those we consulted. We consider that the only fair and practical way forward is to make entitlement to state financial support more universal than now, reflecting the criteria we have identified in Chapters 3 and 4. The aim must be to bring significant help particularly to people with relatively modest means whom the present system does not serve well.

6.28   Against this background we have therefore sought to consider, from first principles, where the balance between collective public provision and personal responsibility should lie in relation to paying for long-term care. What follows represents our analysis and our conclusions, in respect first of residential care and secondly of domiciliary care.

6.29   In principle, people in long-term care incur three kinds of cost (excluding the kind of therapeutic care which is provided by the NHS and is free in any event):

(1) living costs, (food, clothing, heating amenities and so on);

(2) housing costs (the equivalent of rent, mortgage payments and council tax) and;

(3) personal care costs (the additional cost of being looked after arising from frailty or disability).

6.30   It is admittedly a fine point in some cases as to the category into what particular costs should fall. We comment on this in paragraphs 6.43 to 6.48. The key point is that no distinction is currently drawn in principle between these costs in applying the means test. Where the operation of means-testing results in people having to meet some or all of residential or nursing home fees, they are regarded in principle as contributing equally to all three cost elements of the fees. This system is indiscriminate and illogical.

6.31   We judge instead that a proper distinction should now be drawn for funding purposes between the three cost elements in long-term care. A case has been put to us that the state should meet all three elements, as it does for people in hospital. We do not think however, that this is desirable or necessary. Nor would it be a proper use of limited public funds. People who receive care at home have to meet their living and housing costs themselves. The same should apply for people in residential settings. In our judgement therefore people should be fully responsible for elements (1) and (2), that is, their living and housing costs while in residential care, subject to the normal mechanisms for supporting income, subject to a means test if help is required. These are legitimate items for which people may want to save in their old age.

". . . so many of my contemporaries have had so much NHS money spent on them over the years. Aneurisms, heart operations, orthopaedic . . . they have not been charged at all. Does it seem fair that the mentally ill have to be charged for when someone physically ill can have it free whatever their income?"

6.32   The costs of personal care as such are however quite different. These are the costs which, unpredictably and through no fault of their own, old people have to incur when unfortunately they can no longer be looked after at home or cannot be sent home after hospital treatment. They reflect the true risk and "catastrophic" nature of needing long-term care.

In our judgement it is right for the state to exempt personal care from means-testing altogether. This is our key recommendation.

6.33   The justification for our view is based on considerations of both equity and efficiency. Whereas the state through the NHS pays for all the care needs of sufferers from, for example cancer and heart disease, people who suffer from Alzheimer's disease may get little or no help with the cost of comparable care needs. All these conditions are debilitating, but Alzheimer's disease cannot yet be cured by medical intervention. However, a mixture of all types of care, including personal care will be needed. This is directly analagous to the kind of care provided for cancer sufferers. The latter get their care free. The former have to pay.

6.34   For this reason, the distinction between the way care is offered for different diseases has no justification. The situation must be put right. The proposal to exempt personal care costs from means-testing would do that.

6.35   We believe that this proposal would also enhance the dignity and security of old people, issues key to in our terms of reference. Independence, self-respect, dignity and choice have been highlighted as objectives of community care policy generally, though as we noted in Chapter 4, have rarely been attained in the current system. In evaluating approaches to funding, a key concern of the Commission has been to ensure that funding arrangements do not unduly limit older people's choice of care, distort their preferences through unsatisfactory incentives, or create stigma. The current system all too frequently reveals its poor-law antecedence, which the options set out earlier in this chapter would not wholly dispel. This proposal would go a long way to making services provided for long-term care as valued and as jealously guarded as those provided by the National Health Service. The principle of equal care for equal needs would be properly recognised for the first time.

6.36   From the point of view of efficiency we consider that the extension of universality, through the collective approach entailed by the proposal, is the most efficient way of covering the risks of having to meet long-term care costs. Measured against this, the arbitrariness and practical problems of rigorous means-testing, the market failures of private insurance and the uncertainty of relying on peoples' private incomes or savings do not rank highly. The new certainty conveyed by this proposal as to the nature of future state provision could also enable the insurance industry to develop new financial products to cover the areas of individual responsibility.

6.37   *The Commission's main recommendation is that personal care should be available for those individuals who need it, after an assessment.*
(Recommendation 6.4) The rest of this Chapter discusses how this would work, and how it would apply to Care at Home.

Summary of this option

6.38   In summary, option (6) would mean a radical restructuring of the current residential care means-testing system, first to take personal care costs out of the system altogether, and secondly to apply the current means-testing limits and scales to living and housing costs as a new form of co-payment. This proposal would subsume the means-testing relaxation set out in option (3), because it would be more favourable overall. It would also automatically subsume option (5), because the nursing costs in question would be included as personal care costs.

6.39 In practical terms the proposal would work in one of two ways. Either the Government would determine each year the amount of residential charge to be attributed to personal care as distinct from living and housing costs. This would be a standard, UK wide figure to be applied by all local authorities. This sum would be met by the state. The sum would then be deducted from the actual charges made in individual residential homes, leaving the balance representing living and housing costs. People would be personally responsible for these amounts, to be met from income, savings or insurance along with the rest of the population. We refer to this as co-payment. The existing means-testing limits on benefits would remain, entitling people with little means to help with the charges for living and housing.

6.40 Alternatively, the Government could determine a UK-wide amount to be attributed to living and housing costs, to be met by individuals as in the previous paragraph. This would be the obverse of the approach in paragraph 6.38, as in this event the state would meet the balance of actual – charges representing personal care costs. In principle, the Commission would prefer the approach set out in paragraph 6.38, although acknowledges that there may be practical difficulties to be overcome in doing so. For the purposes of calculating costs, we have assumed average costs – £242 a week in residential care, £337 a week in nursing home care. We have assumed living and housing cost charges of £120 based on current pension and benefit levels, leaving personal care costs of £122 and £217 for residential and nursing home care.

6.41 If necessary, this proposal could be implemented incrementally, by prescribing a lower initial figure for personal care costs which the state would meet, with stepped increases over time as resources become available. Alternatively, should Governments in the future judge that over time, people could and should be expected to meet more care costs from their own resources, the figure could be set initially high with stepped decreases over the years. This would, over time, reduce the public expenditure costs of the option, as richer people would be paying more from their own resources, while poorer people would be subject to a means test for income and housing costs, thus responding to changes in comparative wealth. However, the possible effect of incentives to different authorities should also be considered. We express no views one way or the other on the merits of such options. Clearly however, they and variants on them would be available to the Government.

6.42 The immediate cost of this option is likely to be in the range of £800m–£1.0bn in the base year, assuming a deemed personal care cost of £122 a week in residential care and £217 in nursing home care and a living costs element of £120 per week. We estimate that between 100,000 to 125,000 people would benefit. This is an over-estimate to the extent that not all of them might be assessed under the care definition set out in paragraphs 6.43 to 6.48 as needing long-term care. The medium to long-term cost implications, which assumes that 125,000 people benefit in the first year at a cost of £1.0bn are as set out in Table 6.7. Note that the additional sum represents only 25% of the private resources currently devoted to long term care.

Table 6.7: Estimates of health and social services expenditure where personal care is provided without charge (normal living costs in residential care of £120 per week, personal care costs of £122 in residential care and £217 in nursing home care) UK at 1995 prices

Year	1995 Prices	2010	2021	2031	2051
Cost £billion (figures in brackets refer to base case)	8.1 (7.1)	10.7 (9.0)	14.5 (12.1)	20.5 (17.1)	33.0 (27.0)
Tax base on earnings +pensions +investments %	2.4	2.1	2.1	2.4	2.5
% GDP	1.2	1.1	1.2	1.3	1.3

Source: PSSRU model, Government Actuary's Department.[18]

DEFINITION OF PERSONAL CARE

6.43   By "personal care" in this option the Commission mean the care needs which give rise to the major additional costs of frailty or disability associated with old age. We deliberately do not use the term "health care" or "social care" because of the confusion which now surrounds those terms and their association with particular agencies or forms of funding. Personal care is care that directly involves touching a person's body (and therefore incorporates issues of intimacy, personal dignity and confidentiality), and is distinct both from treatment/therapy (a procedure deliberately intended to cure or ameliorate a pathological condition) and from indirect care such as home-help or the provision of meals. This type of care is the main source of contention in the debate about the distinction between health care and social care. It falls within the internationally recognised definition of nursing, but may be delivered by many people who are not nurses, in particular by care assistants employed by social services departments or agencies.

6.44   Personal care, because it directly involves touching a person's body, incorporates issues of intimacy, personal dignity and confidentiality. Because of risks associated with poor personal care (e.g. risks of infection or skin breakdown), it is important that when the level or type of care needed becomes greater than can normally be provided at home by a relative or informal carer, careful assessment is made of how best it can be provided and by whom. It, therefore, differs qualitatively from living costs and housing costs. In recommending that personal care should be exempted from means testing, we are not recommending that this should happen on demand. Far from it, we have stressed throughout our report the importance of proper assessment of need.

Definition of Personal Care

Personal care would cover all direct care related to:

- personal toilet (washing, bathing, skin care, personal presentation, dressing and undressing and skin care);

- eating and drinking (as opposed to obtaining and preparing food and drink);

- managing urinary and bowel functions (including maintaining continence and managing incontinence);

- managing problems associated with immobility;

- management of prescribed treatment (e.g. administration and monitoring medication),

- behaviour management and ensuring personal safety (for example, for those with cognitive impairment – minimising stress and risk).

Personal care also includes the associated teaching, enabling, psychological support from a knowledgeable and skilled professional, and assistance with cognitive functions (e.g. reminding, for those with dementia) that are needed either to enable a person to do these things for himself/herself or to enable a relative to do them for him/her.

6.45   We acknowledge that this definition could be regarded as on the tight side. It would, for example, exclude costs attributable to:

- cleaning and housework;

- laundry;

- shopping services;

- specialist transport services (e.g. dial-a-ride);

- sitting services where the purpose is company or companionship.

6.46   However, the Commission have had to draw the line in a practical way. We consider it reasonable that the state should not meet such costs other than through means-testing, on the basis that although they may contain an element of care they are in principle "living" costs.

6.47   Housing costs would similarly be the responsibility of individuals (subject to the existing means-test) across all the locations in which long-term care is provided, whether in people's own homes (owned or rented), nursing and residential care homes, and including sheltered and supported housing schemes. These would cover:

- The cost of the place where the person lives;

- The "normal living cost" element in residential care, and where applicable, very sheltered settings, including lighting; heating; laundry; alarms; nonpersonal care related services such as wardens. This latter aspect will need fuller consideration in the light of the response to the Government Consultation Paper *Supporting People*[37].

6.48   The conceptual simplicity of the distinction which we have drawn in paragraph 6.44 between the three different elements of the cost of care, and the rationale underlying our recommendations as to how they should be treated for funding purposes, must not be allowed to be obscured by fine arguments as to the category into which particular costs should fall. The proposal has the potential merit of offering for the first time a logical, understandable, workable and above all just approach to the issue of funding.

CARE AT HOME

6.49   As we have pointed out elsewhere in our Report many recipients of long-term care live at home. As Chapter 8 explains, it should be a policy objective to enable even more people to do so, thus avoiding the trauma and costs of going into residential care. Against this background, and in the light of our proposal to restructure the residential means-test so as to exempt personal care costs, we have considered the issue of charging for care services provided in the home.

6.50   As noted in paragraph 4.6, local authorities have the discretion to charge for the provision of domiciliary care services. However, there are wide variations in both the services charged for and the charges imposed. These charges raised about £160m in 1995/96, representing about 10% of gross costs. Much of this income is in respect of services such as meals on wheels, lunch clubs and relatively simple domestic help. However, about one third represents fees for more intensive care delivered to people who have difficulty with at least one activity of daily living. We acknowledge the Government's view in the Social Services White Paper [23] about the case for expansion of home care charges though the House of Commons Health Select Committee[38] has recently expressed a different view.

6.51   The Commission consider that some distinction should be made between domiciliary services based on the level and type of need and the services provided. In line with our proposal for residential care we consider that what can be regarded as personal care should be exempt from charging, leaving charges to apply only in respect of meals, lunch clubs and domestic help which are more akin to living costs. Given pensioners' incomes, the scope for charging the full costs of domiciliary care is limited in any event. An arrangement under which charges were made for low-level domestic help, but not for the more intensive kind of personal care delivered at home, would be realistic and fair to people as their degree of dependency increased.

6.52   This approach should provide an incentive to the expansion of domiciliary care in the long term, enabling people to stay at home. In this event, however, demand would be likely to rise. This might increase costs depending on how many people currently paying for themselves would want publicly provided home care **and** would meet the assessment criteria. In our view, the proposed restructuring of means-testing for domiciliary services should be accompanied by measures to ensure that whatever charges are levied for domiciliary care are on a nationally consistent basis, with no discretion for local authorities to opt out of the system.

They should be designed in such a way that does not discourage poorer people from seeking or taking help. Any means test should be income based and take no account of capital. Flat rate charges would need to be set very low if the poorest were not to be discouraged, and for this reason are probably not the most practical solution.

6.53 The Commission's view is therefore that charges for domiciliary care should apply to the elements which amount to practical help only and set on a consistent basis across the United Kingdom. Charges for more intense personal care at home should be discontinued. The cost would be likely to be between £50m and £110m a year, depending on the take-up of services. Assessment of need would control use and therefore costs. Therefore, total costs for both residential and domiciliary care would be £1,120m. Figures in Table 6.8 shows the full estimated cost of the proposal to exempt personal care from means-testing.

Table 6.8: Estimates of health and social services expenditure where personal care is provided without charge in residential and domiciliary settings.(normal living costs in residential care of £120 per week, personal care costs of £122 in residential care and £217 in nursing home care) UK at 1995 prices

Year	1995 Prices	2010	2021	2031	2051
Cost £billion (figures in brackets refer to base case)	8.2 (7.1)	10.9 (9.0)	14.7 (12.1)	20.8 (17.1)	33.4 (27.0)
Tax base on earnings +pensions +investments %	2.5	2.1	2.1	2.4	2.6
% GDP	1.2	1.1	1.2	1.3	1.4

Source: PSSRU model, Government Actuary's Department.[18]

AIDS AND ADAPTATIONS

6.54 For the sake of completeness, we have considered our proposal for personal care costs in option (6) in relation to the provision of aids and home adaptations. These include items such as ramps, stairlifts, showers, special baths raised toilet seats, bath rails, kitchen aids, emergency and fire alarms. Who provides such items to those in need and whether or not they are subject to charges varies widely across the country. Some aids and adaptations are subject to co-payment while others are free at the point of use. The Audit Commission's Report, *Home Alone* (1998)[39] details the complex and confusing funding streams of which this forms part. It also points to the cost effectiveness of re-using adaptations such as stairlifts. In addition there are well documented problems with the length of time it can take to apply for and obtain a disabled facilities grant.

6.55   In Appendix 1, we set out a table of aids and adaptations, together with suggestions as to what should be charged for and what should not be charged for, on the broad principle consistent with our other recommendations that those which contribute to personal care should not be charged for.

WILL THE EXEMPTION OF PERSONAL CARE FROM MEANS-TESTING LEAD TO AN INCREASE IN DEMAND?

6.56   The simple assumption might be made that if something is made free which an individual was previously responsible out of their own pocket, demand for what was being offered might increase. The argument could be run that people might demand more care at home, they might want to go into a home if they are not responsible for meeting all the costs, and unpaid carers may decide not to provide care any more.

6.57   The nature of the commodity which is being offered should be considered. People will receive personal care who have a high level of need resulting from an exceptional level of disability.   Personal care is not something which can be viewed as a desirable consumer good in itself. To use another example, just because expensive open heart surgery is available on the NHS does not mean that people are claiming it as a right – they get it when their doctor deems they need it as a result of an exceptional medical condition. In the case of personal care, people will have access to it following an assessment of need.

6.58   In the case of Domiciliary Care, the levels of charging which relate to personal care are relatively small (£50 million) and so removing these charges is unlikely to bring about an enormous increase in demand.

6.59   In making estimates we have built in an assumed switch of all private expenditure on personal care to public sources – but we cannot estimate how much of this private expenditure would actually become publicly funded following assessment. Therefore, this over-estimate has within it an element for possible hidden demand – people who do not receive services now who might need them. There is no evidence available as to the amount of "hidden demand" which might exist.

6.60   International experience of changes in demand when public entitlements are increased is mixed, with examples of increased demand (Canada) and of no increase in demand (the Netherlands).

6.61   On carers, studies in the United States, France and England[40][41] suggest that there is limited substitution between informally provided services and those provided by the formal sector.

6.62   Therefore, it is difficult to tell whether or not demand will increase as a result of our proposals. We need to re-emphasis the problems which we have identified in the current system of providing this kind of care, and the role of the assessment system, which will aim to make the best use of resources without the perverse incentives of the current system.

RISING EXPECTATIONS

6.63   It could be argued that as expectations rise, people will demand more from the care system and demand more spending from the state. However, it can also be argued that the rise in expectations will occur in those elements of long-term care which can be offered to a variety of standards – such as accommodation, food, domestic help and other non-care elements. The nature of "personal care" is likely to stay the same. The costs related to rising expectations will continue to be paid by individuals according to their means.

FURTHER OBSERVATIONS ON THE METHOD OF FUNDING THE COMMISSION'S APPROACH

6.64   The earlier part of this chapter set out the Commission's options and proposals for improving the system of funding long-term care, so as to help redefine the relationship between the state and its citizens and remove the uncertainties and injustices of the present system. It remains to be considered how these proposals should be financed, in particular whether the system should be, as some argue, pre-funded in some way, or "pay as you go". If the latter, there is then the further question as to whether funding of long-term care should be via a hypothecated tax or based on general taxation.

6.65   Pre-funding involves the working generation paying into a fund (either voluntarily or compulsorily) which accumulates resources from which they will receive long-term care in the future. It offers an appearance of security in that the fund will pay out as required, providing enough is paid in. The Government Actuary's Department has calculated that, assuming a return on investment of 4% and other assumptions on growth as in the straight unfunded projections in the model, a contribution rate of 1.6% for a 20-year-old would be required if all long-term care were on a funded basis. The rates go up to 2.3% for a 30-year-old, 3.9% for a 40-year-old and 10.1% for a 50-year-old. This is in addition to the 2.17% they currently pay for people receiving services now – they therefore fund the transition from an unfunded to a funded system. Given the burdens on young people to make provision for pensions, to fund their own higher education, and the uncertainty of employment patterns, pre-funding of long-term care would arguably place an unacceptable burden on them.

6.66   There are other potential difficulties with pre-funding. The UK has a much larger element of pre-funding of its pension arrangements than most countries. To do the same for long-term care would add to the pool of pre-funding – adding burdens to the young and increasing the claims of the old on future consumption. Moreover, there is no certainty that pre-funding buys security. Such funds can be "raided" in various ways by future generations, but if the funds prove to be inadequate, potential beneficiaries will be left high and dry. Whatever the funding arrangements, real resource transfer from the working to the non-working population must take place at the point when resources are needed. Pre-funding makes no difference. In short, there is no guarantee that pre-funding, would provide what is required when care is needed.

6.67   We conclude therefore that, given the problems with pre-funding, provision for long-term care costs should in principle be on a "pay as you go" basis, under which current costs are paid for out of current taxes or contributions, as with state retirement pensions. This leaves the issue of whether "pay as you go" should operate through a hypothecated levy (specifically "ear marked") or simply rely on general taxation.

6.68   The arguments advanced in *favour* of hypothecation are that people might have the possibility of knowing how much they were paying for their long-term care and, how much money there was in the "fund" to pay for it. The money would be very visible – it would be there to pay for long-term care and nothing else. People would know what they were entitled to and would know when the entitlements were being changed by the Government. Finally, the introduction of hypothecation might appear as a clean break with the past and might therefore be a way of securing the trust of those who would rely on the system in the future.

6.69   Against hypothecation, it can be argued that it is inconsistent with the approach of successive Governments to funding public services. It reduces flexibility in budgeting and sets priorities in stone. There might be calls for hypothecation in other areas, notably the NHS. There would be no particular justification for long-term care being the first public service to be financed by such a mechanism. Moreover, financing long-term care through hypothecation might make it a target for cuts if for example, a Government were seeking to reduce the tax burden. Also, one Parliament cannot bind another, and so promises made in one Parliament cannot be changed by another. Finally, there would be an issue for people on low incomes. They would either have to have contributions paid in for them or services paid for out of general taxation. This would be an added complication.

6.70   The advantages of general taxation on the other hand are that it provides a generally progressively based source of revenue which can be attributed according to the decisions of democratically elected and accountable politicians. If there are problems in the economy the level of funding of long-term care has a broader base of support than a single levy. Funding long-term care in this way would seem more familiar in the UK system. Moreover, if the whole nature of future care were to change, for example, if a medical cure for Alzheimer's Disease were found, then money could be shifted relatively easily. Finally, general taxation is relatively cheap to administer and would not require any new bureaucratic apparatus. It is a generally accepted and fairly transparent system of public funding which commands wide support.

6.71   On balance, the Commission concluded that non-hypothecated general taxation offers the best way of financing state help for people who need long-term care. It is broadly based, largely progressive, and easily understood. The Government would have an opportunity to re-establish a degree of faith in the tax system and to strengthen the public's willingness to pay for public services, assuming that the money is spent well and efficiently and people can see that it this is so.

6.72   The uncertainty of future long-term care costs has been mentioned a number of times. As Chapter 2 discussed, uncertainty about future numbers of disabled elderly people and the uncertainty about future costs of long-term care taken together could result in a very large funnel of doubt. Whatever future total costs turn out to be, the public collectively or individually will have to pay for them. As we discussed in Chapter 5 private insurance, which is designed to deal with quantifiable risk, is expensive, partly because of the extent of this uncertainty. This adds to the unaffordablility of high premiums for the majority, increasing the importance of public provision. By providing public cover for long-term care for all, these uncertainties can be spread amongst many.

6.73   In the next chapter, we make a further proposal to ensure that a tax based system has within it the right degree of transparency and security for this generation of older people and for generations of older people to come.

Notes

(x)   These have behind them a number of assumptions for the future based on the experience of the past. These are an annual increase in GDP over the period of 2.25%, an increase in earnings of 2%, an increase in health care costs of 1.5% above inflation, and an increase in social care costs of 1% above inflation.

WITH RESPECT TO OLD AGE

Chapter 7
Underpinning the Commission's Proposals — The National Care Commission

This chapter proposes the establishment of a National Care Commission which might have responsibility for a range of matters to do with long-term care for older people, and looks at other measures which would be required to make the Royal Commission's proposals work more effectively.

A NATIONAL CARE COMMISSION

7   Our proposals for improving the funding system will, inter alia, make clear what people are responsible for themselves and what they can expect the state to provide if they need long-term care. However, the Commission are clear that this in itself will not deliver the degree of security which people feel to be lacking in the current system. We rejected the notion of hypothecated revenues on account of their lack of flexibility and inability to provide real security. In coming to this view, we also highlighted the lack of security in funding from general taxation. The Commission concluded, therefore, that if the bulk of the pooling of risk is to be met from taxation, some other visible safeguard is needed for people to have confidence in the system.

7.1   *We therefore recommend the establishment of an independent body to be known as the National Care Commission.* **(Recommendation 7.1)** This body, which could be a non-Ministerial Government Department, or a Non-Departmental Public Body, would have the tasks of looking at the whole care system in a strategic way, stewarding the interests of older people who receive services and reporting on spending on long-term care on a three yearly cycle to Government and Parliament. This cycle would need to be in tune with the cycle for reviewing public expenditure, so that Government could make informed decisions on the resources required to fund long-term care. It would be essential to have a UK-wide focus, but the Commission recognise that arrangements for each of the countries of the United Kingdom would need to be devolved appropriately.

7.2   We see the National Care Commission as a vital way of sustaining the momentum of our own work and monitoring the progress which we hope our Report will set in hand. It should fit into existing structures, but will provide a new level of strategic leadership and stewardship which has hitherto been lacking. Its main responsibilities might be as follows:

A Monitoring Role:

- to monitor long-term trends in the demography of old age, and to ensure that the systems in place nationally to measure trends are appropriate; this is the reason for a UK wide emphasis;

- to produce reports on the resourcing of long-term care, to assess its appropriateness in general terms, and to monitor the way in which resources are spent across the responsibilities of different Government departments;

- to keep under review the market in residential care, and to consider whether it could be managed better in order to provide domiciliary care so as to reduce reliance on residential care;

- to monitor and make recommendations for action on issues relating to housing for older people in a way which brings together other interests such as Health and Social Services;

- to look at wider matters which impact on long-term care, such as the availability of transport and the impact of the built environment (see paragraphs 7.4 and 8.23) in making it possible for people to stay at home as well as the availability of appropriate housing stock and its proper maintenance.

Representing the consumer:

- to bring together different mechanisms for dealing with complaints and to act as an ombudsman in this regard;

- to act as a voice to Ministers for older consumers of the various types of care;

- to ensure that consumers, whether as clients or carers, have the right information easily available and clearly set out to make informed decisions about their own future.

National Benchmarks:

- to publish material which makes clear to the public what they are entitled to in general terms, including standards of performance, and a general but not overly prescriptive set of eligibility criteria, and to develop national systems of assessment;

- to take an overall independent view on national quality standards;

- to monitor quality, working with others nationally through proper and easily comprehensible output measures.

Encouraging the development of better services:

- to ensure the existence of a network of helplines for all older users and their carers which can tell them how to get help locally;

- to encourage improvements in quality and innovation by disseminating good practice and by devices such as league tables;

- to offer advice on technical innovation, to encourage innovation and the transfer of technology developed for younger disabled people which might be useful for older people;

- to ensure that better co-ordinated joint working becomes a reality working hand in hand with others, including the national representatives of local government and the NHS;

- to develop in due course recommendations to Government for a new system of resource allocation nationally which takes account of the role of the benefit system, is more transparent and related to assessed need than the current system;

- to look across different professional boundaries at the training for care workers in a way which would bring together the interests of different professional bodies. This would complement recent Government proposals for a new body to regulate standards and training in social work.

7.3 The Care Commission would not be responsible for day to day regulation of care homes or of workers who provide care in peoples' homes. In England the Government have in any case made proposals for arms-length regulatory bodies separate from Local Authorities in *Modernising Social Services*[23]. The Commission would however work with existing bodies, such as the Audit Commission, the Social Services Inspectorate and equivalent bodies in Scotland, Wales and Northern Ireland commissioning particular investigations as required. The Commission could interact with existing frameworks in a number of ways: the key requirement is that it should be a body with a strategic overview of the whole business for delivering long-term care for older people.

Housing

7.4 Housing is included as one of the key areas on which the Commission should have an overview. If the Government adopts our recommendations, the role of housing will be central to the future of long-term care. We suggest that a number of initiatives are required to enable joined-up thinking across Government. We later mention what needs to be done in respect of budgets for aids and adaptations and the prospect of a small loans scheme (paragraph 8.23). Other, wider actions which may need to be taken forward include:

- Now that lifetime home standards are mandatory for all new house building, these should provide some in-built capacity for people to be able to grow old with the minimum of difficulty, with the facilities for alterations in order to accommodate changing needs with age. To go further in the future, the necessary cabling should be easily fitted and the use of smart technology easily accommodated. Such forward thinking in the approach to the design of homes with ageing in mind was observed by the Commission in Denmark. The Government should take a lead in this regard.

- Government might further consider how it might work in partnership with the private sector to develop housing schemes for purchase which will have some element of care built into them. This might be taken forward across Government in partnership with the private sector.

- The Commission's recommendation in Chapter 6 for the division of the elements of care to be funded by the state and those which should be the responsibility of the individual, contains new opportunities, for example, for a new form of relationship between the client and a care home, along the lines of purchasing a lease on an accommodation unit which can be sold on after death. The Government should work in partnership with the private sector in developing such new products, which might be along the lines of some of the developments which have taken place in Denmark, or of the "bonds" in residential care in Australia, which have helped redefine what residential care is and could become (see Research Volume 1). Given the changing nature of the models of care which the Commission hopes to encourage (see Chapter 8), the development of new products along these lines, which better meet peoples' needs might be a way in which the residential sector could change and develop.

7.5 The paper *Supporting People*[37] is currently out for consultation. This is exactly the sort of area where an informed and independent Care Commission could make a valuable input to Government thinking.

The role of the Care Commission in respect of the Independent Sector

7.6 The independent sector is responsible for providing the majority of all residential and nursing home care beds. It is estimated that in the last 10 to 15 years the independent sector has invested between £10 – £12bn into the long-term care sector, much of it provided by fees paid by the public sector. Additionally, the independent sector is funded by local authorities to provide 43% of their home care and home help hours.

7.7 This market share will increase. A purchaser/commissioner relationship similar in many respects to the NHS is already emerging with the local authorities as commissioners of care and the independent sector as major providers of that care. For this to work requires a constructive on-going partnership between local authorities and the independent sector.

7.8 When in the early 1980s older people became entitled, without the application of eligibility criteria, to claim Social Security benefits to pay for their care in residential or nursing homes the provision of long-term care by the independent sector became highly profitable with a large number of independent providers entering the market. However, since 1993, with the introduction of capped budgets under which local authorities were made principally responsible for publicly funded long-term care, the sector tells us that profitability has been dramatically eroded. Analysis shows[4] that there are too many providers, often in the wrong place. Local authorities have used their purchasing power to drive down fees to a level where providers say it is increasingly difficult for them to achieve an adequate return on their investment. They say this has been exacerbated by increasing costs (primarily labour costs), the national shortage of qualified nursing staff, the fact that many local authorities have not increased prices even to allow for inflation and they face the additional costs of implementing the national minimum wage. The result is that there are few incentives for high quality entrants into the market for residential or nursing home care.

7.9   The effect of this might be two-fold:

■ In the short term, in order to survive, many providers may cut standards;

■ In the longer term, there is the danger that the independent sector will not be willing to provide the extra capacity of residential, nursing or other provision required.

7.10   The providers tell us that in the short to medium term, the squeeze on profitability will be reflected in a fall in standards as it is unlikely that there will be a shortage of available beds. However, as the number of elderly people continues to increase they estimate that the need for beds will rise from the current level of just under 500,000 to just over 1,000,000 in 2050. Based on a current estimated capital cost of £30,000 per bed, 500,000 beds will require a capital investment of £15bn and unless a reasonable return on capital can be achieved, the independent sector say they will not provide it.

7.11   While no immediate crisis is looming, the Government should not simply wait for the crisis to happen but plan to make sure it does not. The solutions are not necessarily price increases for the independent sector. Careful use of the contracting process could enable planned expansion (or contraction) to take place, capital to be raised and encourage innovation which is just as important. In addition, the development of new arrangements for paying for the housing element of care in residential settings which we mention above, such as the purchase of leases by individuals, will be another way of ensuring a supply of capital which pays for provision which reflects people's needs.

The Market for Care

7.12   It will also be important not to get locked into existing models of care if these are inappropriate. In Australia, we saw moves to gradually decrease the numbers of residential beds by issuing fewer licences for bed places and converting them to equivalent home care packages. In Denmark, we saw a ban on the building of new residential homes. If the Commission's wider proposals are accepted, we hope the market for care in residential settings will be quite different. It will need careful managing. That is why we have recommended the National Care Commission having as one of its major functions, the responsibility to look at the market, including the supply of capital in the long term and the high quality provision which will be needed as demand grows. This will require a genuine partnership between Government (both central and local), the NHS, the regulators, the Audit Commission, who have responsibility for monitoring better value, and the independent sector.

Conclusion

7.13   The establishment of the National Care Commission, whatever form or forms it may take, is a key part of the Commission's recommendations. It is in our view essential if long-term care is to be managed properly nationally both now and in the future. It will be instrumental in providing a sense of security as to how the UK will make arrangements for the appropriate degree of risk pooling to be in place to meet the needs of older people. It will also, as has been suggested, be a key way of ensuring that the models of care which the Commission advocates are to be realised, improving standards and acting as an effective steward to the system on behalf of consumers. In the next chapter we discuss what those models are, and outline developments we would like to see in their delivery.

Chapter 8
Models of Care

This chapter looks at the models of care the Commission would like to see emerging, and says something about the structural changes which will be required to ensure these models can be achieved. Research Volume 2 contains some research by the Age Concern Institute of Gerontology at King's College London that has informed our work. This chapter is a summary of the Commission's favoured approach based on that work and many other pieces of evidence.

8   Older people wish to retain their independence and autonomy for as long as possible and generally would prefer to remain in their own homes. This was made clear to us by the written and oral evidence we received and also by focus groups of older people and their carers carried out on behalf of the Commission. These are summarised in Research Volume 2. This is an approach the Commission want to encourage. The Government, in their general approach to welfare reform have expressed their view that *independence* as opposed to *dependence* is an overriding policy aim. The Commission endorses that view.

8.1   Perhaps the very term "care" within the context of promoting continued independence of older people is unhelpful, suggesting actions and services that are done *to* people rather than providing them with help and assistance to maintain independence. Many younger disabled people articulate this view, and such views are likely to be reflected in the attitude of future generations of older people.

8.2   Making independence a reality requires a change in attitude across society. Improved access to some of the components of normal life such as housing, education, transport, shopping, social and leisure activities will be essential in an ageing society. Such an approach, which represents normalisation, will enhance opportunities for social inclusion and allow innovative and appropriate models of care.

8.3   Most older people do not need any formalised long-term care. They continue to live in their own homes and to enjoy independent lives. A large number of older people receive informal or unpaid care from spouses, relatives, friends and neighbours – a form of active communitarianism. This places some moral responsibility on society to offer unpaid carers support and assistance where it may be wanted or needed and to making clear where the boundaries of expectation should lie. We return to this later.

8.4   Our overall conclusions on models of care are:

- A larger proportion of care than now should be provided in peoples' own homes, either in the houses in which they live or in new settings which are closer to the community and which allow a greater degree of independence than traditional residential or nursing care;

- The quality of care must increase so that older people will continue to share in the improvements, choice and greater flexibility which the rest of society will enjoy over the same period;

- There should be greater flexibility in care provision, with a variety of models allowed to develop, with a mixture of providers;

- If the delivery of care is organised coherently, the system could provide better value for money overall;

- A proper system of assessment will be needed for the system to deliver what is required. The assessment process is particularly critical if the Commission's recommendation for personal care is accepted. It puts a premium on joint working and commissioning.

8.5   Research and experience in this country and elsewhere suggest that, as well as being what people want, providing a larger proportion of care in peoples' own homes is a practical objective. Research Volume 2 contains a review of models of care for older people[42] which could provide alternatives to institutional care. This report contains much of the evidence that underpins our conclusion that a much greater degree of care at home could take place, within current resources. To meet the objective of more home based care, the current in-built perverse incentives to residential care which have been outlined in Chapter 4 need to be removed.

8.6   Keeping more people in their own homes will demand much greater attention to and investment in housing as an essential component of long-term care needs. This will entail much greater flexibility of provision. Already £2bn is spent on housing related community care services for 1.3 million people in England. The Consultation Paper, *Supporting People*[37] has just been published. The outcome of this will have a major impact on supported housing and innovative forms of housing provision. We must emphasise that work to establish a sustainable arrangement for the long-term funding of supported accommodation is critical. It is of increasing importance in the light of our recommendations.

8.7   The Commission believe, with the Audit Commission for England and Wales[27], that better value for money can be obtained within the existing system, but in recognising the different circumstances, needs and wishes of individuals we do not advocate a single model. There should be a tapestry of accessible provision from which, within limitations, people may choose, confident that their needs can be met.

Care settings explained

Care is provided in a range of settings by the public, private and voluntary sectors. The explanations of each are general as there is wide variation in practice and form within each, and increasing overlap as innovative approaches are developed.

Care at home	Personal care and practical help provided to older people in their own homes.
Adult placement	Placing older people with selectively matched carers in the carer's own home.
Day care	This includes NHS day hospitals, Local Authority, and independent sector day centres.
Sheltered Housing	Individual housing within a setting which offers different degrees of monitoring, protection or support. It can be owned or rented. Within this there are the following variations:
	Very sheltered housing or housing with extra care
	Retirement communities/Care Villages
Residential care	Care for older people in an institutional setting, that is, either in a residential or a nursing home
NHS continuing care	in nursing homes, hospices and hospitals
NHS Acute services	in NHS hospitals

THE BACKDROP TO CARE DELIVERY

8.8   In looking at the Delivery of Care, the Commission have concluded that:

- There needs to be more effective joint working and a greater sharing of responsibility between health, social services and housing authorities;

- There should be a greater emphasis on prevention and the promotion of health and independence;

- There should be a greater emphasis on rehabilitation;

- There should be a more consistent framework for assessment and eligibility;

- More opportunities should be available to enable people to stay at home;

- More support should be offered to carers;

- There should be more real choice offered;

- Services offered should be culturally sensitive;

- There should be a greater emphasis on quality;

- The system should be easier to access;

- A new relationship of trust between clients, carers and services must be created.

Joint Working

8.9   The House of Commons Health Select Committee in its recent report[38] has criticised separation of Health and Social care in this way, and has made a number of recommendations in this regard. We endorse the thrust of the Committee's report, and agree with most of its recommendations.

8.10   Mention has been made of the different organisational approach in Northern Ireland where the responsibility for both health and social services comes within area Health and Social Service Boards. Here, as in other parts of the UK, the Commission has seen and was provided with evidence of areas in which joint working arrangements provide effective and responsive services. The best models of professional practice that the Commission has seen bring all the relevant professions and skills together around a single focus on assessment and delivery rather than locking them into separate functions and bureaucracies.

8.11   The Government's plans for *Better Services for Vulnerable People* in England, *Modernising Community Care* in Scotland, and other proposals such as the new *Promoting Independence Grants* in England (£750m over three years), the *Long Term Care Charter* and the development of *National Service Frameworks* should go some way to encourage joint working. The Government's proposals for pooled budgets, commissioning and integrated provision are welcome steps. The Commission have been disturbed by the confusion and distress that older people, their relatives and carers tell us they have experienced because of lack of co-ordination between services at times when they are most vulnerable. We regard this as a key area which, if it worked properly, could improve people's lives dramatically. We note, however, the lack of co-terminosity of local Government and NHS boundaries in England which may hinder proper working and needs to be kept under review (See Appendix 2).

8.12   Two particular aspects of professional working are central to sharing responsibility:

(i) ***Assessment of Needs.*** The request for a needs assessment can come from a variety of sources, from the older person themselves, their carer or family and those working within NHS acute care, primary care (including the screening offered to over 75s), social services, voluntary organisations, charities and others. Evidence indicates that there are wide variations in the approaches to and quality of assessments across the UK[43]. We believe that in each individual case there should be a single point of contact through which the process of assessment is arranged and the necessary care commissioned. Logic suggests that the new Primary Care Groups and their counterparts in Scotland,

Wales and Northern Ireland may in future perform this function. Though they are currently at early stages of development, they offer a great deal of potential for being the first port of call in the future. Whatever the precise arrangements locally, it must be clear to the older person, relative or carer where they should go and for what.

For those with complex needs the assessment should be multi-disciplinary. Experience in both Northern Ireland and Australia suggests that a multi-disciplinary team in which true mutual understanding of skills has been developed to a high degree is a key factor. The multi-disciplinary team might include a geriatrician (or psychogeriatrician as appropriate), general practitioner, nurse, social worker, housing manager and occupational therapist; and may additionally include a physiotherapist, speech therapist, chiropodist and others as appropriate. The administrative practicality of involvement will need to match the needs of each person: what is required is a consistent membership of a team, and for that team to be able to work towards the best arrangements for the older person.

This multi-disciplinary assessment should look to reducing dependency, and improving autonomy and quality of life. This not only involves considering prognosis and providing opportunity for rehabilitation, but must adequately reflect the wishes of the older person, and where appropriate, the carer, in developing a care package. Evidence also points to the importance of the timing of the care assessment – preferably undertaken when the older person's condition has stabilised, allowing time for recovery. It should follow positive action to bring about optimum rehabilitation. Final placement in residential care should only occur after the full potential for rehabilitation has been explored. It should not be a once and for all procedure but provide for a process of review and reassessment. If this is to be effective, it is essential that the older person's normal place of residence is maintained until after the reassessment. A number of people are currently admitted to nursing or residential care as emergencies, sometimes directly from hospital accident and emergency departments. In the event of this happening it is essential that these older people have access to proper and timely assessments and rehabilitation services. A proper period of convalescence allowing for recovery and rehabilitation could diminish the need for long-term residential care. *We believe that opportunity for rehabilitation should be included as an integral and initial part of any care assessment, before any irreversible decisions on long-term care are taken.* **(Recommendation 8.1)**

(ii) *Commissioning of Care Services.* The Department of Health's discussion document *Partnership in Action*[(44)] published in September 1998 made proposals for England on the pooling of health and social care budgets, lead commissioning, integrated provision, and the legislative arrangements necessary to allow for them. A separate action plan has been published by the Scottish Office *Modernising Community Care*[(45)].

8.13 The Government's proposals, which will limit the propensity for cost-shunting between budget responsibilities, are attractive in that they seek to work with the grain of current organisational structures, and do not threaten the upheaval and disruption of a wholesale reorganisation. They are soundly based and pragmatic, and allow for the best solutions to emerge locally. We welcome the proposed

legislation which would enable budget pooling to take place in a way that is not currently possible.

8.14   *We therefore recommend that the Department of Health's proposals on pooled budgets be taken further, and ask that in taking forward its Action Plan the Scottish Office take account of our views.* **(Recommendation 8.2).** There should be clear timetables for pooled budgeting between health and local authorities to be established in all areas and for devolved budgetary responsibility to be given to care managers. It is vital that the decisions made during assessment can be backed up quickly with the appropriate resources from all parties, and not require long negotiations while a person in need awaits a response. Proper pooling arrangements should bring the right mixture of high level commitment from both the NHS and from Local Authorities and encourage the best use of money in respect of the person. This will require the Government to keep a close eye on progress, and to ensure that sufficient resources are devoted at the centre to monitor progress and realise benefits.

Prevention and Health Promotion

8.15   More emphasis should be given to delaying the onset of illness or dependency that eventually leads people to need long-term care. A postponement of the onset of dependency could reduce long-term care costs or assist in ensuring that they were at a lower level. A report from the Continuing Care Conference *Fit for the Future: The Prevention of dependency in Later Life*[46] discusses many of the issues. Health promotion has been an important component of Government policy for many years and should apply equally to older people in the drive to maintain independence. The existing requirement on General Practitioners to offer an annual health review for those over 75, could be used, with modification, to provide an opportunity for identifying unmet needs and initiating preventive measures.

8.16   There has been much recent discussion of "low level" services and their effectiveness in preventing or delaying the onset of dependency. The 1998 report *That Little bit of Help*[47] suggests that help with housework, gardening, laundry, home maintenance and repairs enhance quality of life for older people and help them maintain their independence. It found that such services were central to many older people's sense of well-being and confidence about coping at home. Many older people want and value such help, and would actively choose to have these services. The value that older and younger disabled people have put on help of this nature has been reflected in reports on local authority charging policies,[48] and in the evidence we have received from the general public. We have, however, thought it right to concentrate on making personal care, where it is assessed as being required, free at the point of use, while recognising the need to make these "low level" but fundamentally important services more accessible with a fair and transparent system of charges and co-payments.

8.17   Most modelling of the costs of long-term care for older people, including our own assumes that age specific morbidity and disability rates remain constant. It has been put to us that this assumption should be challenged and that age-specific morbidity and disability could be reduced if more attention were given to prevention. Preventive strategies are supported by two arguments; firstly that by delaying the onset of disability and dependency they prevent, or at least postpone, the need for more intensive, and therefore more costly forms of care; and secondly that they improve the well-being and quality of life of older people. While there is more research evidence to support the second argument than the first, we believe that both arguments are valid, but *we recommend further longitudinal research is required to track the processes and outcomes of preventive interventions and to assess their impact both on quality of life and long-term costs.* **(Recommendation. 8.3)**

Rehabilitation

8.18   We welcome the increasing awareness of the role of rehabilitation as an integral part of long-term care, but it is clear that there are marked disparities in provision between geographical areas. Although there are examples of innovation, individual initiatives and good practice, we have been particularly concerned to find that access to rehabilitation services may be denied to people who live in residential and nursing homes.

8.19   There is positive evidence to support the clinical effectiveness of many rehabilitation interventions, though the strength of the evidence on some is mixed[49]. Many of the submissions we received drew our attention to two reports from the Kings Fund[50][51]. These reports, together with a seminar we held to look at the evidence of therapeutic interventions, emphasised that rehabilitation needs to draw on clinical, therapeutic and social interventions across all settings.

8.20   In chapter 6 we have recommended an option (option 1) which would provide a breathing space before irrevocable decisions on residential care are made. This will assist the development of rehabilitation: its effectiveness should be evaluated. *We recommend that further research on the cost effectiveness of rehabilitation should be treated as a priority* **(Recommendation 8.4)**, *but that this should not prevent the development of a national strategy on rehabilitation led by the Government to be emphasised in the performance framework for the NHS and Social Services.*

Better Framework for Assessment and Eligibility

8.21   The Commission have received many calls in written evidence for national standards in the assessment of needs. Others have pointed out the difficulties of such an approach. We believe that people are entitled to know in broad terms what to expect from the system wherever they live. The variation in access to services which currently exists because of geographical location is not acceptable. In the recent Social Services White Paper in England, the Government have recognised this need for stronger direction at national level. The next National Service Framework to be developed will be on services for older people (para 2.35), providing explicit standards and principles for the pattern and level of services required. The Commission also wants to see more consistency in practice.

8.22   We have discussed in paragraph 8.12 the need for a greater degree of consistency and clear objectives for the system of assessment. Transparency seems to have been achieved within the national system developed in Australia[52]. Multi-disciplinary Aged Care Assessment Teams provide assessments which relate to dependency scales that attract different levels of subsidy or funding for those who need or are at the margins of needing institutional care. The existence of such teams, coupled with regulation of the institutional care market's size, has been used to provide more people with the choice of receiving care in their own homes. The Commission suggest the Australian model might be worth further

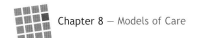

consideration, and has already recommended that the proposed National Care Commission might look in the future at the issue of supply in the private sector.

More people should be able to stay in their own homes

8.23   The thrust of the Commission's recommendations call for improvements in housing to make staying-put a more practical option and for changes in financing to tilt where possible towards the individual in their own home rather than towards residential forms of care. Of course some people may actively choose to live in residential settings as opposed to their own homes and their wishes should be respected. However, if a radical shift reflecting people's general wishes from the institutional to the domiciliary setting is to be achieved, the following conditions are needed:

"If you have got an older person who is taken into care, sometimes the only hope that they have to live for is that someday they'll go back to their house. You take that away and their life ends."

(a) ***A more supportive housing environment.*** We have received evidence on and seen for ourselves many examples of new and innovative solutions to traditional housing issues. We have seen the future in pilot schemes incorporating the new changes to building regulations, in newly built "lifetime" homes – more easily adapted to meet a range of future needs, and the application of new technologies from alarm systems to systems that control any number of household appliances and functions. Nevertheless, for the majority of people such changes will take many years to work through and at the moment such initiatives tend to be confined to social housing providers and the top end of the private market. This is particularly important as research undertaken for Anchor[53] indicates that ownership rates for households headed by people in the 60 – 74 age group will approach 80% by 2011. In England, two thirds of households headed by a person in their late 70s will also be home owners. Only for those aged 80 or more will rates remain below this level at about 68%. Over time we would expect this proportion to increase.

The Anchor research shows that most older home owners (66%) wish to stay in their existing homes with only a minority (30%) preferring the option of moving. This has implications for how the care and repair of their homes is managed. The extension of local "care and repair" and "handyman" schemes across the UK offering advice, support and carrying out work for older people will be essential if a larger number are to remain in their own home. The Government should consider extending these schemes and look at funding schemes with the Housing Corporation.

There are a number of new initiatives increasing choice for those people who wish to move and trade their current homes. These include care communities, retirement flats with wardens or flats that are part of very sheltered housing schemes. Homes in these types of settings have traditionally been offered for rent and have, in part, been financially dependent on initiatives which have pushed at the boundaries of "care" that might be paid for through Housing Benefits. These will be of increasing importance in the social housing sector.

Whether owner-occupied or rented, the unsuitability of a house and the inability to undertake adaptations quickly and effectively is one of the factors that may lead people to need residential care earlier than might otherwise be required. The timely availability of appropriate aids and adaptations to enable individuals to live in their own homes for longer is therefore of vital importance. The cost of these adaptations may be small in comparison to the cost of sending paid staff to do things that, with adaptations, the individual or family may be able and willing to do. The relevant budgets should be brought together with those who are charged with commissioning care packages, and easily and quickly accessible to care managers. We have heard over and over again how a quick intervention with the appropriate aid or appliance could ensure independence and improve quality of life – small amounts of money preventing the later expenditure of larger sums. *We recommend that budgets for aids and adaptations should be included in and accessible from a single pool.* **(Recommendation 8.5)** This pooling refers to existing budgets.

Although, as we discussed in Chapter 5, we do not think that the large-scale release of housing equity is a practical proposition to pay for long-term care, we do think that there might be scope for small scale release to help with the costs of aids and adaptations, and that such an initiative could complement existing budgets for aids and adaptations. Small loans could be available, possibly from local authorities, to pay for aids and adaptations which would be repayable on death or when the house is sold on entering a residential home. The commercial sector might be able to provide such loans, but evidence submitted by the Joseph Rowntree Foundation found older people unwilling to use the equity on their homes with commercial lenders, even for small amounts, therefore a Local Authority scheme may have merit. It will be local authority money that is saved in the long term. Legislation governing Local Authorities' ability to offer loans would need to be introduced, and there may need to be an exemption for Local Authorities from the Consumer Credit Act. *We recommend the development of a scheme which would enable Local Authorities to make loans for aids and adaptations be investigated by Government or the National Care Commission.* **(Recommendation 8.6)**

(b) *A better balance between the provision of residential and home-based forms of care.* We have discussed in Chapter 4 (recommendation 4.6) the transfer of Residential Allowance to Local Authorities. This will remove a major perverse incentive towards residential care. We also advocated in Chapter 7 that the National Care Commission should look at the supply of residential care from the private sector, and consider the extent to which there would need to be a more active management of the market at national level. The National Care Commission may want to see some analysis of the supply of provision in local community care plans, which would enable them to get a better picture nationally.

. . it is . . . unfair that . . . a son or daughter caring for their elderly relatives and parents ⸱ the family home, and, perhaps, foregoing ⸱art of their own lives for a number of years . . ⸱e elderly person may get so infirm that it is no ⸱nger possible for the carer to work. Having ⸱ut in all that time and energy, not only do they ⸱ot get thanked for it, but if they are not ⸱ctually thrown out of the house that the elderly ⸱erson owned, a charge is made on it and they ⸱re, in effect, penalised for . . . taking on the ⸱overnment's role, the major caring role for ⸱at time."

More Support to Carers

8.24   On the grounds of equity and justice we believe carers need more support. They need to be actively engaged in the process of needs assessment, and where possible services to support them must be considered. Evidence given to the Commission supports the view that better outcomes, in the sense of more people receiving good quality care at home, depend crucially on the contribution of unpaid carers. They bear a very great share of the total care burden, many without adequate support. Caring involves a complex mix of social and moral obligation. The evidence from carers' organisations to a large extent focuses on the need for additional, more responsive service provision and some financial recompense for those taking on a caring role who lose not only earning capacity but potential pension contributions. We welcome the proposals in the recent Pensions Green Paper[9] for pensions to help those who give up work to undertake a caring role. There are also other real costs involved in caring. A research review undertaken for the Commission on the policy options for increasing choice for carers is published in Research Volume 3, and has informed our considerations.

8.25 Our evidence suggests that a large number of older people being cared for by informal carers receive no services at all. Some of them ask for respite care, others ask for other kinds of support, advice, or help with the practicalities of caring. It was put to the Commission that offering extra services to individuals who were being looked after by a carer would provide a welcome degree of flexible help. For example, to offer domiciliary services to the most dependent older people who do not live alone and who do not receive services, at the same level as those who live alone (about 80,000 people, at about five hours a week). We estimate this would cost £290m. The help might emerge as some form of respite care – not necessarily traditional residential respite, but support at home which might enable carers to have a break of a few hours a week, if that is what they choose. We would be asking the assessment process to be "carer blind" in the best sense: so that the existence of a carer will not lead to the failure to offer services, or lead to their withdrawal.

8.26 The Government have ring-fenced resources from next year's local authority settlement to provide services geared towards providing a break for carers. This resource represents £20 million in the first year, rising to £70 million in the third year, and was announced as part of the Government's Strategy for Carers. The Commission welcome this and think that their proposals for "carer-blind services" complement the approach being taken by the Government in their strategy. Therefore, we suggest that additional sums of up to £220 million be made available for services which will give the carers the support they need. *We recommend that the Government ensure services become increasingly "carer blind", offering flexible support services where carers currently take on caring unaided by publicly provided services.* (**Recommendation 8.7**) The illustrative costs in future years are as follows:

Table 8.1: Costs implications of services for older people with carers

	1995 Prices (base)	2010	2021	2031	2051
Cost billion £	0.2	0.3	0.4	0.5	0.7

Source: PSSRU model[18].

8.27 Much of what carers want is information about where to get help. Even the most articulate and capable can encounter great difficulty in the current system. Straightforward advice should be available. This could include the telephone information helpline for which we recommend the National Care Commission be responsible, to a single point of contact in the GP practice or health centre. Links could be made to NHS Direct.

"On the needs of elderly carers, it is not obvious what is available. You have to dig around. Nobody comes to you and says, "Look, your mother has been looking after your father in this situation for a number of years, this is what is available."

8.28 The Australian experience with carer support which is detailed in Research Volume 1[52] is an interesting example. The Federal Government's initiative provides a range of basic advice targeted at supporting carers (e.g. health and safety, legal and financial) with an explanation of how and where to obtain more information. It places an emphasis on the support available and suggests that carers should not wait for a crisis to occur before they seek help. ***A national carer support package should be considered by Government (Recommendation 8.8)***.

8.29 The precise nature of a package for carers should be discussed further with carers' organisations. The proposals for "carer-blind" services represents an attempt to meet some needs which are currently not being met. Taken with the Government's proposals, this represents a funding boost to the system of nearly £300m.

"My mum has 24-hour care in her own home. When she was first assessed, the Social Services allocated me a sum of money and said to me, 'How would you like the help?' and I said 'In the evening would be the best time for me' and that was when it was provided. 'Get in touch, please, if you need any more care' . . . over three and a half years I have gradually got more and more care provided when I wanted it, not when the Social Services said I could have it."

Real Choice

8.30 If housing and speed of access to aids and adaptations were improved, financial incentives towards residential care removed and more help provided for carers, people could be offered greater choice. Above this, there should be transparency and flexibility as to what people are offered. People should be given the option of direct payments to arrange the care themselves as a growing number of younger disabled people do. The Government have agreed to remove the age limit and make people aged 65 and over eligible for direct payments. We welcome this, though we suggest the arrangements should be subject to monitoring by a Care Manager at six monthly intervals to ensure the individual is receiving the care that they need and to provide the necessary safeguards against abuse, both financial and personal. The care managers' role should not simply disappear once money has been handed over. ***We recommend that the system for making direct payments is extended to the over 65s, subject to proper safeguards and monitoring. (Recommendation 8.9)***

8.31 Older people, like everyone in society, have rights to make their own choices of lifestyle. There can be no doubt that there will be times when people's choices will conflict with the views of their carer or the care manager. It will be essential for potential risks to be properly and sensitively managed within formal arrangements.

Services for Ethnic Minority Elders

8.32   Many services for ethnic minority elders are run by voluntary organisations as, in many cases, mainstream services have been slow to provide the kind of services that these elders want and which meet their expectations.

8.33   In Research Volume 1 we publish work we commissioned by the Policy Research Institute on Ageing and Ethnicity at the University of Bradford[54] on the needs of older people from ethnic minorities. Groups met to consider these issues in Edinburgh, London and Leeds, and there were other consultations in other cities in other parts of the UK. This research, and the work that went into it, has been valuable and has clear lessons for the whole care system, much of which is reflected throughout this report.

8.34   In looking at services for Ethnic Minority Elders, we observed that voluntary organisations providing services for black and ethnic minority older people seem to have been much more successful in incorporating a rich cultural component to their services. All services offered to older people should have a greater degree of cultural sensitivity built in. All providers of services should be culturally sensitive while meeting the diverse needs of their communities, and this is especially relevant in areas when black and ethnic minority elders are few in number. There can be no doubt that a greater sense of community and fostering of trust between different communities will only come if services develop in this way.

8.35   The research we commissioned showed clearly that demand for black and ethnic minorities is not for different or special services but for more responsive and culturally sensitive mainstream services, something which will benefit all older people who need long-term care. When mainstream services cater properly for diversity, then clients express a good deal of satisfaction with them. ***We recommend that it should be a priority for Government to improve cultural awareness in services offered to black and ethnic minority elders.*** **(Recommendation 8.10)**

8.36   There are also specific observations on how various mechanisms for payment might affect different communities in different ways. The role of housing assets, for example, can be more problematic in a multi-generational household, and the likelihood of formal services making incorrect assumptions about the availability of informal care increased. Overall the research indicated complex attributes towards paying for care, and feelings of betrayal which reflect those in the population as a whole.

Quality

8.37   The Social Services Inspectorate (and Social Work Inspectors in Scotland) have described and mapped out trends in quality in recent years. We welcome the emphasis on better performance contained in *Modernising Social Services*[23], and the targets for quality via the National Priorities Guidance in England. We also welcome the active approach to performance management envisaged in the Scottish Office document *Modernising Community Care*[45].

8.38   Smaller issues, such as the current practice of sending in numbers of different staff for short periods of time, is generally regarded as disturbing by older people. It does not represent good quality care. Continuity of personnel will assume a greater importance if more care is to be provided in peoples' homes.

8.39   We also want to encourage innovation and good practice and the lessons learned
        to be disseminated. The National Care Commission should monitor and
        encourage the development of good practice in commissioning, and work with
        other bodies and departments across government to ensue a coordinated and cost-
        effective approach to long-term care.

8.40   The Government's commitment to introduce a Long-Term Care Charter should
        assist the process of ensuring the development of quality services.

8.41   We are aware of a number of initiatives within the private residential home sector,
        working with a number of local authorities to develop care quality ratings for
        individual establishments, aimed at improving the services and provision of care
        within residential homes. If current pilots are successful they could also play an
        important role not only in maintaining standards, but in informing people's
        choices. We encourage the consideration and evaluation of such schemes by the
        private sector and local authorities.

Ease of access

8.42   Many people find the current system hard to navigate. Many of those who have
        written to us detail their own accounts of the difficulties and frustrations they
        face. While a great number of older people will want to and are capable of
        obtaining relevant information themselves, informing and making their own
        choices, it will assist everyone to have access to independent and comprehensive
        information. The availability of independent advice and information is one of the
        most important factors in delivering a client centred approach to long-term care
        provision. We have mentioned earlier the potential use of the proposed Primary
        Care Groups as an entry point to this system, and this is an obvious location not
        only for service provision but for advice. Many health centres are now giving
        space to independent advice workers and Citizens Advice Bureaux.

8.43   Information on the full range of long-term care provision, health and
        rehabilitation, social and housing needs, aids and adaptations, leisure needs,
        transport and education should be available from one point of contact. This could
        be available at a neighbourhood centre, perhaps a health centre, where
        geographical proximity of staff helps closer working, paid from public, private and
        voluntary resources. In rural areas where population and staff are dispersed
        geographically it will be necessary to key into existing structures for the
        dissemination of information. Centres such as the EPICs Centre in Marlowe or
        the Care Connect Centre in the London Borough of Merton provide models which
        are worth further study.

8.44   We are impressed by the role of advocacy and would like to see it developed. In
        situations where there may be some conflict between the wishes and needs of the
        client, their family or carers, and those arranging care, the availability of an
        independent intermediary to act for and on behalf of the older person or others
        concerned about an older person can be extremely helpful. There are many
        examples of advocacy schemes in which advocates act as the interface between an
        older person and Social Services. *We recommend that such a role of representation
        should be developed locally, with backing from central Government.*
        (Recommendation 8.12)

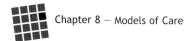

A Climate of Trust

8.45   We have noted the breakdown of trust, and the confusion which exists in the current system. The main improvement which would assist the client's and carer's need for security would be a ***national regulatory system***. The Government's Better Regulation Task Force[55] recommended that all care providers should be brought within the scope of regulation, domiciliary care should be subject to regulation, the registration and inspection of residential nursing and domiciliary care (including registration and appropriate checks on all care workers) should be unified, and complaints and appeals mechanisms should be reviewed as regards residential/domiciliary care/supported housing provision. Proposals have been set out in the English Social Services White Paper[23]. We agree with these proposals, and that the regulation of domiciliary, residential and nursing care should be undertaken by one body.

8.46   The unification of registration and inspection of residential and nursing care homes adds additional weight to the arguments against their continuing separate classification. These two separate classifications will be increasingly inappropriate, although regulators would have to be satisfied of a home's ability to meet all the requirements of particular needs. Our proposals for restructuring the payments system for residential care will further reduce the distinction.

MODELS OF CARE: CONCLUSIONS

8.47   The environment in which the future older people will be living should in time become more user-friendly. Twenty-five per cent of the population will be over 60 within the next ten years, and with this growth should come accessibility not just in the built environment and access to transport, but to a wider recognition of the determination and right of older people to enjoy arts and leisure activities. Lifetime learning opportunities nurture the spirit not just the mind. Living in a stress and crime-free environment are other issues to be addressed to ensure that older people are enabled to live a full and active life. Investment in people will be repaid by an active, wiser and healthier society.

8.48   We have sought not to be prescriptive about the settings in which care may be offered in the future. The needs and wishes of today's and tomorrow's older population will be varied and the provision of long-term care needs to reflect this. Overall we have sought to illustrate a system which, within its financial operation, will not produce incentives that oppose the general wish of older people to remain in their own homes, nor penalise those who may wish to receive care in institutional settings.

8.49   The continued rise in numbers of very old people in itself may indicate an increase in need and the total cost of long-term care for older people. In Chapter 2 we discussed the complex nature of future demand for long-term care, costs and the relationships between demographic trends, health expectancy, the levels of unpaid care and potential changes in the use of formal services. We explain how this leads to uncertainties in levels of future costs, and what has been termed the "funnel of doubt". On the other side of the equation, prevention, health promotion, rehabilitation and the promotion of independence all appear to offer opportunities by which long-term costs may be contained. There is little research available to date on the long-term cost effectiveness of approaches within these areas.   This is partly because the demonstration of cost-effectiveness in this field requires longitudinal studies which are not easily sustainable under the current funding system, and is a role for the National Care Commission.

8.50 We also make a number of recommendations that aim to bring together health care, social care and housing into a cohesive approach to rehabilitation assessment of needs and commissioning. We have taken the view that current initiatives to allow pooled budgets will only be established uniformly across the UK if there are clear targets set and there is joint accountability. In this respect we are greatly encouraged by the Social Services White Paper for England[23]. We believe that the establishment of broad national eligibility and quality criteria will encourage cross-agency working.

8.51 We have taken on board views presented in evidence that in the short-term major structural changes would be counter-productive, but consider that a judgement on the effectiveness of pooled budgets needs to be made following their introduction. Most significantly we believe that services should be directed to and for older people themselves. The supply of informal care is an unknown quantity in the future, which makes it even more important that the wishes of the individual receiving care must be paramount. Direct payments increase the choice available, including the choice not to have to ask family or friends for help.

8.52 In the next chapter we look at the implications of our proposals for younger disabled people, before making some final remarks about our overall proposals and their implementation.

Chapter 9

Younger Disabled People

This chapter considers the implications of the Commission's proposals for younger disabled people.

INTRODUCTION

9   In our terms of reference we were asked to have regard to the implications of our recommendations for younger people who by reason of illness or disability have long-term care needs. By younger disabled people we mean those aged 18–64 who are effectively subject to the same community care legislation as older people[(xi)]. We included in our Reference Group organisations of and for younger disabled people and received from them both written and oral evidence relating to their particular concerns. As well as this evidence the Commission visited residential, training and rehabilitation schemes for younger people with disabilities and talked directly to younger disabled people of their experiences with the care system – especially to those receiving and advocating direct payments. If we have not gone as far in our discussion or recommendations as those with a specific concern for younger disabled people would like, it is because we have had to balance this part of our remit with our main remit to concentrate on the funding of long-term care of older people and to report within 12 months.

9.1 We are encouraged that many of the developments in the care of younger disabled people now find ready echoes in the way care should be provided to older people, especially through ways to offer people greater choice about their care arrangements; there are many similarities, although there are also important differences between people whose disability arises later in life and younger disabled people. We expect that many of our recommendations will be directly relevant to younger disabled people, although for different reasons, and could be implemented with little or no modification.

VALUES

9.2   It is fundamental to our values and to this Report that older people must not be socially excluded from society by reason of either their age or their disability. This has a clear link with the continuing debate about younger disabled people. Many younger disabled people are showing that impairment is not necessarily a barrier to an active and fulfilling life, but more could be done to improve social arrangements and the physical environment. The Government are currently consulting on strengthened anti-discrimination legislation and on the creation of a Disability Rights Commission. We are pleased that the Government are taking steps to improve the economic position of younger disabled people through its "New Deal" and other incentive programmes.

9.3   We are pleased with the Government's announcement in *Modernising Social Services*[23] that direct payments, which were pioneered in social services by younger disabled people, are to be extended to people aged 65 and over.

CHARACTERISTICS OF YOUNGER DISABLED PEOPLE

9.4   In order to provide a background to our considerations we now look at the characteristics of younger disabled people in terms of their numbers, type of support they receive and the financial arrangements which underpin that support.

9.5   The most comprehensive survey of disablement that is currently available[56] shows that the risk of disablement is closely related to age. Most disabled people are older people and most severely disabled people are older too. While the risk of disablement is low among the population aged under 60, it becomes greater at each successive age group thereafter, and 7 in 10 of those aged 80 or over have some disability[xii].

9.6   Tables 9.1 and 9.2 illustrate this conclusion. As Table 9.1 shows, the risk of disablement is very low at younger age groups, and even those in middle age have significantly lower rates of disability that older groups; for example, the prevalence of disablement in the 40–49 age group is one-tenth that of those aged 80 and over. However, as there are more people in the younger age groups, the numbers of those disabled is relatively higher as a proportion of the older groups; there are, as Table 9.2 shows, only around five times as many severely disabled people aged 80 or over as there are in the 40–49 age group, by contrast with the 1 in 10 ratio of prevalence. In total there were estimated to be around three times as many severely disabled older people (aged 60 or over) as there were in the younger population, about a million as against one-third of a million.

Table 9.1: Estimate of number of disabled adults in Great Britain by age

Age group	Numbers disabled 000's	Rate per thousand
16–19	76	21
20–29	264	31
30–39	342	44
40–49	453	70
50–59	793	133
60–69	1,334	240
70–79	1,687	408
80+	1,254	714
Total	**6,202**	**142**

Source OPCS 1985–1988. * (56)

* Disability was defined for the purposes of the Survey as "a restriction or lack of ability to
perform normal activities, which has resulted from the impairment of a
structure or function of the body or mind".

Table 9.2: Estimate of number of severely disabled adults in Great Britain by age

Age group	Numbers 000's	Subtotals 000's
16–19	22	
20–29	64	
30–39	68	
40–49	83	
50–59	131	369 (ages 16-59)
60–69	231	
70–79	361	
80+	497	1,089 (Aged 60+)
Total	**1,457**	

*Source OPCS 1995 – 1988. Severe disability defined as OPCS categories
7-10* (56)

9.7   Of course, the experience of disablement will have a different impact on different age groups. For the great majority of older people it is an episode, albeit a painful one, at the end of life, when family ties, employment and other life events have been experienced. Younger people must try to negotiate their lives while disabled and when the vast majority of their peers, who set the standards of normal behaviour, are able-bodied. By comparison, as 7 in 10 people aged 80 or over have some level of disability, being unable to do some things or needing help with others is a common and anticipated experience. This perception may be behind the differences in the policy approach to supporting younger and older disabled people, both in service terms and financially[xiii].

9.8   The service pattern for younger and older disabled people is significantly different. The predominant trend in policy for younger people has been to move services outside institutions and maintain younger disabled people at home. So, for example, in England for every one younger disabled person in a care home there are 14 households with a younger disabled person receiving home care. The comparable ratio for older people is nearer to two in a care home for every five households with home care[58].

9.9   There are also differences in the financial arrangements for supporting long term care as between younger and older people, both in terms of average service expenditure and social security entitlements. One example is Disability Living Allowance covering a wider spectrum of care needs and including help with mobility needs. In England the standard spending assessments for social services are calculated separately and local authorities appear to operate separate budgetary arrangements too. In another context we have already commented on the bias in local authority spending on care for younger disabled people compared with older people (paragraph 4.21). Perhaps this is a manifestation of the greatest difference we have come across which are the limits which local authorities use as a yardstick for the costs of home care packages before offering residential care. For younger disabled people we have heard of upper limits of around £300 – £400 per week, but for older people much lower limits of about £100 – £200 are reported [59].

9.10   Younger disabled people also have access to the resources of the Independent Living (1993) Fund (ILF) which currently provides an extra £50 million across the UK to supplement the cost of home care packages in conjunction with local authorities and the clients themselves who are also expected to make a contribution. On average the ILF pays a supplement of about £189 per week, but we are told (personal communication from Independent Living Funds) that this average disguises a spread of contributions from around £10 per week to a maximum permitted of £300 per week with just under half of all payments being £200 per week or more. This is on top of a minimum local authority contribution of £200 per week.

9.11   We note that although there may be a strong desire to work, younger disabled people are far less likely to be in work or in well-paid work than their able-bodied peers. Many of them find themselves reliant on social security benefits for long periods of time as their main source of income and this has wider consequences. We are pleased that the Government are making changes to the social security and tax system to help here.

9.12   We were told that there was a dearth of information to allow proper planning of services for younger disabled people, including information on life expectancy. We have already commented on the lack of information in relation to our main deliberations so we naturally urge Government to ensure that information of relevance to younger disabled people is also made available to assist in planning and managing services for them.

IMPLICATIONS OF OUR RECOMMENDATIONS FOR YOUNGER DISABLED PEOPLE.

9.13   We think our recommendations can apply in general to all adults with disabilities who may need long-term care.

9.14   All adults should have protection from the catastrophic costs of needing long-term care. If the need for long-term care is a random event for older people, it is an even more random event for younger people given the lower incidence of disability in younger age groups and the arguments for collectively organised protection are as strong if not stronger.

9.15   We think younger disabled people should and would wish to be responsible for making decisions about and meeting their own living expenses because such responsibility is, as for older people, a normal part of everyday living. The social security system is intended to help disabled people of all ages with the extra costs of day-to-day living arising out of disability. However the inconsistency in local authority provision between different parts of the country, and the wide variation in charging regimes seems to be a factor in reducing access to personal care for younger disabled people. We have also received evidence that means tested charges for personal care are one factor in providing disincentives to work or seeking better paid work. This point is also made in research for the Joseph Rowntree Foundation[60]. Effectively these charges add to the financial burden of disabled people when they enter work or receive a wage increase.

9.16   We think that our recommendation that there should be greater consistency over the provision of services, that personal care should be provided free of charge at the point of use, and for a nationally consistent system of charges for publicly provided help with living costs (i.e. domestic help or help with tasks like shopping) will be of value to younger disabled people in all these areas.

9.17   We note that the ILF takes account of an applicant's means in determining its contribution to the costs of the care package which may include an element towards the costs of personal care. If it were no longer to have regard to an applicant's means for this element of its care packages the Funds would require an additional £9 million this year to meet demands on it[61]. We would like to think that our recommendation that personal care should be free at the point of use would be applied consistently across all public provision and *we therefore recommend that the Government should consider how the Commission's principle of personal care, subject to assessment, free at the point of use, could be achieved in relation to ILF provision for personal care needs.* **(Recommendation 9.1)**

9.18   Many of our other recommendations about improved rehabilitation services for older people, pooling of budgets, provision of aids and adaptations etc apply equally to younger disabled people. The recommendations should improve the provision and coordination of services for younger disabled people and help to promote independence.

9.19   Our recommendations for increased support for carers, but mainly focused on supporting disabled people themselves, seem appropriate for younger disabled people too, although we have already commented on the fact that younger disabled people may have quite a different relationship with family carers than do older people – born of the very different circumstances in which caring may be required and this must be taken into account when considering the needs of younger disabled people.

9.20   The role we envisage for the National Care Commission is specifically designed to address the long-term care needs of older disabled people. Younger disabled people have a much wider range of needs and requirements which includes education, training and work as well as long-term care. We think that the Government should consider with younger disabled people themselves the best way to manage and co-ordinate all these diverse needs across the totality of Government policy

9.21   This has been inevitably a fairly brief analysis of a complex set of issues. We recommend that the Government consider further, the read across of the Commission's findings to Younger Disabled People and to consult the relevant bodies.

Notes

(xi)   Disabled children are subject to a different legislative framework.

(xii)   There is no reason to suppose that the overall picture will have changed since this survey was carried out in the mid-1980s. A more recent survey using the same questionnaire (Craig and Greenslade, 1998)[57] found the same general pattern. Analysis of this more recent survey is continuing and full results are not yet available.

(xiii) There are, of course, legitimate questions about the validity of these different policy approaches which we do not examine here in detail but which we do examine in Chapter 8 (Models of Care) and elsewhere in our report.

Chapter 10
Concluding Remarks

This chapter draws together the various strands of the Commission's report and makes some suggestions on implementation. It also considers the possible impact of the Government's pensions review.

IMPLEMENTING THE COMMISSION'S PROPOSALS

10   If our proposals are to be implemented in full some aspects of our recommendations will require legislation and others can be implemented administratively to a much quicker timescale.

10.1   For example, establishing the National Care Commission and related entities in all of the home countries is clearly a priority no matter what else the Government choose to do. It is important that a body gets underway very quickly to re-establish confidence in the system and begin the work of carrying out research, identifying the resources spent on long-term care and pulling together some of the interests of older people across the system. This could be established initially as a shadow body within a Government Department – either one of the sponsoring Departments or a central Department with cross-cutting responsibilities such as the Cabinet Office. They would also be responsible for the swift setting up of information lines and other information support for carers.

10.2   Some of the proposed financial changes could be implemented quickly because secondary legislation or guidance is all that is required. This would include the disregarding of assets for the first three months (Option 1) or extending the provision of free nursing care (Option 5). Changing the means test limits as such (Option 3) would also require secondary legislation, as would the provision of extra funds to provide services to people with carers.

10.3   Other measures which should be taken forward quickly by Central Government or a shadow Care Commission are:

- The proper identification of the resources which go into long-term care – bringing this together into an identifiable, cross-governmental programme for what is spent on long-term care;

- The establishment of clear lines of accountability for spending across Government;

- The setting of proper performance targets for the programme which are measured against cross-departmental aims;

- A review of the role of housing in long-term care which will come up with practical proposals for making sure that housing makes a proper contribution to keeping people at home when this is possible, including the development of new approaches to residential care, new tenancy agreements or leasing arrangements.

10.4   There is much in our report which can be achieved quickly and without legislation. We urge the Government to do as much as they can while considering some of the recommendations which raise wider issues. One thing we are quite clear about: there is no such thing as a do-nothing option.

10.5   Primary legislation would be needed in the following areas:

- To allow the separation of personal care costs from living and housing costs for means testing purposes, to define what Local Authorities and Health Authorities would pay for within the new system, and to underpin the relevant flows of money from central Government to Local Authorities in particular;

- To allow the creation of a National Care Commission with the functions and remit as set out in Chapter 7;

- To allow Local Authorities to make small loans for aids and adaptations secured against part of the value of a house;

- To allow for the kind of pooled budgets we recommend, including putting money for aids and adaptions into any budget pool. The Government have already made proposals along these lines. We hope that the legislative changes they propose for Health and Social Services can take account of our recommendations.

10.6   The Commission wish to re-emphasise that, although our projections of trends and costs look far ahead to 2051, our policy recommendations should be seen over a much shorter timescale.

10.7   No Government can realistically expect to set policies for more than say 10 to 15 years at a time. We can see no good reason to make any exception in this respect for the funding of long-term care. Against this background, we believe our proposals to be measured, reasonable and practicable. We urge the Government to consider them in the spirit in which they are put forward.

OLDER PEOPLES' WIDER INTERESTS

10.8   Our recommendations should make a significant difference to the way in which society responds to older people's care needs. More broadly however, we believe that stronger leadership is needed within Government across a whole range of issues affecting older people, with the aim of truly combating social exclusion and encouraging older people to make a strong and independent contribution as active citizens in a modern Britain which does not ignore the talents or potential of any of its people. The Ministerial group on older people which currently exists should ensure that the wider interests of older people are taken into account across Government Departments. The work of this group is important. The potential of technology should be developed to make the lives of older people better, and the Government should do everything it can to help with this. More leadership is also needed in the provision of opportunities for older people to take part in volunteering and to make an active contribution to society.

10.9   Opportunities for education and access to leisure opportunities for older people should continue to be a high priority in all aspects of public provision. The Ministerial Group must take a lead on this, and ensure that opportunities for older people are high on the agenda of every Government department involved in this area, particular Department for Education and Employment and Department for Culture, Media and Sport. Consideration should be given to the progress of the Better Government for Older People Initiative and its expansion considered.

THE GOVERNMENT'S PENSION REVIEW

10.10   Our Terms of Reference require us to have regard to the Government's Pensions Review. The outcome of this review was published in December 1998 under the title: *A New Contract for Welfare: Partnership in Pensions*[9].

10.11   We acknowledge that, in focusing entitlement to the second state pension over and above the basic retirement pension on people with relatively low earnings, with higher earners expected to make their own provision, the Government are arguably moving in a contrary philosophical direction to that taken by us in respect of long-term care. In our view however, any such comparison would fail to take account of important differences between pension provision on the one hand and provision for long-term care on the other, which we have already touched on briefly in paragraph 3.2.

10.12   For example, the Government (rightly in our view) propose to keep the basic pension as a universal entitlement paid for by today's national insurance contributors. We too propose a universal element in state provision for long-term care, namely entitlement to personal care costs, with individuals responsible for living and housing costs from their own resources or means-tested state support. In this sense, therefore, both the Commission in relation to long-term care and the Government in relation to pensions envisage a role for universal state provision supplemented from other resources.

10.13 From another standpoint there is in our view, a strong argument for, on the one hand, the limitation of the second state pension to those of moderate means and, on the other, for the state to meet the care costs of long-term care irrespective of means. Virtually everyone of working age can reasonably assume that they will reach pension age and need a pension to live on thereafter. It is reasonable for people to have some choice over the level of their future provision and to make financial provision for it accordingly, and in relation to those who might not otherwise be able to provide at a sensible level, for the state in effect to do this for them (through the supplementary pension). Long-term care however, is a contingency, not a probability. Neither its incidence nor the scale of care needed are predictable. As we have maintained through this report, it is equitable and proper for the state to meet at least one element of these "catastrophic" costs for everyone. And the costs in the future, in relation to people's likely means, will remain catastrophic. We anticipate a shift in the partnership between Government and the individual with regard to pensions, not an increase in the amount of wealth available to the majority of the pensioner population. As is demonstrated in the Government's own "PENSIM" model, pensioners' incomes will increase overall, but most of the increase will be with richer pensioners, not across the board. In this respect, our proposals for a new Partnership for Care, based on need, looks even more appropriate.

10.14 Had the Government chosen to make second-tier pension provision compulsory, with everyone in employment statutorily required to contribute, the Commission would have needed to consider the case for adding a long-term care "insurance" contribution to the pension contribution. This would not have affected our conclusion in paragraph 6.65 that pre-funding of long-term care costs is not appropriate. It might however, have strengthened the argument in paragraph 6.68 in favour of a hypothecated long-term care contribution as distinct from the general taxation approach which we recommend.

AFFORDABILITY OF THE COMMISSION'S RECOMMENDATIONS

10.15 Our Terms of Reference require us to have regard to public spending constraints. We have done so. As a group of people with wide direct experiences of a range of public services we are well aware of the need for (and seek to put into practice,) such a responsible use of public money. None of us would wish, or intend, that our Report should lead to any kind of spending spree. The need for proper limitation of public spending is a reality which we readily acknowledge.

10.16 But there are other realities at play here. First, the reality of the issue we have been asked to address – if the issue were not real, then Government would clearly have wasted its time and money in setting up the Commission. Secondly, what is in our judgement the realistic nature of our main recommendation in proposing proper and decent public support for the genuinely catastrophic costs of care while making people responsible for their normal living costs. Thirdly, there is the reality of what we are certain is strong public support for our proposal deriving from our extensive public consultation.

10.17 Taking all these considerations together, and recognising that public expenditure decisions and any related taxation implications are ultimately for Government, we consider that our main recommendation, entailing estimated additional costs of up to £1.1bn, is affordable. By definition our less-cost proposals are also affordable. By this we mean that a decision by Government to devote this amount of additional resources to long-term care would be proper and reasonable in our judgement. It is on this judgement that our recommendations ultimately rest.

SCOPE FOR SAVINGS

10.18 We also judge, based on the evidence we have studied, that a number of aspects of the current system offer considerable scope for getting more value for the resources invested. The resulting savings would mitigate some of the extra costs and help to enhance the affordability of our recommendations. We have not sought to put a price on savings which are achieveable, as this would be misleading.

10.19 It has been put to us (by the Audit Commission and by others) that in arranging packages of care individuals are much more likely to be offered services based on provision which has been paid for by the commissioning authority already – either because they own the provision or have entered into block contracts at the beginning of the year. If packages of care were better linked to what people need, more modest packages could meet individuals' needs more effectively and at less cost. This approach is at the heart of our proposals (see Chapter 8) and needs developing further as part of the implementation of "best value" throughout the public services.

10.20 The approach could be facilitated in a number of ways. The Government is developing a new regime of Best Value under which the economy and efficiency of services should be considered alongside effectiveness and quality. Where local authorities continue to be providers as well as commissioners they should subject that provision to a rigorous audit under the best value regime, with proper and realistic costings. Such facilities should not be used unless it can be demonstrated that they represent best value to the care system overall.

10.21 There may be an argument for establishing such facilities as public sector trusts which would compete on cost and quality with the private and voluntary sectors, thus facilitating savings. This would require legislation. In Northern Ireland, all social services are already provided and commissioned by Health and Social Services Trusts. Where inappropriate provision can be disposed of, we suggest that savings in running costs be ploughed back into commissioning services, and that capital receipts be used in innovative partnerships with other sectors to enable more care to take place outside residential settings.

10.22 Second, there should be a greater awareness at all levels of the real costs of packages of care which are suggested for individuals, wherever the public money which goes to support them comes from. Where local authorities' own provision is used, the real costs should be taken into account, so that a proper assessment can be made of the relative cost effectiveness of different care packages.

10.23 We have found no conclusive evidence on how much money could be saved in this way. Evidence submitted by the Independant Healthcare Association[62] suggested £500m. This is something for the National Care Commission together with the Audit Commission, to take forward with central Government.

MORE EFFECTIVE BUDGET MANAGEMENT

10.24 The need for more sophisticated purchasing, with a proper sense of the real values and costs of various options, suggests that a greater degree of flexibility should be offered to those responsible for arranging care. Budgets should be less centralised and held by those who are responsible for arranging the care. More importantly, responsibility for arranging patterns of care for an individual should ideally rest with one person. This too should help to drive down costs. The resulting efficiencies could be taken further by budget pooling on the lines proposed in Chapter 8. This is all part of a renewed emphasis on the system coming together around the client rather than the client fitting into particular services.

10.25 Pooled budgets will be essential to ensuring cost effectiveness and to the successful working of the client centred approach outlined in Chapter 8. We are not seeking a new statutory body to commission care locally, but it is essential that existing bodies work better together, that a single budget is placed somewhere, and that individual clients are not the innocent victims of budgetary disputes. Such disputes ill serve the client and, we believe, take budget holders' eye off the aim of ensuring proper value for money – in the real sense of providing what is most appropriate to the individual at the best cost.

Summary on Savings

10.26 While the case for numerous increased efficiencies (some of them summarised above), has been put to us very forcibly, there have been no studies which have been able to price those efficiencies effectively. The Government, as part of the Comprehensive Spending Review settlement, have established efficiency targets of 2% for 1999–2001 and 3% in 2002. Applied to the baseline spend on health and social services for older people, this produces an efficiency saving of nearly £500m, some of which would arrive in the field of long-term care. However, to achieve this level of improved efficiency will require a step change in practice nationwide, which will take time. It is integral to our recommendations overall that the Government, working with the NHS and local authorities, takes firm steps through the best value programme and other measures to ensure that the efficiency savings are delivered.

DISTRIBUTIONAL IMPLICATIONS OF THE COMMISSION'S PROPOSALS

10.27 It is important to consider how our main recommendation will affect different groups in society. The immediate beneficiaries of our main recommendation - that those who require personal care should be exempt from means-testing for that care - will clearly be those who are in need of care AND currently pay for their care from their own resources. This is a varied group, many of whom have low value houses and income not very different from those who are publicly supported. Therefore not all the self-payers are in the top end of the income distribution. In Table 2.3 in Chapter 2 we set out details on the income distribution of older people.

10.28 The overall distributional implications of our recommendation do not depend only on the beneficiaries and their incomes. The overall net implications also depend on those who pay the taxes currently and their incomes. This is a fundamental point: the overall net distributional effect depends on how monies are raised and not only on how they are spent. We argue that long-term care should continue to be funded from general taxation. Existing taxes that pay for public services are redistributive. The better off will contribute more for benefits which will be realised only if they are in need.

10.29   In addition, the largely progressive nature of taxation as a way of raising money, means that overall distributional consequences are in favour of those in need, with the wealthy paying proportionately more than those on lower incomes. Therefore, we consider that any concern about distributional consequences do not undermine the soundness of our proposals.

A FINAL WORD - ACHIEVING A NEW SECURE CHOICE

10.30   This Report is not about helping the well off – although some of the people who benefit may incidentally be considered "better-off". It is about helping those in need of care. It is about a better and fairer split between costs met by the individual and the state. It is about allowing people to stay in their own homes for as long as they are able, and improving the lives of those older people who need care, and those who care for them.

10.31   In the Commission's considered view, our main recommendations taken as a whole represent an opportunity for a new contract between Government and people and between all generations of society, so that not only will the nations' resources be spent on the care of older people in a more effective way, they will be spent with an aim of promoting increased social cohesion and inclusiveness. We recognise that our proposals do not come without some costs. But they are none the less valid and important. If the state resources we envisage are spent wisely, so that people once more have confidence in the system, this money will have been well spent. It may indeed buy something beyond price. The nation will have demonstrated that it values its older citizens, and will have given them in large measure the best thing any society can offer – freedom from fear, and a new security in old age.

ALL OF WHICH WE HUMBLY SUBMIT FOR YOUR MAJESTY'S GRACIOUS CONSIDERATION

Sir Stewart Sutherland,

Knight (Chairman)

Dame June Clark,

Dame Commander of Our Most Excellent Order of the British Empire

Sir Nicholas Goodison,

Knight

Iona Heath

Joel Joffe,

Commander of Our Most Excellent Order of the British Empire

David Lipsey

Mary Marshall,

Officer of Our Most Excellent Order of the British Empire

Claire Rayner,

Officer of Our Most Excellent Order of the British Empire

Paula Ridley,

Officer of Our Most Excellent Order of the British Empire

Robert Stout

Robin Wendt,

Commander of Our Most Excellent Order of the British Empire

Leonard Woodley,

One of Our Counsel learned in the Law

Alan Davey *(Secretary)*   **Howard Leigh** *(Deputy Secretary)*

Subject to the signed note of dissent which follows this report.

Royal Commission on Long-Term Care of the Elderly
Hannibal House, London, SE1 6TE

WITH RESPECT TO OLD AGE

Note of Dissent

by Joel Joffe and David Lipsey

CHAPTER 1 INTRODUCTION

1.   We have worked closely with fellow Commissioners over the past 14 months. Most of the analysis and recommendations in the Commission's report we enthusiastically endorse. We are therefore profoundly sorry that we cannot go along with one of the two central recommendations of the majority Report, namely that personal care should be provided free of charge, paid for from general taxation, on the basis of an assessment of need.   This is the context in which our note of dissent must be read.

2   The standard of care for old people is not good. Care in residential settings is at best patchy; and in individuals' homes, both of variable quality and inadequate quantity. Given demographic pressures, the cost of formal care could, on perfectly plausible assumptions, rise to five or six times what it is now (Figure 3 Chapter 2). When you add the likely demand of future generations for better care standards, you have a potentially explosive mix.

3.   To make personal care free for all those who are assessed as needing it would make matters worse. In essence, it would transfer initially at least £1.1 billion rising to at least £6 billion in 2051from the private to the public purse[a]. This huge addition to the burden on public expenditure would not, however, increase spending on services for elderly people by a single penny.

4.   Because it would make personal care free for those who qualify for it, it would add to the demand for such care, imposing an additional cost on top of that driven by demographics. Because it would provide public funds irrespective of income, it would weaken the incentive for people to provide for themselves privately. It

(a)   Effect of the proposal for free personal care on public/private costs.

£ billions	Currently	Personal care paid by state
Public costs	7.1 (64%)	8.2 (74%)
Private costs	4.0 (36%)	2.9 (26%)

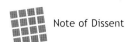

would transfer income and wealth to the better-off members of society and their heirs, at the expense of those most in need. It would pre-empt the state's resources in this area so that it unlikely that some of the Commission's other proposals would be funded.

5.   For it is important to remember a central problem which this Royal Commission was set up to address. Essentially it is this: that there is a clash in Britain today between the resources available to the state and the nation to pay for the long-term care of elderly people, and the expectations of its people in terms of the services they should receive and who should pay for them.

6.   In the course of its work, Commission has witnessed the pain many older people and their relatives feel at the workings of the present system. We heard from many elderly people and their families who thought that the state would provide them with care from cradle to grave. Many were distressed that they could not leave their property in full to their children. Many felt resentful that, while those who had spent their money during their lifetime received care free after a means-test, those who had been frugal had to pay. And indeed there are anomalies caused by the fact that people facing essentially the same problems in their later years may have to pay more or less for their own care depending on where they happen to be receiving it, and whether they are under the health service or local authority care. Something must be done.

7.   At the same time, resources – particularly for public expenditure – are under severe pressure in this as in other fields. Services for elderly people are under-funded. Because scarce resources are focused on those with the most serious disabilities, nothing like enough is done by way of prevention and rehabilitation. The needs of carers and those they care for are neglected. Moreover, expenditure is set to grow rapidly in the future even without any changes in policy. As we explain later, if the standards of care for older people are to rise in line with growing living standards, the percentage of the nation's income devoted to them will have to multiply. In theory, the whole of this cost could be borne by the state. In practice, it will not be. So present tensions, on present policies, will get worse. Something must be done.

8.   But how should these conflicting priorities be balanced? Our approach is as follows. First, the state must estimate and cost the minimum standards of care that it believes to be acceptable and then fund these costs. Second, it must decide what is to be funded by the state and what by elderly people themselves.

9.   In an economy where resources are limited money can either be spent on improving services or providing existing services cheaper or free to those who currently pay for them. There is a tension built into our terms of reference which asks us to have regard both to "the expectations of elderly people for dignity and security" and "constraints on public funds". For, self-evidently, the greater the number of better-off elderly people who are supported by the state and the better the standards of care, the greater the pressure on public funds.

10.   There is a tension too between the need to improve services for those who cannot afford to provide for themselves and the need to make the burden of paying for care more manageable for those of moderate means. It is because of these tensions that priorities are essential. At the end of the day, there is no substitute

for judgement in deciding where the line should be drawn. We set out our judgement in what follows.

11.　Once the need for priorities according to assessed need is accepted we believe that this undermines the case for the free personal care proposal. In its place, however, a practical path for bettering the lot of older people, not just now but to the middle of the next century, opens up. Our full recommendations are listed on page 141 of this Note. In summary we have seven proposals for change which are different from, modify, or add to the proposals made in the main Report:

(a) *Modifying the existing means-test, so that it is less harsh towards people with small amounts of wealth and does not force elderly people to sell their home* **(Chapter 4).**

(b) *Making nursing care (more restrictively defined) in nursing homes free, to get rid of the worst anomaly in the existing system* **(Chapter 4).**

(c) *A genuine public-private partnership in the funding of care, with private savings and private insurance making their contribution* **(Chapter 5).**

(d) *A programme to rescue community care, to prevent disability in old age and to rehabilitate those who can be helped.* **(Chapter 6).**

(e) *Better support for those who care for their elderly relatives and friends themselves* **(Chapter 7).**

(f) *Measures to make sure public spending is used to best effect; and that current waste on inefficiency and bureaucracy is eliminated* **(Chapter 8).**

(g) *Progress towards integrated budgets for the care of elderly people, so that spending reflects real priorities and not perverse financial incentives* **(Chapter 9).**

CHAPTER 2: THE PHILOSOPHICAL CONTEXT

12.　In this Chapter we explain the context of our proposals in terms of the two schools of thought which have dominated the post-war debate about how long term care should be provided. On the one hand, there has been the statist philosophy which dominated "left" thinking roughly from the end of World War II until the mid-1970s. Under this way of thinking, long-term care, like health and social benefits, is the right of every citizen. It should be allocated on the basis of need, not wealth, and paid for from taxation. This, classic welfare socialism, implies universal benefits.

13.　That approach was never coherent, because it was never clear where the necessary funding was to be found. In the 1970s, however, it came to be seen as financially unviable. In the late 1970s and the 1980s, the philosophy of the free market largely took its place. This approach emphasised individual responsibilities, not rights; the inefficiencies of state provision and the virtues of private provision; and the political and economic limits to taxation.

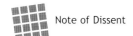

14. There are still extreme free-marketeers today who recommend that the state should stop providing long-term care. But the manifest defects of this thinking have become apparent – most notably that it has never found a way of providing adequately for those not able to provide for themselves. The trend is now away from pure free-market thinking on welfare.

15. This does not herald a return to state welfare socialism. People are groping towards something which is neither wholly statist nor wholly free market but which transcends both approaches. They seek to draw on the insights of both and build from them a policy which is affordable as well as just. Provision should neither be universally public nor universally private. Rather it should be based on a partnership, taking the best from each. We have looked for and found a different solution to the one set out in the main Report within the context of this wider debate.

16. Advocates of the care-through-partnership approach agree with statists that decent care in old age must be available to all who need it. At the same time, they agree with some of the criticisms of state-dictated provision made by the advocates of private provision, for example of the cost and inefficiency of the bureaucratic machinery that supports it and that elderly people who can afford it should accept responsibility to pay for their own care.

17. A number of other broad precepts, though they do not necessarily follow from this philosophical approach, nevertheless underlie our thinking.

   (a) It is not enough merely to focus on public activity in this field. We believe that there is also dignity that comes from providing for oneself in old age if one can afford to do so. As Professor Anthony Giddens says in his book "The Third Way", "old age shouldn't be seen as a time of rights without responsibilities". Universal welfare provision discourages thrift and self-reliance. The central role of families and friends in caring for elderly people should be recognised. The state should nurture that contribution, not merely because otherwise the burden on the public purse will rise – although it will – but also as a compelling matter of social justice.

   (b) There should be no distorting ideological preference for publicly-provided over privately-provided activity or *vice versa*. The skills of the non-state sector must be harnessed, both in the provision of insurance and, even more important, in the provision of care itself; but subject to appropriate regulation which ensures that it does not exploit the old and vulnerable.

   (c) Elderly people, within budgetary limits, should be given what they want. They should be empowered and their priorities met. Individual professions such as nurses, social workers, and doctors all have contributions to make in caring for elderly people, but professional vested interests often erect costly barriers, and should be demolished. Where elderly people prefer to make the decisions, perhaps by receiving cash to buy services rather than services directly, that is what should happen.

   (d) The Commission's terms of reference enjoin it to have regard to "the constraints on public funds". These should be concentrated on those who are least able to provide for themselves. It follows that those who can afford to provide for themselves, in whole or in part, should do so. It is also vital that public money is used to best effect so as to concentrate funds on productive expenditure. The state's contribution needs to be clearly targeted and perverse budgetary incentives must be eliminated.

(e) Policy should not be formulated on the assumption that central projections on costs will be fulfilled. Where there is doubt, it is usually best to err on the side of caution, particularly where huge amounts of the taxpayers' money are involved.

CHAPTER 3: THE CHIMERA OF FREE PERSONAL CARE

18.   The solution to the tensions in Chapter 1 of this Note, favoured by the majority of the Commission, is that personal care should be provided free of charge, paid for from general taxation, on the basis of an assessment of need. This deals at a convenient stroke with half the problem faced by the Commission, by meeting expectations. Unfortunately, it does so only by ignoring the other half: the problem of limited resources.

19.   Any discussion of costs must be set in the context of what would happen to them, if the existing system of care continued. It is true that it is possible to exaggerate the impact of the rising numbers of elderly people on the costs of caring for them. In real terms the cost is set to rise, according to the Commission's report, from some £11 billion for formal care now to £45 billion in 2051. But GDP should also rise, and so, to fund the existing system for long-term care would require, only a relatively gentle increase in expenditure from 1.6% of GDP now to 1.9% of GDP in the year 2051.

20.   Over such a long period relatively small changes in the assumptions can make a big difference to the cost: hence the "funnel of doubt" in the majority report. In particular, if wages of care workers rise faster than the model assumes, or if informal care drops off, then much higher expenditures may be incurred. This alone should lead to great caution in embracing more spending. The Commission's relatively optimistic projections may not be fulfilled.

21.   But there is a more serious flaw in these projections. We believe that they do not reflect adequately future expectations of quality. However, unless we are entering an age of callous disregard for our older people, the demand for higher standards will be irresistible.

22.   Think back 50 years. In those days, the expectation of life for men was only 69 years and for women 74. Those without money who lived long enough to need care, and whose families could not or would not provide it, would be put in local authority care of often deplorable standard, or in repellent geriatric wards in hospital. Rightly, today's richer society will not tolerate either. This rise in standards is reflected, for example, in the costs of residential care which, according to Andrew Dilnot, Director of the Institute for Fiscal Studies, have been rising annually not at the 1%–1.5% above inflation used in the Commission's Report but at 3.5%.

23. Now think forward 50 years, as the Commission has been asked to do. Those generations of older people who grew up before the welfare state, and have modest expectations of the standards of care they should get, will have gone. They will be superceded by new generations brought up to expect more. In 50 years' time, older people will demand support to stay in their own homes, even when their care needs are intensive, and when this is a more expensive way of meeting them than residential care. In residential care, unlike more than half of current residents, they will demand *en suite* facilities, and, unlike more than a quarter of current residents, they will not be prepared to share bedrooms. They will want better than communal lounges to sit in. Endless television will no longer seem sufficient to cater for their recreational and creative needs, and so on. Society then will be much richer than society now; and people in their later years will have a claim on a share of that increased wealth, which they will have helped to create.

24. The report of the Personal Social Services Research Unit "Demand for Long-term care: projections of long-term care finance for elderly people" is relied on by the Commission for all its projections. It puts the point clearly. "It does seem sensible", it says, "to start from the present levels and patterns of care. It needs to be recognised, however, that elderly people, or society in general, may not be content in the future with 1990s care. Expectations about quantity and quality of care may rise. Rising expectations may even put greater pressure on demand for long-term care than demographic changes". And that means that very large sums of money will have to be found for the long-term care of elderly people in future, whether from public or private resources.

25. Insofar as this money comes from people and their families paying for themselves, finding it is not a problem for society. Individuals can allocate their own money as they wish. If they want better long-term care, they will just have to spend less on other things they could buy, and save the money for their old age. They should then be able to buy the long-term care they want.

26. However, insofar as funding for personal care is to come from the state, it is a problem. There, spending on care will have to compete against other desirable objects of increased public spending; and against the natural desire of taxpayers to keep taxes low. While it is relatively easy to justify state spending on minimal provision, it is harder to argue for it for less spartan standards.

27. It is against this background that the decision of the majority of the Commission to recommend making personal care free must be judged. For this recommendation represents a huge transfer of expenditure from the private to the public purse over a period when the public purse is likely to be severely stretched.

28. The cost is alarming. The proposal would cost (quoting the Commission's higher estimate) £1.1 billion initially at 1995 prices, rising to some £2.6 billion by the year 2021 and to £6.4 billion by the middle of the next century. This would add close to a quarter to public spending in this field. These sums take no account of the general pressure to spend more on long-term care; and of consequential improvements in care standards, both to remedy existing inadequacies and to meet future rising expectations.

29. If you cut the cost of something from a lot to nothing, people will want more of it. The extent to which demand would increase is hard to estimate. Evidence from

countries which have tried it is conflicting: demand rose sharply in Holland, though not in Canada.

30. We expect that that there would be a substantial increase in demand for residential care. During the period after the introduction of special additions to benefits to pay the fees of people taken into private residential homes, it was reckoned that nearly a quarter of people who were in residential care did not need to be there[4]. Expenditure rose from £350m in 1985 to £2.5 billion in 1993, forcing the Government to take steps to phase out the scheme.

31. Contrary to fashionable wisdom, there are older people who prefer the security and predictability of life in residential care to staying in their own home. Some older people might choose to go into residential care if the cost to them were reduced, to avoid burdening their children. As is increasingly the case in America, their children may choose to put them in residential care to avoid burdening themselves.

32. As for domiciliary care, there is no evidence of the likely impact on demand. But the psychological effects of providing an entitlement to a free benefit should not be underestimated. Expenditure on social security benefits in Britain has risen rapidly as past social inhibitions to claiming have been eroded, exceeding year after year the Treasury's estimates of their likely cost.

33. Under the majority report's proposals, one of three things will happen. Either the increased demand they create will be met – in which case the proposals will cost far more than the majority estimates. Or the demand will not be met – in which case they will cause anger among those who expected to benefit from them. In practice, most likely they will achieve an undesirable double: both more spending and more discontent.

34. If the Croesian flood of expenditure required to support the free personal care recommendation went to purchase better care for elderly people, then the case for it would be stronger. But it does not. Practically none of it would benefit the worst off in society – for example, the seven in ten in residential care for whom the state now pays. Rather it goes in the first instance simply to provide free personal care for those who are assessed as needing it and who would currently pay for it. Most of the beneficiaries, it is true, are not by any standard rich, though the rich will also benefit. But the priority for state support should be those least able to fend for themselves.

35. Even relatively well-off older people would not be the true beneficiaries. The true beneficiaries would be their heirs, rich or poor.

36. The effect of the free personal care proposal on poor people will not stop there. We live in the real world of limited financial resources, including resources for the care of elderly people. If more of these are absorbed by making personal care free, this is likely to mean less spending on services for poorer elderly people.

37. Free personal care would leave in place, admittedly with reduced impact, the means test. Indeed, just as many people would be means-tested under the majority's proposal as are now. For living costs would still be underpinned by state support through a means-test, as the expeditionary force of Commissioners who

visited Germany to study their new social insurance for care discovered. People would still be forced to sell their homes and run down their savings to pay living costs just as they are now to pay care costs.

38.   At present Britain has a limited form of social insurance. Everyone is insured against not being cared for, because they will be provided with care free if they cannot afford to pay for it for themselves. That gives people various choices. They can insure themselves privately. They can accumulate savings to pay for their care. They can rely on running down their assets, particularly their housing assets. Or they can do nothing. The argument for moving beyond such individual responsibility to collective provision is weak.

39.   Collective provision means people paying higher taxes, and thus having less to spend on other pressing needs such as buying homes and caring for children. In return, they will not have to pay for their care later on. But why should they not pay for their care later on? Then, care will be their principal need. The only other use for their resources will be as a legacy for their heirs. Leaving legacies is something which many people want to do, and which they can enable themselves to do, by insuring for care costs privately. But it is not a goal which everyone shares and towards which everyone should be forced to contribute. Certainly it is hard to see the government, which has just rejected universal compulsion in the field of pensions, introducing something similar for long-term care.

Health and Social Care: a false analogy

40.   The proposal for free personal care rests heavily on the analogy between health care, usually free, and personal care, means-tested. This analogy is given credibility by some serious anomalies. In particular, nursing care provided by the nursing staff in nursing homes is charged for whereas the same care in a residential home, a hospital or domiciliary setting is not charged for – an anomaly which we propose to remedy. However the analogy does not stand up to close analysis.

41.   Health care is unusual in being largely free. Even so, it is simply not true that all health care is free. Few people get osteopathy or acupuncture on the state. Many have to pay for prescriptions and dentistry.

42.   Just because much health care is free, it does not follow that personal care should be free too. There is no principle that says that because one thing is free, something else should be free. It is a matter of where the balance of advantage lies in each case. And there is no point in moving from one admittedly not very satisfactory dividing line (i.e., that now between health and personal care) to another if the other also proves unsatisfactory. Anyone doubting that the new line would be unsatisfactory should look at Appendix 1 to the main Report, and try to work out why some things on it would be free under the majority's proposal and other things on it not free.

The unreliable state

43.   The majority report rightly insists that people should know clearly what they are entitled to in their old age, so that they can make their dispositions accordingly. However, it does not recognise that this in itself constitutes a decisive argument against its free personal care proposal. For even if some government some day introduced it, people could never be sure it would endure.

44.   In the Scandinavian countries, genuine universal welfare states survive. There, people seem to be happy to allow the state to take around 60% of their incomes in tax and provide services in return. But in Britain, and no matter what they tell opinion pollsters, voters seem to baulk at paying taxes totaling much more than 40% of national income. At that level of taxation, universalism in welfare – whether for long-term care, or for pensions, or for unemployment – is always under pressure. The whole trend of recent years is for universal benefits to disappear in favour of more focused benefits.

45.   Even when the state does make a commitment to expand universal provision, it frequently welshes on that commitment. One example should suffice. The state introduced a second pension for all called SERPS in 1978. It halved its value in 1986. It cut it back again under the 1995 Social Security Act and the government, in its pensions review, has just announced its intention eventually to marginalise it. In practice, few people expect anything different as evidence to the Commission showed: young and old alike displayed a disturbing but understandable distrust of the state.

46.   Against this, the report argues that their recommendation would create a solidarity of all classes in society in favour of the new benefit which would make it effectively sacrosanct. This is a dubious proposition. If everyone was sure to receive precisely the same services, it might have force. But in fact the main Report explicitly recognises that the state will pay only for personal care cover. Anyone wanting more comfort or better facilities will have to pay for themselves. Once different people are receiving different care depending on their different incomes, solidarity evaporates.

47.   The proposal for free personal care would in practice harm the long-term cause of elderly people in Britain by diverting resources from the care they need. The remainder of this note sets out our alternative.

CHAPTER 4: SHARING THE BURDEN, RELIEVING THE MEANS TEST

48.   Nobody likes means-testing. It is redolent of the 1930s where people in poverty, through no fault of their own, were stripped of dignity before receiving state support. Though less stigma attaches to means-testing today, the reality is still not pleasant. And there is a suspicion, sometimes justified, that clever people can cheat means-tests.

49.   The traditional hostility to means-testing was among the poor. In this case, however, as our public meetings showed, that hostility extends to better-off people and their dependents. They believe that they had been given a pledge of care "from cradle to grave"; they believe furthermore that they are due that care free; and they are aggrieved that they are not getting it – especially when people whom they believe to have managed their affairs less prudently are getting care from the state for free.

50.   The alleged fecklessness of those who benefit under the existing system is largely urban myth. Most people are not old and poor because they have been feckless. Most people are old and poor because before that they were young and poor – low earners, unemployed, single parents, unable, even if they were willing, to save

enough for their own old age. Moreover, it is an exaggeration to say-as the majority does – that the present system has a tendency to "require impoverishment". Even under the current flawed system, everyone is allowed to keep at least £10,000 of assets and is entitled, if they need it, to adequate care.

51.   Nor does the means-test, as critics sometimes say, remove the incentive to save. Four in five people will never need long-term care. So most people will keep any savings they may make. Of the remainder, many will want better care than the state provides, and will save with the aim of buying it. Indeed, self-sufficiency in old age is why people save.

52.   Sadly, there is no tool in social policy as powerful as the means-test in concentrating limited public spending on those who most need it. That is why the trend under governments of both parties has been for more means-testing. The Government's pensions review published in December 1998, to which we were asked to have regard, is only the latest example.

53.   Current hostility to the means-test for care for older people may prove primarily a generational phenomenon. Anyone in need of care today is likely to have spent their formative years in the immediate post-war era, where state provision reached its apogee. Many now hoping to inherit a house now spent their formative years in the early 1980s, when the Conservative Government was lauding the benefits of home-ownership. Attitudes are changing. New and more realistic generations are coming along: of older people who see in time that they cannot expect the state to pay for everything and younger people who understand that they cannot hope to achieve through inheritance what previous generations have generally achieved only through the sweat of their own brows. Though our own survey of younger people suggests that they want the state to play a major role, it also suggests that they believe that the state cannot and will not pay for everything. In 20, 30, 40 years time it will be accepted that older people draw on their assets to fund their care in the same way, as they now draw on their pensions to pay for their food.

54.   Should we therefore conclude that nothing should be done now? That would be to fail to address the present resentment. We therefore recommend affordable measures which, at more modest cost, would remove the sting of the current means-test and allow people who have accumulated modest assets to retain them. These should be combined with stronger measures to combat the devices used by some people to evade the means-test, and action by local authorities to make sure that they work.

55.   The first of these measures involves little, or perhaps even no cost to the state. Much of the fear of the means-test revolves around people's concerns that their homes will be taken away from them willy-nilly, making a decision to enter residential or nursing care irrevocable.

56.   The extent to which this fear reflects reality is moot. The evidence in support of the often-quoted estimate of 40,000 elderly people losing their homes each year is not strong. Local authorities already have discretion to postpone the sale of an old person's home to pay for care. In any case, of those elderly people who do sell their homes, many do so voluntarily. What matters is less what happens, and more what elderly people fear might happen.

57. We therefore propose that the state offers a virtual guarantee that no old person will have to sell their home against their will. This would be put into practice by a state-sponsored loan against the value of the home of any older person in need of care who does not want to sell, so long as they have equity in it. An appropriate rate of interest would be charged on this loan. When the equity of the borrower reduced to the proposed upper capital limit of £30,000, the usual means-testing rules would apply and additionally the interest on the loan would continue to accrue. The loan would become repayable on death or on the sale of the home.

58. We would expect the cost to the Exchequer to be low. In a few cases, it is true, the loan might turn out in the end to be more than the total value of the house, and thus not prove recoverable from the borrowers' estate. In most cases, however, the scheme would merely involve a funding gap, between making the advance and its repayment.

59. It may well prove possible to get the private sector to fund the requirement over that gap; and to treat it, for public expenditure purposes, as an off-balance sheet expenditure. There is an analogy here with the student loans scheme, though there is also an important difference. A care loan would be secured against a tangible asset, the value of a house, rather than an intangible asset, a student's future income stream. Private finance for the scheme may therefore be more easily achieved than was the case for the student loan scheme. We would not expect the scheme to be used by more than a few of those eligible for it. We would expect that most people, having concluded that they would not be returning home from residential care, would then decide to sell their home rather than to continue to worry about maintaining it. And we would expect some offsetting savings because some older people, enabled by our measure to keep their homes, would return to them, where their care might cost less than in a residential setting. We would be surprised if as many as 1,000 people a year availed themselves of the scheme, though it will alleviate the anxieties of many more. It would initially require around £40 million funding for each of the first two years and a gradual top up each year to £230 million in 2051 but virtually all the money would eventually be recovered with interest.

60. Our second proposal relates to the impact of the present means-test on people with relatively low levels of assets. At the moment, the first £10,000 of a person's assets are disregarded for means-test purposes. For assets between £10,000 and £16,000 they lose £1 a week for every £250 in assets (the "tariff income"), which represents a charge on capital of 20% pa. Above £16,000, they receive no help from the state at all.

61. We believe this is too severe a test in two regards. First, £16,000 is not a high enough top level. We think that people should be allowed to own more than that before being entirely deprived of all help from the state. Secondly, the tariff income is punitive. It far exceeds the rate of interest that could be earned on the excess over £10,000 and therefore means that capital is rapidly eroded.

62. We therefore propose that the band for favoured treatment should be widened from the present £10,000–£16,000 to £10,000–£30,000. We further propose that the tariff income in this band should be halved so it is at a rate of £1 per week per £500 of capital, not £1 per £250. The estimated cost to the Exchequer is £85m

rising to £230 million in 2051. This combination would concentrate help on those with more modest assets.

63. A third proposal is designed to get rid of one glaring anomaly in the present system. While nursing care provided in a hospital, residential home or community setting is free, it has to be paid for by people who pay for their own care in nursing homes. It is impossible to justify this in a society which claims to provide health care free for all, but which in practice denies it to elderly people in nursing homes. It reeks of ageism, and causes understandable distress.

64. The main Report sets out the option of making nursing care free in nursing homes at a cost of £220 million.

65. However, it has been suggested to us by Dr Chai Patel, chair of the Continuing Care Conference, that it could be done for less. This would require that such care was strictly defined as that care which requires the specific knowledge and skill which only registered nurses can provide. Such nursing care would for example include the assessment of health-care needs and specific interventions which require technical competence and knowledge of disease states in such matters as tissue and skin care, administration of drugs, complex medication, incontinence, stoma care and parenteral nutrition.

66. We would envisage such nursing care being provided free as a component of packages of care tailored to the specific, assessed needs of the individual elderly person and provided in regulated accommodation. The cost would be borne by the National Health Service. This would require changes to make the existing regulations governing nursing homes more flexible. These would be consistent with the recent White Paper *Modernising Social Services* and with the recommendations on long-term care of the Better Regulation Taskforce.

67. Dr Patel estimates the cost at an average of £50 per patient per week, resulting in an annual cost of £110m. This seems to us to be of the right order of magnitude. Dr Patel, however, also argues that the changes in regulation would enable more efficient use to be made of nurses' time. This would enable changes to be made in the skills mix between nurses and other staff in nursing homes, which could lead to savings in state spending in nursing homes two or three times as great as this extra cost. This could perhaps free nurses up to meet the shortages at present being experienced by the National Health Service.

68. If Dr Patel is right, it would clearly make sense to introduce the change as soon as is practicable. However, while we are firm that the anomaly should be dealt with, the priority that should be attached to that change must depend on a more detailed examination of its cost and other ramifications by the government, in conjuction with the nursing profession and others.

69. Is this enough? On the one hand, our priority for any state funding available beyond this is the improvement of services for elderly people, particularly elderly people in poverty. On the other hand, we recognise the political pressures to make the means-test less harsh. Therefore, one further proposal is put forward for consideration if ministers take the view that more must be done, now or at some future date when present pressures on spending may be less acute, to reduce the cost of care to individuals.

70.   The proposal concerns those elderly people who, because of the nature of their condition and their longevity, spend a long time in residential care. Although the average length of stay in residential and nursing homes is two years, some 10% of people who pay their own fees are there for four years or more and such people account for around 25% of total bed-years. A proposal designed to address their problems would be that no one with substantial and demonstrable personal care needs should have to pay for more than four years personal care in a residential or nursing home out of their own resources.

71.   This proposal has great virtues. Whereas to have to fund a period of care at the end of your life is a common experience, to have to fund a very long period of care is not. This therefore is insurance against an unpredictable and (from a wealth point of view) potentially catastrophic event. With this underpinning, it will become reasonably possible for many more people, including a majority of home owners, to put themselves in a position where they have enough assets to be self-sufficient in old age, no matter what misfortune then befalls them. Saving to look after oneself would become, for many better-off people, an attainable goal.

72.   Secondly, this proposal brings reassurance. The life of many elderly people in residential and nursing care is not always a happy one. This proposal would enable them, in those earlier years of care, to dip into their savings, knowing that in doing so, they are not eating away a supply of capital they might eventually need to pay for their own care.

73.   Thirdly, it would have a beneficial effect on the market for private insurance (see Chapter 5). Private insurance companies would no longer have to allow in their premiums for the possibility that some policyholders will claim for a very long time. They would also no longer need to conduct their business with one eye on the risk that longevity will increase; and that what seems like profitable business today might turn out to be disastrously loss-making. The price of private insurance would fall. The more people who, as a result, insure privately, the less would be the burden on the state

74.   Fourthly, our proposal would reduce the incentive to abuse the means test. Well-off people are increasingly resorting to various devices to get around means-tests – for example giving their property to their children. These are worthwhile when the sums involved are large. The four-year rule would mean that most of these people would lose only a proportion of their wealth before qualifying for state funding. This would reduce the incentive for abuse.

75.   But there are also powerful arguments against this proposal. It bears a family resemblance to the proposal for free personal care of which we are so critical. It applies without test of need. Its benefits too would go entirely to better-off people; it would do nothing for the poor. Most people who are in care for more than four years will be state-funded because they have exhausted their assets. For residential and nursing care, few who had assets of less than £70,000–£80,000 when they first went into care would benefit. And the cost, at around £250m for nursing and residential care is high, though it would be rather less if it was combined with the free nursing care proposal above. It would absorb state spending that might otherwise go to improve care standards.

76.   For these reasons, Joel Joffe feels strongly that this proposal should not be adopted. There would only be about 5,000 new beneficiaries each year, and the richer they were, the more they would gain. So it is a benefit for the rich and undermines the rationale of the minority case against free personal care, namely that it does nothing to improve services and the effect would be to transfer income and wealth to the better-off in society and their heirs at the expense of those most in need.

77.   David Lipsey appreciates the force of these arguments. Nevertheless he thinks that the case for this proposition, set out above, means that it merits further consideration by government.

CHAPTER 5: THE ROLE OF PRIVATE INSURANCE

78.   Our vision of the future of long-term care is based on a partnership of the state and the individual. The right balance must be struck between what the state provides and what is provided privately. Some private provision will take the form of people spending their savings or running down their assets. Some more will take the form of private insurance. It is on the role of the latter that this chapter concentrates.

79.   Under the majority's proposals, the primary role of private insurance would be to pay living costs for elderly people with disabilities. However, this would do little to cut the state's bill for long-term care. Under our proposals, the more private insurance is used, the more state resources will be available for improving services.

80.   The role of private insurance will always be limited. The reasons why were explained to the Commission in evidence by Professor John Hills of the London School of Economics. Professor Hills does not rest his case on any ideological opposition to private insurance. Rather, he cites a number of technical reasons which limit the provision of attractive policies in this field. They include problems of moral hazard (having policies may encourage people to claim); adverse selection (those most likely to need care may be most likely to insure); uncertainty (people may claim for longer than expected, causing insurance companies to make losses); and inequity (insurance may not be available to some people at greater risk).

81.   These are substantial problems, and quite enough to scupper the arguments of those (for example Professor Patrick Minford of Cardiff Business School) who have argued that state provision in this field should be abolished in favour of private provision. For private provision is no panacea. Policies will remain expensive. They will never provide for everyone; for example, they will not be available to those who are in ill health before they enter old age. They will never provide for everything; low-level care for those with less severe disabilities is unlikely to be met by private insurance. Most provision for the long-term care of elderly people will be either directly funded by the state or directly funded by them out of their own resources.

82.   However, Professor Hill's objections are not necessarily decisive. Many of them also apply to life insurance, which has not stopped insurance companies building thriving businesses selling life and critical illness policies. Moreover, somewhat counter to Professor Hills's analysis, the long-term care market is growing,

admittedly from a low base. According to Laing and Buisson, the leading authorities on care, there are some 23,000 policies in force. Fourteen companies now offer long-term care policies. Commissioners were deluged with submissions from private companies eager and willing to design and market such policies.

83.   There are already policies which can be taken out later in life, when the prospect of needing care becomes more real. Companies offer "point of use" policies whereby you insure on entering residential care, based on the likely length of your stay, and are therefore protected against the costs of living for a long time. Some offer 24-hour "hotlines" for advice and counsel for their customers, something on which the public sector is only just starting. As competition intensifies, it is likely that policies will become cheaper.

84.   Private provision offers an answer to an otherwise difficult conundrum. At present better-off people say: "Why should I pay when the state promised to?" Part of the answer is to say for the future: "The state doesn't promise to pay. If you want to protect your assets for your children, by all means do so – but privately."

85.   The main obstacle to the development of private insurance in this area lies less with the supply than with the demand. People are myopic about old age. David Laibson, a young Harvard economist, has developed the theory of "hyperbolic discounting" which shows that individual have a higher discount rate for events far into the future than for those likely to occur sooner. Thus they will tend to fail to insure against long-term care when they are young and policies would be cheap, and instead will wait until they are old, when policies are relatively expensive. The more state provision there is, the greater will be the temptation to rely on it, with all its inadequacies, rather than to insure privately.

86.   As private insurance is hard to sell, it is worth considering ways in which the state could help encourage take-up. We would not like to see an across-the-board subsidy from taxpayers to purchasers of such policies. For one thing, most of the subsidy would go to those who would have bought policies anyway without the subsidy. However, we would like thought to be given to the existing limitations on the use of pension funds to buy policies. For example, one firm, Cannon Lincoln, in 1991 offered a policy whereby 10% of a pension annuity could be commuted in return for a large increase in the annuity if certain criteria for long-term care were met. This was originally approved by the Inland Revenue, but subsequently disapproved on the grounds that pensions, which are tax-privileged, should not be used in this way. We think this is precisely one way in which they should be used. Detailed policies would require an across-the-board look at policy on the taxation of pensions. We recommend that the government should institute such a review.

87.   Affordability is a big obstacle to private insurance. But, over time, the wealth of better off elderly people is likely to increase substantially-a point that the majority report, which concentrates on their average incomes, misses. According to PENSIM, the government's projections of future pensioner earnings, the incomes of the bottom 20% of pensioners will rise by only 10% in real terms between 1994 and 2025. However those of the top 20% will rise by two-thirds for a couple and more than double for single pensioners. These richer pensioners will be well placed to afford their own care.

88.   Moreover high home ownership will help solve the problem of affordability. There are ingenious schemes available even now which allow people with substantial equity in their homes to release part of that equity during their lives.

89.   In America, around 5% of elderly people have long-term care policies. If by the year 2051 the same were true in Britain, an extra £2 billion at today's prices would be available for long-term care from this source.

90.   All this is subject to one important proviso: that those who buy such products should be fully informed of their costs and benefits and of the alternatives available to them. This requires that their sale should be regulated.

91.   However, the Treasury and the Financial Services Authority are dragging their feet. The FSA's evidence, indeed, could serve as an exemplar of bureaucratic foot-dragging. The market, the FSA told us, "is still at a formative stage". There is "little or no evidence of misselling". Though the FSA Board "considers that the LTCI market has several characteristics that make a strong case for considering an extension", it "is not in a position to commit now to bring conduct of business of all long-term care insurance into regulation". Rather "we will review the position once the Royal Commission has reported and the Government has formulated its response". Even then it will have to conduct a cost-benefit analysis of regulation and "assess the case".

92.   We are disturbed (David Lipsey writing as a member of the board of an existing regulatory authority, the Personal Investment Authority, which favours regulation of long-term care products) by this *insouciance*. As the horse prepares to bolt, the best the FSA can do is to say that it might, one day, get round to looking at the latch on the stable door.

93.   This will not do. We accordingly strongly endorse the proposal in the majority report that the Treasury and the FSA urgently begin work designed to bring all private long-term care insurance within the ambit of conduct-of-business regulation at the earliest possible date.

CHAPTER 6: IN PLACE OF SHORT-TERMISM

94.   As this note of dissent has argued, there will be large additional demands on the public purse to finance care of elderly people in future, even without making personal care free. However, there are some aspects of present provision which, quite apart from the need for to improve standards generally, need to be tackled. We do not hesitate to advocate increased public expenditure – indeed, of all the recommendations in this note of dissent, the ones in this chapter are the ones to which we would give the highest priority.

95.   Care in the community is in trouble. Though it has dealt successfully with some of the most urgent failings of the previous system, it is now chalking up serious failings of its own. Though more hours of care are being provided in a domiciliary setting, those hours have been concentrated on those with the greatest needs. So the number of people receiving care services in their own homes has actually fallen.   Extracts from the Community Care Trends Report on the Impact of Funding on Local Authorities[63], make disturbing reading:

> " a number of Authorities have introduced stringent limits on the number of placements they will make and the services they will provide. These have been introduced as emergency measures in response to budget shortfalls."

> "Eligibility criteria, previously not contentious, are being further tightened as a means of controlling demand."

> "The rationing of services to older people and other user groups must cause concern over the kind of service they will receive in future and the quality of life they can look forward to."

96. Even for those who do benefit under the system, the amount of care provided is low. Figures for the Commission show that of those living at home with the most severe care needs half get no services at all. Even those getting help receive on average only five hours of care a week. In our view, this suggests that needs are not being adequately met.

97. Neatly symmetrical evidence of this reached the Commission from two places not generally regarded as amongst Britain's most deprived: Oxford and Cambridge. A study "Unmet Community Care Needs in Oxfordshire" by the University of Oxford's Social Disadvantage Research Group[64] found that "only those in desperate need receive a service … this clearly leaves many needs unmet." And Andrew Lansley, the Conservative MP for South Cambridgshire, told the Commons recently that "117 people are receiving care packages in the community who should be placed in residential or nursing homes places" and that "an increase in core funding for social services is necessary to prevent deterioration in the position"[65].

98. Community care is not a cheap option. Adding up all the costs of social workers, district nurses and emergency admissions to hospitals, domiciliary care can often cost more than residential care. It is often socially desirable; but its ability to achieve its desirable ends depends upon society also giving it the means.

99. Nor is community care an alternative to residential care, which will also be required on an increasing scale. Some dream of a future where all elderly people are cared for in their own homes. But home care is often more expensive than residential care. Frequently residential care will be the preferred choice of frailer older people, who no longer feel able to support the burdens associated with independent living. Those getting residential care usually need it. The PSSRU (in "Resources, Needs and Outcomes in Community Care") recently reported that "needs-related circumstances of users and careers are the primary cause of admission to institutional care, rather than supply-side issues such as a shortage of domiciliary services …".

100. As numbers of older people in need of care rise, in the next millennium, so too will demand for residential care. Up to twice as many residential and nursing home places are likely be needed in the year 2051 as now. Even at the present capital cost per bed of £30,000, this will require investment of the order of £15 billion.

101. Yet all this is endangered by a lack of resources – there is simply insufficient money in the system to provide adequate long-term care. While in itself far from conclusive in the five year period 1992/93 to 1997/98 the basic amount of the

Personal Social Services Standard Spending Assessment has actually decreased by 6.1% in real terms at the same time as the number of elderly people needing such care has progressively increased. We welcome the proposed additional resources Government has decided to make available as a result of the Comprehensive Spending Review for 1999 to 2000-02 but we agree with the Association of Directors of Social Services that "there is still some way to go before the accumulated deficit of the past is eradicated". Age Concern's final paper (of nine papers) to the Commission states unequivocally:

> "However, no matter what the funding or administrative system, the heart of the current problem is inadequate funding. However financed ... more money must be set aside for those who will need care as they age. The result of the failure to take account of this and to plan accordingly is damaging short termism."

The funding of residential care and the independent sector

102. Local authorities are under budgetary pressure. One way of dealing with that pressure is to cut the amount they pay to independent providers of residential care for their services. And this is what they are doing: according to Laing and Buisson, the experts on this market. Fees rose by only 1.8% between 1996–97 and 1997–98, while the retail price index rose 3.1% and hourly earnings for women, who mainly staff the homes, by 5.2%. Nor are local authority commissioning practices optimal. We found strong evidence that, in order to preserve flexibility in budgeting, they tended to purchase too much in "spot" markets, even though they could better control costs and standards by long-term contracting.

103. This problem would be liable to get worse if the recommendations of the majority of the Commission were accepted. Local authorities would then be almost the only purchasers of care, and thus would be in a position to drive fees still lower.

104. At present, demand for residential care is, if anything, falling. In these circumstances authorities should use only the better homes. What they are in fact doing is to use only the cheaper homes. Fees are not sufficient to provide an adequate return on capital, nor an incentive to quality. Except in specialist fields, where profits are still to be made, bigger companies are building few new high-quality homes. According to Andrew Richmond, a leading Long Term Care analyst of stockbrokers Collins Stewart Limited, the corporate sector is being priced out of the market and unless existing returns, presently of the order of 9%, are enhanced through price rises, little, if any, new capital will be invested. This view is supported by the abysmal performance of four of the five quoted long term care quoted companies all of whose prices have fallen over the last three years (by about 30% on average) while the FTSE All Share Index over the same period has risen by 48%[b].

105. These problems will get worse in the years 2001–2004 when, because of the fall in births during the First World War, there will be a fall in the demand for residential care. While it is desirable that short-term excess capacity in the market is eliminated (particulary in areas where there is a significant over-supply), it is even more important that the purchasing of provider capacity should be conducted in a way that ensures that, when demand rises, as it will, the sector will be able and willing to respond.

(b) The period covered is 1 January 1996 - 9 February 1999. The fifth quoted company performed strikingly well but is not directly comparable as it secured lucrative NHS contracts for long stay patients which guarantee occupancy and price increases.

106. Many care home owners feel forced to respond to lower prices by cutting back on those activities which would improve the quality of care of their residents. Indeed, it is not impossible to imagine British residential homes following the trend apparent in the United States, where, in some places, the use of liquid feeding combined with an institutional approach and a cost-cutting environment means that old people are kept alive but nothing more.

107. To some extent, these problems might be resolved by greater efficiency in the sector. Too many providers use underpaid, undermotivated and undertrained workforces, which underperform. There are devoted people working in the field, but there are also too many people who, frankly, should not be entrusted with such duties.

108. The government is in the process of reforming the system of regulation. Greater flexibility would be helpful. In general, there is too great an emphasis on meeting rigid physical standards and too little on quality measures. In particular, it must be doubted if the regulatory division between nursing homes, which must always have a nurse in attendance, and residential homes which need not, makes sense. A broader and more flexible range of provisions and standards might be more appropriate – and cheaper.

109. What is needed are more sensitive local-authority purchasing policies in the short run; and a more stable basis of funding and more flexible regulation around which the industry can increase efficiency in the long run. The precise mechanism for achieving this should be a priority task for the new Care Commission, recommended in the majority's report.

The funding of domiciliary care

110. An analogous set of problems exists for domiciliary care. Because they are strapped for money, local authorities have had to focus domiciliary care on those with the greatest care needs. These people are getting more. The result is that there is less money available for those with lesser needs.

111. This delineation of priorities, though understandable in the short term, is damaging. Often, a little money spent today on someone with a lesser need (e.g. for a minor housing adaptation) could save more being spent tomorrow when they develop a greater need. But the money is not there to spend.

112. That same policy is leading to the purchasing of poor domiciliary care. Private sector providers are offered extremely low rates to provide services. We learnt of one case in Angelsey where a local authority offered a private provider £2.50 to go out and put an old lady to bed.

113. In domiciliary care, as in residential care, firms often can only make a profit at those rates by using cheap, unskilled labour. So elderly people are often faced with poor quality staff, doing to them rather than for them. The problem is compounded because authorities turn the tap on and off for budgetary reasons, cutting back the private sector when funds are short (often partly to ensure that their directly-employed staff are not cut). What are needed are sensible rates; sensible block contracts for care; and a determined effort to drive up standards with better-trained and sometimes better-paid staff.

Paying for prevention

114.   From the shortage of resources stem other failings. More needs to be spent on preventing a loss of capacity to cope among healthy older people and on rehabilitating sicker older people. Timely interventions can save money (e.g., on future hospital admissions) as well as contributing to human happiness amongst elderly people. People who are deprived of basic support, including cleaning and home maintenance, are likely to give up on independent living, as the Joseph Rowntree Report *Meeting the Costs of Continuing Care* eloquently demonstrates. Providing such support would prevent many admissions into expensive residential care, yet the majority does not recommend funding for this purpose.

115.   Though there is much anecdotal evidence of the value of prevention and rehabilitation, hard economic evidence of its value in Britain is limited. In America, however, the American Federation for Aging Research (APAR) has analysed the potential benefits of postponing the onset of the diseases of aging. They find, for example, that $5 billion a year could be saved by delaying hip fractures; and $8 billion a year from delaying urinary incontinence. An important report *Fit for the Future* by the Continuing Care Conference, sets out policies to improve morbidity in Britain, and we commend it to the government

116.   The state has a responsibility here. But there is a role too for individuals. Older people are not powerless to improve their own lives, for example by taking regular exercise appropriate to their capacities and by not smoking. We seek neither the statist model whereby services are provided without obligation; nor the free-market model, whereby it is all down to the individual. We seek a partnership with obligations on both parties.

117.   That said, we believe that there is an urgent need for more spending in these areas. No-one could give us a very convincing answer to the question of how much. The local authority associations have asked the government for an extra £321m for services to elderly people, though this includes an element for inflation. We recommend that the government should inquire further into the scale of provision that would be appropriate. In our provisional judgement, not less than £300m is required to ensure adequate minimum standards of care and it may be considerably more. The government should use its best endeavours to ensure that this money is applied to the purpose for which it is intended. Some part of any extra money might be awarded on a challenge-funding basis to authorities which came up with the most innovative and convincing plans for its deployment.

Paying for their own care

118   In the future there will be a steady increase in the numbers of elderly people able to afford their own care. While no reliable statistics exist on how the numbers will build up William Laing[66] estimates a possible shift away from the current 66:34 ratio of state funding to personal funding outside peoples's homes to something closer to 50:50 over the next 20 years; the PSSRU[67] estimates shifts of 6% by 2031 while the IPPR[11] sees public provision falling by 2031 from 73% to 39%. Whatever the right number turns out to be, the state will be relieved of a significant burden unless it has committed itself to paying for the free personal care proposal in which event it will deprive itself of the benefit arising from the increasing wealth of elderly people.

Note of Dissent

CHAPTER 7. HELPING INFORMAL CARERS

119. Another area in which sensible additional spending is needed is in support for informal carers, and for those for whom they care. Though more help with caring is recommended by the majority in their report too, in their scheme of things, it will have to compete for priority with their free care proposal. As we do not live in a have-it-all world, the likely consequence is that support for the informal care sector will continue to be minimal.

120. One calculation, by the Institute of Actuaries, valued informal caring at £33.9 billion in 1991. Even in their own terms, such calculations should be taken with a pinch of salt; the Institute of Actuaries, for example, valued informal care at a generous £7 an hour. They are misdirected in another sense too. Economics plays an important part in the life of man, but it is not the whole of the life of man. Informal caring is a term which hides a rich variety of human relationships: between spouses, between children and parents; between kith and kin, friends and neighbours. Most care without giving thought to the financial cost of caring. It somehow demeans them to reduce their dedication to cash amounts.

121. The decline in informal caring has long been predicted. The PSSRU report on demand for long-term care itself concludes that "considering all the factors affecting the availability of informal care together, the prospect is likely that the supply of informal care will decline relative to demand". More marital break-ups, more women working and more mobile lifestyles have often been said to threaten it. Many carers say that they are at the end of their tether; that if they are not better supported they will give up; and that the consequence would be vastly greater costs for the state.

122. Attempts to measure these effects (e.g., London Economics recent study for the Carers National Association) have not proved successful. But it would be unwise to take informal care for granted. Twice as much care is provided informally as is provided formally. It follows that a reduction in informal care would tend to mean a more than proportional increase in formal care. The consequences of a reduction in informal care for spending would be alarming. If 20% less informal care than projected by the Commission materialises, then public expenditure in 2051 would be £3.8 billion, and total expenditure £6 billion higher than on the Commission's projection.

123. It is hard to demonstrate any link between any particular package of help for carers and its outcomes. However, equally it must be true that it is more likely that people will continue to care if they are valued, supported and given incentives to do so. And this is particularly so at the crucial point where the carer is struggling to cope. Prompt help then could forestall a breakdown in the caring relationship. Besides its social benefits, this could save many years of expenditure on expensive residential care.

124. Like our fellow Commissioners, we would like to change things so that the fact of informal care no longer stops people from getting formal care if they need it. This will be particularly important in future, when caring will often consist of an elderly person looking after a more elderly person, often their partner.

125.   But it was respite care which emerged as a main priority from the Commission's written evidence. The difficulty with proposed new rights to respite care is that they tend to be expensive: £290m for example for a right to two weeks of respite care for all those with heavy caring duties. What is needed are ways of extending respite care, not as a right but as something which is concentrated on those in most need.

126.   This could be done through an assessment process. Alternatively, or additionally, respite care could take account of the resources available to the carer and the cared-for person. In particular, the carers who need most support are probably poorer carers, in the worst accommodation, who are the least able to buy outside help and the least likely be able to afford a break from their task. By contrast, though better-off carers give as much, they may be in a position to buy a measure of relief for themselves.

127.   Government in its national strategy for carers (Caring for Carers) has just announced a package for carers at a costs of £140 million over three years. We believe this to be inadequate both on the grounds of need and social justice for carers who, voluntarily and often at great personal cost to themselves, save the Government billions of pounds each year. We recommend a budget of £300 million per year (including the funds announced by Government) to support carers. As to the way this further budget is to be allocated as between services and respite care, we would like to see this emerge from an open dialogue between Government and carers on how this money might be used to best effect. We place less importance than the main Report on "carer blind" services and more on those carers with greatest need who can least afford to care.

CHAPTER 8: PRIORITIES FOR SAVING

128.   As we have seen, there is a real danger that the costs of care will rise sharply over the coming half-century. In addition, implementing even the limited initiatives suggested in this note of dissent would cost money, though much less than is suggested by the majority. There is, therefore, a pressing need to try to identify offsetting savings. The manifold inefficiencies of the existing system – ill-targeted benefits, unnecessary costs and perverse incentives – provide plenty of scope.

129.   The system is very wasteful. For example:

(a) Some local authorities prefer to provide residential care themselves to buying it from the private sector. Some do so for ideological reasons. Others do not want to close existing homes and make the residents move. They object to the low wages paid to workers in residential care homes in the private sector. They do not want to be stuck with unused buildings or to make staff redundant. Still, the gap between the average price of a place in a private residential home (£238 a week) and that in a public-sector residential home (£366 a week) is striking. It is the more so since the Audit Commission has found that local authority homes, despite their higher costs, are not providing higher standards of care. The excess cost of local authority homes over private sector homes totals some £500m pa, though, in fairness, this is coming down already.

(b) Local Authority assessments are carried out by highly trained social workers. Much of their time is devoted to telling people that, for budgetary reasons, they cannot have care which they need. Assessing needs is an empty exercise if those needs cannot be met. Social workers are admirable professionals with admirable skills, but caring, not refusing care, is what they are best at. Using them is very expensive. Social workers cost £38 an hour to run. They currently spend 38% of their time in contact with their elderly clients. Some of this work could be devolved to less experienced staff.

(c) There is separately a concern about the range of costs per place in different Local Authorities for residential care. Yet the Audit Commission has found little relationship between costs and standards.

(d) Some Local Authorities make their budgets stretch by delaying assessments of elderly people. However, this often means high costs for other authorities. Professor Nick Morris, Chair of Research into Ageing, estimates that there are more than 6,000 cases a year where discharge from hospital is delayed, due to slowness in assessments or placements, or through budgetary problems. The annual cost of such delays is estimated at £160m.

(e) The scope for savings from integrated care has not adequately been tapped. We heard of one experiment, the Elderly Persons Integrated Care System (EPICS) in South Buckinghamshire which provides a 24-hours-a-day helpline and short-term flexible care to people over 65. It maintains a database of clients in its area and works closely across health, social services and voluntary sector boundaries. From a 1996 audit study, it is estimated that, by preventing hospital admissions and reducing hospital stays, the service could save 1,354 bed days and £220,000 could be left over for other services, even allowing for the cost of EPICS.

(f) Timely provision of sheltered and very sheltered housing could contribute both to the well-being of elderly people and to reducing the costs of their care. In future, we think that there will be increasing scope for imaginative schemes designed to produce solutions for elderly people which bridge the gap between caring for them in their own homes, and the full panoply of residential and nursing care. We are however not convinced that community-care structures, involving as they do health and social-care professionals, give enough weight to the potential contribution to care of positive and innovative housing policies.

(g) We recommend in the following chapter a standard means-test, to apply in all local authorities, for domiciliary care. Data to calculate a yield for this does not exist, but at present, Local Authorities recover only some £150m of the £1,200m they spend here. If it were possible to double the yield, £150m would be saved, which would pay for half what Local Authorities say they need for community care.

(h) As Chapter 6 says, there might be further savings from more flexible regulation of nursing homes

130.   In sum then, we believe there is scope for substantial savings to offset the new expenditure which we recommend (for a summary, see the Appendix). And even

where better practices would not actually cut costs, they would at least lead to greater efficiency and value-for-money which is the key to appropriate use of public resources today.

CHAPTER 9: BRIDGING THE DIVIDE

131.   Finally, we address one of the most serious problems in the care of elderly people, namely the divide between health, social-security and social-services budgets, and the perverse incentives to budget holders which follows from that. Elderly people now find themselves the innocent victims in a bureaucratic game of pass-the-budget. The health service seeks to discharge elderly people as fast as possible from its hospitals to save money – leaving social-service authorities to pick up the bill. Local authorities, if they cannot prevent this, have a strong incentive to put older people in residential homes – where a large part of the bill is picked up by the Department of Social Security – rather than looking after them in their own homes, where the local authority may have to meet the full cost. The metaphor of the level playing field is doubtless overworked; but this particular game is being played on a pitch which yaws crazily this way and that. Not surprisingly, the results are unsatisfactory.

132.   The first task is to level the field for the authority responsible for commissioning social care. (We come to the issue of what that authority should be below.) This requires, first, that broadly the same means-test should apply for domiciliary care as for residential care. A national means-test applies, as we have seen, for residential care. But current means-testing for domiciliary care is a mess. Some authorities charge everyone for domiciliary care whether they can afford it or not. Research for the Commission by Ken Judge and others suggest that this prevents poorer people getting care they need. Some authorities provide domiciliary care free for all. Some impose a means-test but one which is not in any way standardised. These different practices create a dog's breakfast of distorted incentives.

133.   In one regard, it is not possible for the means-test to work in the same way for home and for residential care. For residential care, the value of a person's house is taken into account for the means-test. To do the same thing for a house in which an elderly person was still living would be too harsh. However, with this exception, we recommend that a standard national means-test should be applied to both home and residential care; and that should be combined with a more rational and uniform tariff of charges for home care.

134.   It would also have an incidental advantage. Under a uniform means-test home care would be free for poor people, so they would not longer be prevented by poverty from getting the services they need.

135.   This, combined with the action to deal with distortions caused by particular social security benefits proposed in the Commission's report, would help. It would not, however, deal with the thorniest problem of all. It lies in the divide between the different budgets for health and social care and those who hold them.

136.   We find it hard to believe that, as long as different authorities with different budgets are responsible for different bits of care, a seamless service will emerge.

Without unified budgets, moreover, choices will be made not on the grounds of what old people want nor even of what is the most efficient way of caring for them, but on the basis of the distorted and perverse incentives which apply to individual authorities.

137.   There are in essence three solutions. One is to give all commissioning of care, including health-related care of elderly people to local authorities. The other is to move in another direction and give it to some body within the health service. The compromise is to provide for some form of joint budgeting between the two. In *Partnership in Action*, the Government is now committed to legislate to make this third option possible.

138.   "Every time we were beginning to form up into teams we would be reorganised" remarked Caius Petronius shortly after the birth of Christ. "I was to learn later in life that we tend to meet any new situation by reorganising and a wonderful method it can be for creating the illusion of progress while producing confusion, inefficiency and demoralisation."

139.   Petronius's description will be recognised by every social worker in the country. We too start from a strong prejudice against major institutional upheaval, which always involves heavy transitional costs. We shall therefore be delighted if the Government's joint budgeting plans are adopted widely, and work. But there are real practical difficulties, including the lack of co-terminosity of health and some local authority boundaries and the demanding changes in management that it requires. More important there are strong obstacles, institutional, professional and political, to amalgamation. Though we would expect central pressures to be brought to bear to try to resolve these issues, we are not yet convinced that progress will be sufficient and sufficiently rapid.

140.   So should we return to the spirit of the Griffiths community care recommendations, and give the lead role and full budgetary responsibility over these matters to the local authorities? We also start with a prejudice in favour of giving more powers to democratically elected local authorities and fewer to non-elected health bodies. This has been compounded by witnessing the way some doctors in high-tech fields syphon off limited resources to their specialities, leaving services to elderly people as "Cinderella Services".

141.   On the other hand, evidence, most notably that from the Audit Commission ("The Coming of Age" 1997) suggests that many local authorities are not currently doing a good job in this field. Costs vary hugely (*ibid*, para 128). Standards vary in a way not related to costs (para 128). There is evidence of much waste.

142.   We should like to think that Local Authorities will themselves tackle these problems in a determined way, and quickly. We should like also to think that joint budgeting will soon become the norm rather than the exception, and work in a way that renders redundant further institutional upheaval. However, we are not entirely convinced that either of these things will happen. Given that we were asked to look ahead, we also looked for a solution which would apply if they did not.

143.   And one big change, proposed by the government, gave us a model to examine. The Government's health service reforms are to create a new level of provider in

and around this field. The new primary care groups, covering areas of around 100,000 population will deal with a wide range of health needs, including GP services. Social care of elderly people would be a natural and important add-on.

144.   We therefore commend in this regard the evidence given to the Commission by Professor Howard Glennerster of the London School of Economics, which proposes that it is at primary health group level in the health service that social and health care should be unified. We envisage the creation of multi-skilled teams including nursing, social work and benefits expertise. They would provide a single point of contact and a single commissioning authority for social care with a single budget. They would be free to move resources from (for example) residential care to domiciliary care; to provide more rehabilitation for those recovering for illness and health advice for those who are still well; and generally to adopt a holistic policy towards the needs of elderly people in their areas.

145.   There are some serious difficulties to overcome before that would be an appropriate solution. Primary care provision is itself highly variable. It will be a long job to get primary care groups working, particularly in deprived urban areas, and they must master their healthcare work before taking on social care too. Because the health service is not used to charging better-off people, it would not be easy to get primary care groups to the point where they able and willing to undertake the necessary means-testing for care. And the use of primary health groups would tend still further to separate social care from housing provision. Even if this proposal was adopted, it would be necessary to create partnership arrangements embracing local authorities and the voluntary housing movement to deal with this aspect of provision.

144.   Realistically, then, this is a long-term approach, as befits a long-term commission. Yet even now, we are permitted one glimpse into that future. In Northern Ireland, where local authorities do not have many powers, social care and health care are in principal integrated. The results are not perfect, but they are encouraging. The Commission visited one area where what would apply in Britain under this suggestion was already in place: the South and East Belfast Health and Social Services Trust. There for example, it was proving possible to keep frail old lady of 102 in her own home, at lower cost than if she had been in a nursing home. That is a tale of hope-which is an appropriate note on which to end this note of dissent.

Summary of main conclusions and recommendations

1. *The Government should allocate additional funding, which we provisionally estimate at not less than £300m, to deal with the present shortfall of funding for nursing homes, residential homes and community care, including more money for home care, prevention and rehabilitation* (**Chapter 6**). *This is our top priority.*

2. *The Government should alleviate the worst effects of means testing* (**Chapter 4**) *by:*

   (a) *Putting in place a loans scheme which would virtually guarantee that no elderly person would be forced to sell their home to pay for care while they retain equity in it.*

   (b) *Raising the ceiling for the means-test from £16,000 to £30,000 and reduce the tariff income for by those with assets over £10,000 from £1 a week per £250 of capital to £1 a week per £500 of capital.*

   (c) *Removing the anomaly that those in nursing homes pay for their nursing care, whereas those in hospitals, residential homes and in their own homes do not, following a detailed examination of the cost and other ramifications of such a change.*

   (d) *(David Lipsey only) Considering further whether to make personal care free to those who have been in residential or nursing care for four years or more.*

3. *To promote a more genuine public-private partnership in the provision of care, the Government should review the tax treatment of pensions, with a view to removing obstacles to the use of pensions to fund policies providing for long-term care, and make the sale of long-term care insurance policies subject to conduct of business regulation* (**Chapter 5**).

4. *The Government should provide an extra £300m (inclusive of the funds already committed under "Caring for Carers") annually to provide help to carers, focusing the extra money on those with the greatest needs, and on poorer elderly people and carers* (**Chapter 7**).

5. *The various options for specific savings set out above, including the phasing out of uncompetitive Local Authority direct provision of residential and nursing care, measures to tackle bed-blocking and the introduction of a universal charging regime and means-test for home care, should be energetically pursued* (**Chapter 8**).

6. *The Government should devote further effort to promoting joint health and social service budgets for care; and consider in due course whether these budgets should be invested in its proposed primary health groups* (**Chapter 9**).

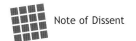

Appendix

Summary of costs and savings

The following table summarises the costs and savings in the Note of Dissent.

COSTS

	Base (% GDP)	2021 (% GDP)	2051 (%GDP)
Means-test made less onerous	£85m	£200m	£490m
Nursing home nursing free	£110m	£280m	£730m
Community care addition	£300m	£620m	£1,425m
Carer's package	£230m	£385m	£725m
Total	**£725m (0.1)**	**£1,485(0.12)**	**£3,370(0.14)**

SAVINGS

Run-down in Local Authority's own residential homes	£500m
End of bed blocking	£160m
Uniform national means-test for domiciliary care	£150m
Total	**£810m**

Notes:

1. *It should not be read into these figures that this is a nil cost package. The savings are more speculative and may arise over a longer time period than the items of extra spending.*

2. *Spending would rise by a further £200m-£250m if David Lipsey's tentative suggestion of free care after four years was accepted.*

3. *There might be a further saving of getting on for £300m if the changes in the use of nurses in nursing homes do indeed produce the savings projected by Dr Patel.*

4. *The Guarantee against home repossession is not a cost because it is recoverable against the security of the home.*

COST COMPARISON

This table is a comparison of base year and projected costs as between the main Report and the Note of Dissent

		1995	2021	2051
Base case (cost of current system projected as in Chapter 2 of Main Report) (note 1)	£bn	7.1	12.1	27.0
	%GDP	1.0	1.0	1.1
Cost including Main Report recommendation for free personal care (note 2)	£bn	8.2	14.7	33.4
	%GDP	1.2	1.2	1.4
Cost including Main Report recommendation for free personal care plus carer package (note 3)	£bn	8.4	15.0	34.1
	%GDP	1.2	1.2	1.4
Cost including Note of Dissent recommendations (note 4)	£bn	7.8	13.6	30.4
	%GDP	1.1	1.1	1.2
Cost including Note of Dissent recommendations plus David Lipsey's proposal for state funding after four years	£bn	8.0	14.2	31.9
	%GDP	1.1	1.1	1.3

Notes:

1. *Total of first two rows in table 2.6 main Report - Base case; projections of long term care costs for older people, UK at 1995/96 prices*

2. *Table 6.8 main Report*

3. *Tables 6.8 and Table 8.1 main Report. The main Report does not combine the figures in these two tables.*

4. *The cost elements included here are*
    Means test made less onerous
    Nursing care free in nursing homes
    Community care addition
    Carer's package

WITH RESPECT TO OLD AGE

DISSENTIENT NOTE BY JOEL JOFFE AND DAVID LIPSEY

Joel Joffe,
Commander of Our Most Excellent Order of the British Empire

David Lipsey

WITH RESPECT TO OLD AGE

References

1. Report of the Pensions Provision Group, Department of Social Security (1998), *We all need pensions – the prospects for pension provision*. The Stationery Office Ltd.

2. Wittenberg R., Pickard L., Comas-Herrera A., Davies B., and Darton R. (1998), *Demand for Long-Term Care: Projections of Long-Term Care Finance for Elderly People*. Personal Social Services Research Unit, London School of Economics/Kent University/University of Manchester.

3. Netten A and Dennett J (1997), *Unit Costs of Health and Social Care*. Personal Social Services Research Unit, University of Kent at Canterbury .

4. Laing and Buisson (1997), *Care of elderly people – Market Survey 1997*. Laing and Buisson.

5. Government Memorandum to Royal Commission and communication from Department of Health and Social Services for Northern Ireland.

6. Goodman A., Johnson P. and Webb S. (1997), *Inequality in the UK*; pp. 64–66. Oxford University Press.

7. Swiss Re Life & Health (1998), *Long Term Care Data Pack*. Swiss Re Life and Health Ltd.

8. Department of Social Security (1997), *Family Resources Survey: Great Britain 1995/96*. The Stationery Office Ltd.

9. Department of Social Security (1998), *A New Contract for Welfare: Partnership in Pensions*. The Stationery Office Ltd.

10. Nuttall S., Blackwood R., Bussell B., Cliff J., Cornall M., Crowley A., Gatenby P., and Webber J. (1994), *Financing long term care in Great Britain*. Journal of the Institute of Actuaries, 121, 1, 1–68.

11. Richards E with Wilsdon T and Lyons S. (1996), *Paying for Long-Term Care*. Institute for Public Policy Research.

12. Office for National Statistics (1998). *Informal Carers: Results of an independent study carried out on behalf of the Department of Social Security as part of the 1995 General Household Survey*. The Stationery Office Ltd.

13. Pickard L. (1998), *The Demand and Supply in the Informal Sector*. Personal Social Services Research Unit, internal paper.

14. London Economics (1998), *The Economics of Informal Care*. A report by London Economics to the Carers National Association. London Economics/Carers National Association.

15. Office for National Statistics (1996), *Living in Britain: Results from the 1994 General Household Survey 1994*. HMSO.

16. Netten A., Bebbington A., Darton R., Forder J., and Miles K (1998), *1996 Survey of Care Homes for Elderly People: Final Report*. Personal Social Services Research Unit; Discussion Paper 1423/2, University of Kent at Canterbury/ London School of Economics/ University of Manchester.

17. Health Committee (1996), *Long Term Care: Future Provision and Funding*. Third Report, Volume 1, HC 59-1. The Stationery Office Ltd.

18. Analysis undertaken by Personal Social Services Research Unit (see 2 above) for Royal Commission.

19. Bebbington A. C. and Darton R. (1996), *Healthy Life Expectancy in England and Wales: Recent Evidence*. Personal Social Services Research Unit, Kent University.

20. Millard P. *et al.* (1998), *Discussion document on the interactions and costs between health and social care*. Submitted as evidence to the Royal Commission.

21. Fenn P. (1999), *Financing Long Term Care; The Potential for Insurance*. Research Volume 1 of the Report by The Royal Commission on Long Term Care. The Stationery office Ltd.

22. Wittenberg R. (1999), *Economics of Long Term Care Finance; Review of literature and issues*. Research Volume 1 of the Report by The Royal Commission on Long Term Care. The Stationery Office Ltd.

23. Department of Health (1998), *Modernising Social Services*. The Stationery Office Ltd.

24. Wright F. (1998), *The effect on carers of a frail, older person's admission to a care home*. JRF Findings No. 478; Joseph Rowntree Foundation.

25. Sir R. Griffiths (1988), *Community Care: Agenda for Action*. HMSO.

26. Department of Health (1989), *Caring for People: Community Care in the Next Decade and Beyond*. HMSO.

27. Audit Commission (1997), *The Coming of Age: improving care services for older people*. Audit Commission.

28. Burchardt T. and Hills J. (1997), *Private welfare insurance and social security: Pushing the boundaries*. YPS for the Joseph Rowntree Foundation.

29. Clarke H. and Parker G. (1997), *Attitudes and Behaviour Towards Purchasing Long Term Care Insurance*. Nuffield Community Care Studies Centre, University of Leicester.

30. Dr W. Scanlon of US General Accounting Office in testimony to Senate Special Committee on Aging, 9 March 1998.

31. CML Research (1997), *Ageing, Home Ownership and the Mortgage Market*. Forrest & Leather.

32. Department of Environment (1993); *English House Condition Survey 1991*, HMSO.

33. Hancock R. (1998), *Can Housing Wealth Alleviate Poverty Among Britain's Older Population?* Fiscal Studies.

34. Joseph Rowntree Foundation/Joseph Rowntree Housing Trust (1998), *Failure: Equity Release*. Joseph Rowntree Foundation.

35.   Henwood M. and Wistow G. (1999), *Evaluating the Impact of "Caring for People"*. Research Volume 3 of the Report by The Royal Commission on Long Term Care. The Stationery Office Ltd.

36.   Department of Social Security analysis of Family Resources Survey: Great Britain 1995/96.

37.   Department of Social Security (1998), *Supporting People: A new policy and funding framework for support services*. Department of Social Security.

38.   Health Committee (1999), *The Relationship Between Health and Social Services*. First Report, Volume 1, HC 74-1. The Stationery Office Ltd.

39.   The Audit Commission (1998), *Home Alone: the role of housing in community care*. The Audit Commission.

40.   Tennstedt S., Crawford S. and McKinley J. (1993), *Is Family Care on the Decline? A longitudinal investigation of the substitution of formal long-term care services for informal care*. Millbank Quarterly 71, 4, 601-24.

41.   Davies B, Fernandez J-L and Saunders R (1998), *Community Care in England and France: Reforms and the Improvement of Equity and Efficiency*. Ashgate.

42.   Tinker A., Wright F., McCreadie C., Askham J., Hancock R. and Holmans A. (1999), *Alternative Models of Care for Older People*. Research Volume 2 of the Report by The Royal Commission on Long Term Care. The Stationery Office Ltd.

43.   Challis D. (1999), *Assessment and Care Management: Developments since the Community Care Act Reforms in the UK*. Research Volume 3 of the Report by The Royal Commission on Long Term Care. The Stationery Office Ltd.

44.   Department of Health (1998), *Partnership in Action – New Opportunities for Joint Working between Health and Social Services*. Department of Health.

45.   The Scottish Office (1998), *Modernising Community Care – An Action Plan*. Scottish Office.

46.   Continuing Care Conference, Prevention of Dependency in later Life Study Group (1998), *Fit for the Future; The prevention of dependency in later life*. Continuing Care Conference.

47.   Clark H., Dyer S., Horwood J. (1998), *That Little Bit of Help: The high value of low level preventative services for older people*. The Policy Press.

48.   Joseph Rowntree Foundation and Community Care (1996), *The Cost of Care; The impact of charging policy on the lives of disabled people*. The Policy Press.

49.   Wistow G. and Lewis H. for Anchor Research (1997), *Preventative Services for Older People: Current approaches and future opportunities*. Anchor Trust.

50.   Nocon A. and Baldwin S. (1998), *Effective Practice in Rehabilitation: The evidence of systematic reviews*. King's Fund.

51.   Sinclair S. and Dickinson E. (1998), *Trends in Rehabilitation policy; A review of literature*. King's Fund.

52.   Royal Commission Secretariat (1999), *Lessons from international experience*. Research Volume 1 of the Report by The Royal Commission on Long Term. The Stationery Office Ltd.

53. Forrest R., Leather P. and Pantazis C. (1998), *Home Ownership in Old Age; The future of owner occupation in an aging society.* Anchor Research.

54. Patel N. (1999), *Black and Minority Ethnic Elderly: Perspectives on long term care.* Research Volume 1 of the Report by The Royal Commission on Long Term Care. The Stationery Office Ltd.

55. Better Regulation Task Force (1998), *Long Term Care; Review.* Central Office of Information.

56. Martin J., Meltzer H and Elliot D (1988), *OPCS Surveys of Disability in Great Britain 1985.* HMSO.

57. Craig P. and Greenslade M. (1998), *First Findings from the Disability Follow-up to the Family Resources Survey.* Research Summary No. 5; Analytical Services Division, Department of Social Security.

58. Department of Health, *Department of Health Personal Social Services Statistics. March 1996 for care homes; September 1996 for home care:* Department of Health.

59. Information provided by Professor B. Davies, PSSRU, University of Kent at Canterbury – from the Evaluating Community Care Project.

60. Kestenbaum A. (1998), *Work, rest and play.* York Publishing Services.

61. Estimated figure provided by the Independent Living Funds.

62. Figure quoted by the Independent Health Care Association.

63. Edwards P. and Kenny D. (1997), *Community Care Trends 1997: The Impact of Funding on Local Authorities.* London Research Centre.

64. Coren E. and Noble M. (1995), *Unmet Community Care Needs in Oxfordshire.* Oxford University Social Disadvantage Research Group.

65. *Hansard*, House of Commons, Col. 326, 11 November 1998.

66. Laing W. (1993), *Financing Long-Term Care: The Crucial Debate.* Age Concern England.

67. *Evaluating Community Care for Elderly People*, PSSRU Newsletter, September 1998. Personal Social Services Research Unit, University of Kent.

Appendix 1

AIDS AND ADAPTATIONS – HOW THEY SHOULD BE PAID FOR

Examples of where some aids and adaptation may fit within any charging structure						
Item	**Usually Assessed by**	**Care****			**To be Charged?**	
		H	PC	LC	No	Co-Pay
Mobility						
Wheelchair	Physiotherapist or GP		✔		✔	
Zimmer frame	Physiotherapist		✔		✔	
Walking Stick	Physiotherapist		✔		✔	
Ramp	Occupational Therapist			✔		✔
Stair lift	Occupational Therapist			✔		✔
Outside rails	Occupational Therapist			✔		✔
Riser chair	Occupational Therapist			✔		✔
Bedfast at home						
Bed	Nurse	✔			✔	
Commode	Nurse		✔		✔	
Special mattress	Nurse	✔			✔	
Pressure cushions	Nurse	✔			✔	
Kitchen aids						
Safety devices (eg. cut-off for cooker)	Occupational Therapist			✔		✔
Raised/lowered surfaces or sink	Occupational Therapist			✔		✔
Special cutlery	Occupational Therapist		✔		✔	
Bathroom aids						
Raised toilet seat	Occupational Therapist		✔		✔	
Bath seat	Occupational Therapist		✔		✔	
Hoist (fixed or mobile)	Occupational Therapist/Nurse		✔		✔	
Shower	Occupational Therapist			✔		✔
Downstairs WC	Occupational Therapist			✔		✔
Toilet frame	Occupational Therapist		✔		✔	
Bath boards	Occupational Therapist		✔		✔	
Bath rail	Occupational Therapist		✔		✔	
Incontinence pads	Nurse		✔		✔	
Technology						
Alarm systems	Social Worker		✔			✔
Possum	Hospital			✔		✔
Safety devices for people with dementia	Social worker or Occupational Therapist		✔		✔	
Compliance aids for drugs	Nurse	✔			✔	

*   *Procedures for assessment, and the practice of who it is undertaken by currently varies from area to area*
** H   = *Health care – to do with therapy or treatment*
     PC = *Personal Care – to do with the promotion of personal care*
     LC = *Living costs – aids to daily living*

Appendix 2

MAPS SHOWING CO-TERMINOSITY

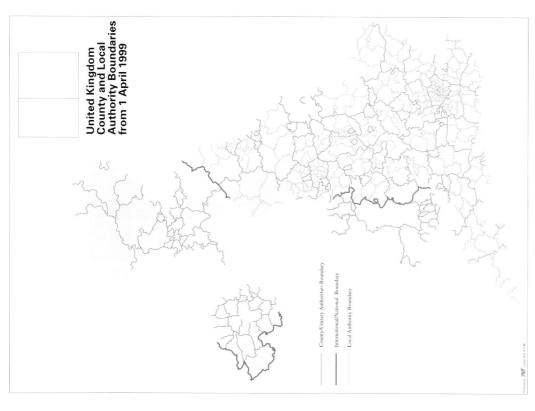

United Kingdom County and Local Authority Boundaries from 1 April 1999

County/Unitary Authorities Boundary

International/National Boundary

Local Authority Boundary

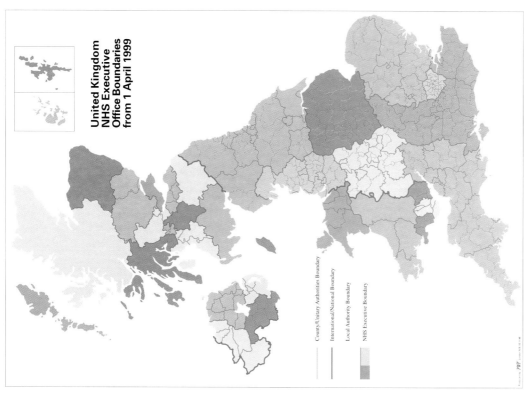

United Kingdom NHS Executive Office Boundaries from 1 April 1999

County/Unitary Authorities Boundary

International/National Boundary

Local Authority Boundary

NHS Executive Boundary

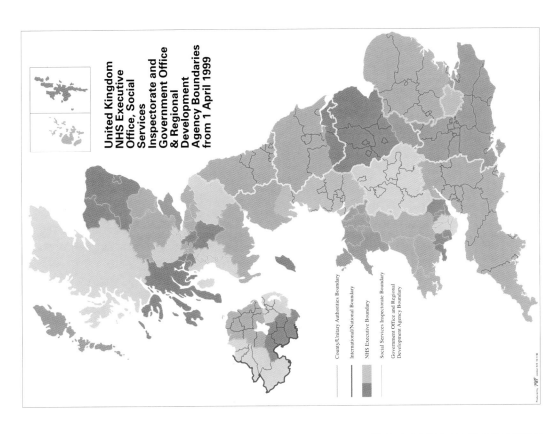

United Kingdom
NHS Executive
Office, Social
Services
Inspectorate and
Government Office
& Regional
Development
Agency Boundaries
from 1 April 1999

County/Unitary Authorities Boundary

International/National Boundary

NHS Executive Boundary

Social Services Inspectorate Boundary

Government Office and Regional
Development Agency Boundary

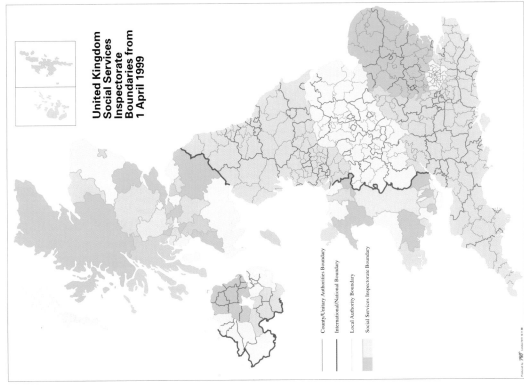

United Kingdom
Social Services
Inspectorate
Boundaries from
1 April 1999

County/Unitary Authorities Boundary

International/National Boundary

Local Authority Boundary

Social Services Inspectorate Boundary

Appendix 3

MEMBERS OF THE SECRETARIAT

- Liz Baldock

- Stephen Bateman

- Alan Davey

- Carl Evans

- Gillian Farnfield

- Patrick Hennessy

- Stephen Hillcoat

- Howard Leigh

- James Morbin (until May 1998)

- Becky Sandhu

- Silroy Silvera

- Roz Vialva

Appendix 4

PLACES VISITED BY THE COMMISSION

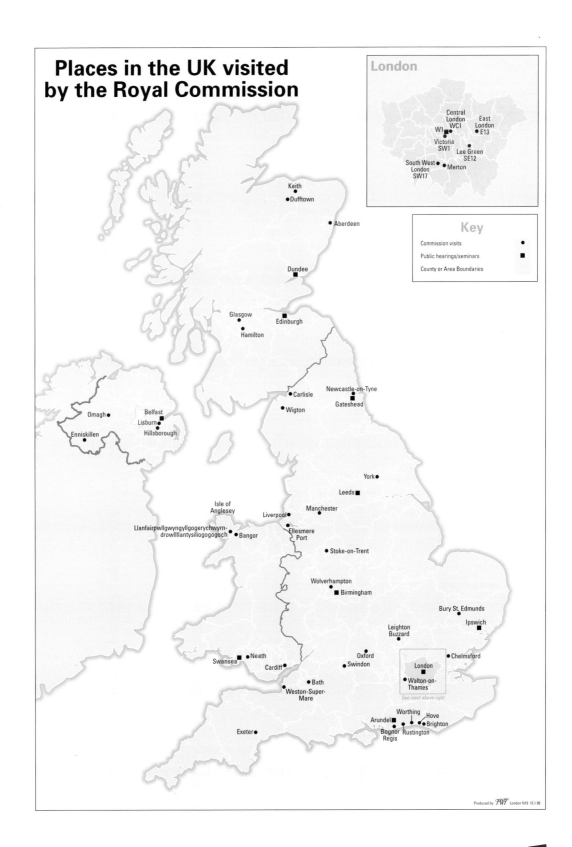

Places in the UK visited by the Royal Commission

London

Central London WC1
W1
East London E13
Victoria SW1
Lee Green SE12
South West London SW17
Merton

Key
Commission visits ●
Public hearings/seminars ■
County or Area Boundaries

Keith
● Dufftown
● Aberdeen
Dundee ■
Glasgow ●
Edinburgh ■
Hamilton ●
● Carlisle
Newcastle-on-Tyne ■
● Wigton
Gateshead ■
Omagh ●
Belfast ■
Lisburn ●
Enniskillen ●
Hillsborough ●
York ●
Leeds ■
Isle of Anglesey
Liverpool ●
Manchester ●
Llanfairpwllgwyngyllgogerychwyrn-drowllllantysiliogogogoch ● Bangor
Ellesmere Port
● Stoke-on-Trent
Wolverhampton
■ Birmingham
Bury St. Edmunds ●
Ipswich ■
Leighton Buzzard
Neath ●
Oxford ●
● Chelmsford
Swansea ■
Swindon ●
Cardiff ●
London ■
● Bath
Walton-on-Thames ●
Weston-Super-Mare
See inset above right
Worthing
Arundel ■
Hove
Brighton ●
Bognor Regis
Rustington
Exeter ●

Produced by *TWT* London N19 15.1.99

Appendix 5

EVIDENCE TAKEN BY THE COMMISSION

1.   The Royal Commission has been greatly helped by the information and evidence provided by organisations and individual members of the public. As well as this written evidence, the Commission held six well attended public hearings around the country and an oral hearing in London with a number of national representative organisations; made a number of visits across the UK to see how care is delivered and spoke directly to older people, carers and those providing care within the formal sector; made a number of visits to other countries; set up a Reference Group of larger, national organisations with an interest in long-term care with which we held an initial conference and whom we consulted on particular points. We held a number of seminars bringing together researchers and experts in relevant fields and commissioned specific research. We have consulted with organisations like the Audit Commission for England and Wales and Agencies like the Housing Corporation and the Northern Ireland Housing Executive. During the year we have also been in regular contact and held meetings with Government Departments.

2.   We cannot thank enough those who contributed to our work.

SUMMARY OF WRITTEN EVIDENCE SUBMITTED TO THE ROYAL COMMISSION

3.   Written submissions were sent by 1,438 individual members of the public. People from a wide range of backgrounds have written to us. These include health professionals, care home owners, carers, social workers, financial consultants, researchers, academics and most importantly, members of the public with an interest in long-term care of older people, either directly or within their family. A full list of all the individuals and organisations who submitted evidence is provided at Appendix 6.

4.   We found the submissions to be detailed, clear, well thought through and helpful to our work. We have deposited the submissions from organisations with the Public Records Office so they can be viewed by those interested in our work, except where organisations indicated their submissions should be confidential.

5.   As promised in our call for evidence we have not made direct reference to individual submissions within our Report, although a number have been quoted anonymously to highlight specific areas of concern. People from many backgrounds have given us their views and conclusions which reflect their experiences with the current system of long-term care provision. While they do not represent a random sample we were struck by the consistency of many of the messages presented including:

- people find it hard to find information on which they can make reasoned judgements and choices; many of the decisions taken that effect their own and their families lives seem to be taken out of their hands;

- the process for questioning decisions is labyrinthine, and takes so long that a satisfactory resolution is unlikely;

- charging policies are unfair and seen to penalise the thrifty and those who have shown the foresight to provide themselves with some financial security in their later years.

6.   Long-term care, as we have shown, covers a wide range of interests and issues. This is also reflected in the submissions. Each submission has been considered by the Commission individually in terms of its content and as part of the weight of views which have directed our deliberations to some of the issues of most concern. In this short report, rather than provide a summary of the general content of evidence, we have indicated some of the main areas of concern on which there was a general agreement.

WRITTEN EVIDENCE SUBMITTED BY INDIVIDUAL MEMBERS OF THE PUBLIC

7   Submissions of written evidence from individual members of the public have been separated from those provided on behalf of local and national organisations.

8.   Submissions from the public received by the Commission cover a wide range of issues and concerns and these are set out on page 165. They cover:

- *The funding and financing of long-term care;* how care is or should be paid for and the wide ranging problems this has created and how these can or should be addressed.

- *Cost of care;* the actual cost of care provision to the user and how the Commission should address this.

- *Care/carers;* who provides the care by whom, where, how and why; problems experienced in delivering care; ideas on how such problems can be overcome.

- *Other issues;* ideas that are new, or have yet to be exploited within long-term care systems for older people, including international perspectives on long-term care for older people.

FUNDING

The sale of assets

9.   A great many people have expressed concern about being forced to sell their family homes to raise sufficient funds to pay for residential and nursing home care. As a consequence, they have little choice but to take irreversible actions and decisions, and are denied the opportunity to pass on their estate to children or relatives. However, although fewer, a number of people indicate their willingness

to finance care from all available sources including the sale of their home as well as the use of other personal assets and savings.

10.   Others, have suggested methods of raising capital without having to resort to selling their homes such as endowments, equity release schemes (based on the value of a property), and inheritance tax.

Long-term care insurance

11.   There have been a wide range of views on whether a insurance scheme for long-term care should be private or public. Of those who have addressed the issue a higher number were in favour of public provision (46%), a significant proportion suggested a shared responsibility (36%) and some suggested that all should take out private insurance (17%). Many indicated that they would prefer an extension of the National Insurance scheme or funding through income tax to enable the state to finance long-term care provision. Other submissions suggest the introduction of compulsory state and private long-term care insurance. We were told that in our approach we needed to take account of the needs of today's older people who had expected, through their own contributions to receive "cradle to grave" care free at the point of delivery. To avoid expensive premiums in later life, some suggested that younger people could be educated on the need to make provision by taking out long-term care insurance policies earlier in their lives, and that tax relief on premiums could be introduced as an incentive.

Extending capital disregard

12.   Many submissions asked the Commission to consider recommending a substantial increase in the practical approach of the current ceiling of £16,000 in personal savings, capital and other assets, including a persons former home, above which help with care home fees is not available.

Unfairness of current system

13.   The unfairness of the current system is number of submissions. These indicate a general dissatisfaction at the manner in which those who have saved and made financial provision for their later years appear to be penalised by having to pay for their own care. While most point to the moral imperative of meeting the needs of those who have been unable to provide financially for themselves, there is what can only be described as an expression of outrage against those who should have been able to provide themselves with more financial security, but have chosen not to do so.

Welfare benefits

14.   A number of comments were made on entitlements to Social Security benefits and other state financial assistance schemes:

- there remains a lack of awareness of entitlement to welfare benefits;

- ineligibility for Attendance Allowance while in local authority residential care homes;

- the inadequacy of Income Support payments for those with "preserved rights";

- a number of unpaid carers asked the Commission to take account of the financial cost of caring, in terms of income foregone and future pension rights.

COST OF CARE

Residential and nursing home fees

15. Many submissions commented on the level of fees for long-term care in residential and nursing homes. There were two very opposite views expressed. Members of the public, families with a member in institutional care, generally expressed the view that the weekly charges were too high, while those running residential care and nursing homes suggested that the power local authorities have as purchasers had driven down charges too far. Several contributions expressed the need for independent audits and inspections to be carried out to ensure homes were providing value for money. There were a number of moving personal accounts of the difficulties encountered when people moved from one local authority jurisdiction to another, where the fees the new authority would meet were lower. The Commission were asked to consider the introduction of national flat rate fees.

Nursing

16. A great number of people pointed to the apparent contradiction in charging which means that care provided by nurses is free at point of delivery across all settings apart from when a person is placed in a nursing home. Many of the people who addressed this topic referred again to the National Health Service, and what they felt had been promised by successive governments in terms of "cradle to grave" care. There were many clear calls for nursing to be made free across all care settings.

DELIVERY OF CARE

Health and social care divide

17. Evidence relating to the differentiation of health care, free at the point of use and social care, usually subject to a means-test, was submitted by many individual members of the public as well as those involved in providing services. The evidence was indicative of a wide debate and knowledge of the practical difficulties faced on the ground. Submissions were wide ranging and, surprisingly consistent at pointing to problems in the existing system, these included:

   - Duplication of responsibilities assessments and provision of care services;

   - Confusion for the user in finding a clear gateway to services created by too much bureaucracy;

   - A perceived waste of resources;

   - The need for an integrated 'seamless' service;

   - Joint health and social care budgets; and

   - Clear lines of responsibility.

Residential and nursing home care

18. Submissions that included a view on institutional care were generally consistent in their messages. A number of people made the point that all care in residential

and nursing homes should be provided by suitably qualified staff, and there was some recognition that the low pay and status attributed to care assistants, together with a lack of a career structure caused problems in some establishments. Many suggested that national care standards should also be used to determine what are good and bad homes. There were a significant number of submissions from relatives and friends of those in residential care homes that recounted bad experiences related to the general treatment of residents. These included a perceived lack of care, distress caused through inadequate laundry arrangements and the disappearance of personal clothing. They highlighted perceived difficulties and fears many people face if they attempt to complain or question staff on such issues.

Domiciliary care

19.   The generally expressed preference for older people to receive care while in their own home and for as long as practicable was clearly backed up by the evidence received from the public. A number of submissions address particular areas of concern with domiciliary care; the irregular timing of visits and the time formal carers can provide within tight schedules, the number of different staff that might undertake such duties, and the lack of regulation of care staff.

Respite care

20.   As an issue, this was included in the submissions of a number of unpaid carers. They expressed the view that respite care should be more widely and frequently available to meet the needs of carers and families, reducing the stress that caring for a disabled person without any opportunity of a break can cause.

Care for those with dementia

21.   The evidence received particularly from those working in the caring services pointed to the growing demand for specialised care in residential and nursing homes for older people with Alzheimer's Disease. Other contributions ask the Commission to record that additional care provision should also be provided for the terminally ill and the physically disabled.

Charitable and voluntary organisations

22.   The Commission has received a great many examples of residential homes and other services run through charities and voluntary organisations that were viewed by those who worked with them or received services as providing good quality care.

Sheltered housing

23.   Many submissions containing positive accounts of innovative sheltered housing projects operating throughout the country have been received. There is a clear feeling that such schemes can enable older people to retain their independence and autonomy while providing care services and personal security.

Older people as part of the community

24.   A significant number of submissions of evidence recounted the benefits that can flow from and to older people who remain and are active within the community. Details and support for various independent living and active lifestyle initiatives set up by local authorities and voluntary organisations were received. These not only enable older people to achieve their maximum independence, but also allow

them the opportunity to participate in wide ranging activities including physical exercise, mentoring, arts & crafts, and working within the community for the benefit of themeselves and the community.

New technology/Information technology

25.   Most evidence concerning new technology and information technology have come within submissions from the academic, and scientific community. The Commission were asked to consider the availability and potential of new technologies, particularly advances in information technology, and how these might enhance the current and future quality of life. Mention was made of a number of initiatives that already exist in this area and those seen as possible in future; from community alarms to more complex interactive information systems. This evidence clearly indicated that such innovations are likely to be applied further and become increasingly important.

International comparisons

26.   A few respondents drew on their knowledge and experience of long-term care provision in other countries, often pointing to particular aspects they might like to see adopted in the UK. The countries referred to were Australia, Scandinavia, Germany, France, New Zealand, Japan and Hong Kong.

WRITTEN EVIDENCE RECEIVED FROM ORGANISATIONS

27.   In this summary, organisations have been listed by broad area of interest.

CARERS

28.   Evidence has been received from organisations representing carers such as the Carers National Association and the Princess Royal Trust for Carers, as well as many of their local branches, carer initiatives, and carers' support groups. Issues surrounding unpaid care were often central to the evidence provided from a wide range of organisations, in particular the Alzheimer's Disease Society and Alzheimer Scotland – Action on Dementia and the National Federation of Women's Institutes. Evidence stressed the importance of the carers' role – to the individual, to society in general and to formal care provision. Carer organisations made the point that, in their view, the caring undertaken by unpaid carers saves the country billions of pounds and that support for carers can prevent or delay admission of older people to residential care or nursing homes. Particular emphasis was given to informing the Commission on carer's direct experience with the current arrangements for formal care services at the local and national level.

29.   This evidence reinforced many of the concerns by the general public, such as the availability of and access to information and advice. In general there was a balanced approach to the help that carers may themselves require to help them and with formal assistance and provision directed at older people themselves. The provision of respite care, at minimum cost, was the single most common issue raised. Other prominent concerns were the decline in emphasis on rehabilitation, the neglect of continence issues, and the need for flexible care services. Submissions also addressed specific concerns about the stress and health of carers,

and the financial burden that caring placed on them while caring and its effect on their pensions position in later life.

30. The uncertainty of the future was stressed in much of the evidence. The changes in the make-up of society, the growing evidence of looser family ties, and number of divorced older people were suggested as factors that may cause a reduction in the future availability of informal care. This argued for greater recognition within society of the carers' role and the importance of providing the information and support they require.

FINANCIAL SECTOR

31. Evidence was received from the financial sector; insurance and reinsurance companies, banks, building societies and their associations, pensions organisations, independent financial advisers and friendly societies. These provided detailed information on the availability of and costings behind current long-term care insurance policies, demographics and public attitudes and motivations. All considered that the private financial sector had an important role in the future funding of long-term care, though many recognised current difficulties with the pricing of insurance policies and the affordability of equity release schemes. A number of specific approaches were suggested including linking long-term care insurance to pension policies and limiting the years of liability.

32. There was a general belief that fiscal incentives should be considered to encourage self provision and reduce costs, and that proper regulation would be important for public confidence.

HEALTHCARE ORGANISATIONS

33. We received evidence from organisations across the UK who have a particular interest in healthcare including the Royal Colleges, the NHS Confederation, UNISON, the Independent Healthcare Association, health authorities, NHS Trust hospitals, GPs and Community Health Councils. The evidence concentrated mainly on the delivery of health and care services. They provided much detail, comment and analysis on the current system of long-term care delivery and gave examples from across the UK of innovative approaches being undertaken, tested and researched. Many of these included joint working and partnership arrangements with local authority social services around hospital discharge arrangements funded by "winter pressures" money in 1997. A number of organisations addressed the complex issues surrounding the health and social care divide in more detail. There was widespread agreement that partnership between health and social care authorities was the way forward rather than a major reorganisation of responsibilities.

34. Organisations placed great emphasis on the process of assessment for long-term care needs. There was particular agreement on the application of a multi-disciplinary approach, though their views occasionally differed on the relative importance/leadership of the individual professions involved. There was a consensus that there was a current lack and need to increase the role of

rehabilitation in the care of older people. Within domiciliary settings many pointed to the important role that community nurses play and the particular public confidence they generate.

LOCAL AUTHORITIES

35. We received evidence from individual local authorities from all parts of the UK as well as umbrella organisations such as the County Councils Network, the Local Government Management Board, the Local Government Association, and the Convention of Scottish Local Authorities. Associations representing Directors of Social Services Directors and Social Workers and UNISON who provided detailed and comprehensive submissions. Like health related organisations many provided detailed comment and analysis on the current system of long-term care delivery and gave examples from across the UK of innovative approaches being undertaken, tested and researched. Again, there was a general agreement that the way forward was through joint working and partnership arrangements.

36. Many submissions highlighted the importance of joint local planning arrangements between health and local authorities and the need for these to incorporate housing issues. It was pointed out by some that joint planning arrangements were improving. Some organisations considered that national assessment tools and eligibility criteria would assist in providing a greater degree of equality of access to provision around the country. Most organisations were concerned that many of the current difficulties arose through insufficient funding. Other issues that were addressed included the need for additional support for carers, the quality of care being offered and the introduction of national framework of care standards across health and social care.

HOUSING

37. Detailed submissions were received from the National Housing Federation and the social housing funding bodies with responsibilities in all areas of the UK. A large number of housing associations provided evidence, and submissions were also received from property consultants and companies/charitable trusts involved in developing retirement communities and very sheltered housing as well as those operating care and repair schemes for existing housing. Submissions from local authorities also emphasised the importance of housing in the long-term care of older people. Most recognised that providing suitable housing was a prerequisite of ensuring that older people could retain their independence and remain in their own home in the community for as long as possible.

38. Many organisations provided a wide range of reports, surveys and research that provided a depth of information on practical concerns, public attitudes and future trends in housing that were invaluable to the Commission. Submissions provided detail on the innovatory approaches to mixing housing and care, and to funding/purchasing arrangements. Concern over the current review of Housing Benefit in supported housing schemes was raised by many. A number of organisations involved in sheltered housing reflected on the increasing dependency of tenants.

39.   The state of repair of owner occupied houses was an issue for a number of organisations. Many argued for the cost effectiveness of minor repairs and maintenance and providing cash for aids and adaptations for older and disabled people, but pointed to lack of information, difficulties in procedure and the length of time arrangements can take as being major drawbacks. Details on "care and repair" and "handyman" schemes from all parts of the UK were submitted as a means by which some of these concerns might be better addressed.

PENSIONERS' GROUPS

40.   We received evidence from several pensioners' associations and retirement fellowships as well as the National Pensioners Convention. Their evidence and views tended to mirror the themes in the public evidence and included individual member's experience and a number of local surveys on long-term care and community care issues. Submissions expressed the fact that pensioners had been sold "cradle to grave" care as part of the welfare state, had kept their side of the bargain by paying taxes throughout their lives and were now being let down. There were many comments about the level of retirement pension and pensioner's incomes, and on the current system of funding long term care often involving the sale of houses. Great emphasis was placed on preserving the independence, autonomy and dignity of older people who need care.

41.   Many made the point that more emphasis should be placed on health promotion, rehabilitation and health maintenance for older people. Many remarked that the means-test in itself was humiliating. Where mentioned the preference was for a state run system of long-term care funded through general taxation.

42.   Other points of concern were the variation of charging arrangements for home care in the UK, standards of care provided in both homecare and institutional care situations and the general underfunding of long-term care.

VOLUNTARY BODIES

43.   A range of National and local voluntary bodies concerned with long-term care for older and younger disabled people provided evidence. Evidence was submitted about detailed research projects, national and local surveys, opinion based on experience and accounts of older people's direct experience of the current system of long-term care delivery. This highlighted the special needs of mentally ill people and people with learning disabilities particularly when they are in need of long-term care, the needs of people caring for them as well as the cost of good quality care. Attention was drawn to the difference in approaches between the funding and operation of services for younger disabled people and older people.

44.   Submissions tended to agree that older people want to stay in their own homes as long as possible and that funding should be targeted to achieve this. There was an emphasis on the equality of access to services and the quality of care provision. There was a general agreement that the current levels of service provision were inadequate and a number of organisations expressed concern that some local authorities were delaying referrals as a method of rationing their resources, and

restricting choice by giving preference to their own services. A number of organisations reflected the general public's concerns about the sale of homes, but like the public, some suggested that it was an appropriate use of financial assets to pay for institutional care. There was also a general belief that people required more information and guidance to steer their way through a complex system, and many detailed examples of large and small care-related initiatives from around the UK.

45. Many submissions covered detailed concerns about the current split and differences in charging between health and social care. There were a number of calls for national care standards, and national approaches to assessment of needs and eligibility criteria. It was suggested that within Government there should be a Minister for older people.

PRIVATE SECTOR CARE HOMES

46. We received evidence from owners of residential care homes, nursing homes and dual-registered homes. A number of national representative bodies also provided submissions in writing and orally. Overall, there was great emphasis on trying to ensure that older people got the services and quality of care that they wanted. There was a recognition that the private sector has a poor public image but said that as a sector they were providing high standards of care at competitive prices.

47. The role of Local Authorities was a general concern. Many indicated that they would prefer to see Local Authorities as enablers of care rather than enablers and direct providers. A number suggested that Local Authorities provided more expensive placements in their own homes before using private residential homes and that there dependency levels of clients referred to them was increasing. There was also a general concern about the present levels of fees that would be met by Local Authorities. Submissions indicated that in many areas there was a shortfall of funding between the Local Authority fee and their running costs at the expense of quality of care and financial viability of some. Examples of a number of industry led initiatives being taken forward with Local Authorities, that sought to reassure the public on quality, provide better information, and reflect the cost of good quality care provision in the Local Authority's contracting process were detailed.

48. Most submissions recognised that there was a need to register care homes and indicated a strong preference for a single registration process for residential and nursing homes that would reduce bureaucracy.

VOLUNTARY SECTOR CARE HOMES

49. A number of detailed submissions of evidence were received from voluntary and charitable providers, running care homes and offering a range of home care and information services. Similar views to the private sector were expressed on the increasingly grey area between residential and nursing homes, and the level of fees met by Local Authorities. Many made the statement that although their costs were rising fees paid by Local Authorities were not keeping pace or increasing. In these circumstances a number indicated that the shortfall in funding was being

met by charitable donations putting at risk new developments and improvements. A number of submissions raised the issue of culturally-sensitive provision, believed that it should be available as of right, and indicated that there was a growing demand from minority ethnic groups for such provision.

50. Many voluntary and charitable operators detailed particular schemes that emphasised the need for community links and which provided support and services to older people in their homes through the use of volunteers

RESEARCH ORGANISATIONS

51. In addition to research provided and referred to in more general evidence, a number of submissions from Universities, research bodies and individuals were received. These covered a wide range of topics, and addressed the funding of long-term care for the older people in particular, care quality standards, and the use of technology in enabling people to stay at home for as long as possible.

OTHERS

52. A number of submissions of evidence were received from other organisations which do not fall into these general categories. These raised a number of pertinent issues and included elder abuse, medication for older people in general and its use in institutional settings, international comparisons with care provision and funding arrangements, mental and social stimulation particularly in care homes, and employment issues in care homes.

THE ROYAL COMMISSION'S REGIONAL HEARINGS

53. The Commission held public meetings hearings throughout the United Kingdom (Swansea, Dundee, Belfast, Ipswich, Arundel and Gateshead) between April and June 1998. At the same time members of the Commission visited local services and met doctors, nurses, social workers, care managers, purchasers and providers of health and social care services, users – old and young – of care services, their carers and people with academic or other interest in the subject. In all, we saw close to 800 people. We were pleased that the public demonstrated an enthusiasm for our visits by turning out in all weathers and travelling long distances to be with us. We were delighted with their candour and their ability to get their points across in such a clear way. We should like them to know that we have weighed their views very carefully in reaching our recommendations.

54. While we acknowledge that the views of those who did attend should not be regarded as strictly representative of the public as a whole, we cannot ignore the remarkable consistency of the views we heard between these meetings and in our written evidence. The public are certainly not content with things the way they are and there was clear demand for and consensus in favour of change.

55. There were many personal and harrowing accounts of neglect of older people. The public were dismayed by how complex the system was and how difficult it was to navigate through it. The public could not understand the difference in distinction

WITH RESPECT TO OLD AGE

between health and social care and why this had to continue; for the public care was care no matter where it came from and who gave it. The sense of betrayal or "cradle to grave" care was palpable.

56. The plead for more care, compassion and respect for older people was clear. Society had to change its perceptions of older people – they should not be marginalised or old age seen as "boring", but rather older people should be seen as people who can and do continue contribute in a very active way to the well-being of their families and of society in general.

57. When it came to the *provision of services*, there were low expectations of the availability of both health and social care services. The public were in no doubt that with adequate provision of home care services – often just help with domestic tasks or supervision and proper rehabilitation after serious illness, people could and would wish to remain in their own homes for as long as possible rather than move into residential care or nursing homes.

58. On the key question of how to *pay for long-term care* there was a general willingness to pay more into the system (either through contributions or taxes) provided it was seen to be spent on long-term care. There was undoubted opposition to means testing for care costs, although there was a willingness to accept means testing when it came to things like help with accommodation costs in care homes. The public were adamant that the way funding was organised at local level needed to be simplified.

59. There was unanimous support for more help for unpaid *carers*. There needed to be more recognition of the valuable role they played; more support by way of short breaks and more financial support to compensate them for loss of income now and in the future.

60. For *future generations*, the public expressed the views that there was a need to create incentives and remove the present disincentives for the younger generation to provide financially for their own long-term care.

THE COMMISSION'S VISITS IN THE UK

61. Many of the organisations and individuals who wrote to us giving evidence invited the Commission to see the care services that they were involved in supplying or were receiving. We were sorry not to have been able to take up all the invitations we received. However we were able to make almost a hundred visits during the year. We considered it particularly important to see the range of services and provision currently available and seek the views of older people, their unpaid carers and those engaged in the providing formal care. We thank all those who we met for their time and the forthright views they expressed. The Commission were struck by the commitment and enthusiasm shown by those we met in the caring professions, and the liveliness and independence of the older people we talked with.

62. Every effort was made to include an appropriate range of visits to all parts of the UK. We wanted to include as wide a range of service provision as possible, taking in generally available services as well as the more innovative approaches, an

appropriate balance of providers, public, private and voluntary. As part of this we included some wider aspects looking at arts and education projects set up for older and younger disabled people. We have not detailed each visit we made but provide a map (Appendix 4) showing the locations of our visits around the UK.

63.   Again, we would wish to thank all those who we met, particularly those people whose time and homes we intruded upon. The information and evidence they provided formed much of the background to our discussions and remained at the forefront of our minds as we formed our recommendations.

THE COMMISSION'S INTERNATIONAL VISITS

64.   The Commission made a number of visits to gather evidence and discuss the experience of other countries. Visits were made to Germany, Australia, New Zealand and Denmark. A full account of these is provided in Research Volume 1.

THE COMMISSION'S ORAL EVIDENCE DAY

65.   The Commission held an oral evidence day on 24 September 1998 which took evidence from some of the larger nationally representative organisations in the UK. This was held in public. A full record of the hearing is available on the Commission's Web Site (www.open.gov.uk/royal-commission-elderly/). The organisations invited to give evidence and be question by the Commission were:

Age Concern

Lady Sally Greengross (Director General)

Evelyn McEwen (Director of Information & Policy Services)

Lorna Easterbrook (Community Care Services Policy Officer)

Pauline Thompson (Community Care Finance Policy Officer)

Help the Aged

Mervyn Kohler (Head of Public Affairs)

Michael Lake (Director General)

Tessa Harding (Head of Planning & Development)

Carers National Association

Francine Bate (Assistant Director of Public Affairs)

Tia Khan (Board of Trustees)

Malcolm Wicks Esq MP (Vice President)

Joanna Wood (Policy Researcher)

Tim Willesden (London Economics)

Alzheimer's Disease Society

Brian Roycroft (Chair)

Clive Evers (Director of Information & Education)

Dr Julia Cream (Research & Policy Officer)

Emily Holzhausen

Jeremy Holmes (Economists Advisory Group)

Alzheimer Scotland/Action on Dementia

Mary Hope (Convenor)

Dr Alan Jacques (Vice Convenor)

Prof Alison Petch (Council Member)

Jean Henderson (Council Member)

Jan Killeen (Assistant Director of Public Policy)

Continuing Care Conference

Desmond Le Grys (Chairman)

Terry Bamford (Royal Borough of Kensington & Chelsea)

Barry Hassell (Independent Healthcare Association)

Sandy Johnstone (Commercial Union)

Dr Chai Patel (Chai Patel Associates)

THE COMMISSION'S REFERENCE GROUP

66.   The Commission recognised that to fulfil its task within the timescale it had been given it would need to draw on the considerable expertise of organisations with a direct interest in long-term care. A range of organisations were invited to join the Commission's Reference Group that could facilitate discussion, give their particular views on issues, and provide background information, evidence and research. A list of the Reference Group membership is at Appendix 7.

67.   The Commission began its dialogue with the Reference Group at a special conference on 12 February 1998. This provided the opportunity for the Commission to explain the way in which it would work generally and the values that would underpin its considerations. It also provided many of the Reference Group member organisations with their first opportunity to discuss issues directly with the Commission. A record of that meeting was published afterwards and is available on the Commission's Web Site.

68.   Following the Conference, the Commission proceeded to have contact with individual members of the group asking for views, evidence, explanation and detailed information on specific issues. We would like to take this final opportunity to thank all the members of the Reference Group for their assistance over the past year. We asked them some complex questions, often at short notice.

Their replies were clear and concise and always contained the offer of further explanation – an offer we took up on more than one occasion.

RESEARCH

69   There was already an extensive body of research available on issues that relate to long-term care of older people. Our attention was drawn to a great deal of this by the submissions of written evidence and our contact with members of the Reference Group. There were issues on which the Commission thought it would be necessary and advantageous to arrange for particular reviews, symposia of experts and commission specific research. The short timescale we had to work in imposed difficulties with those we asked to undertake such work. All put aside other work and priorities to provide us with the evidence that we needed. The reports and research we commissioned have all been published in our three Research Volumes – the contents of which are listed in Appendix 8. We commend it to those who have an interest in long-term care of older people.

Appendix 6

NAMES OF THOSE WHO SUBMITTED EVIDENCE

Abbeyfield Northern Ireland
Abbeyfield Oban Society Ltd, The
Abbeyfield Society, The
Abbotsford Nursing Homes
Aberdeen Committee for the Elderly
Abuel-Ealeh, Muhammod (Mr)
Accounts Commission for Scotland
Aconley, M (Mrs)
Action for Dysphasic Adults
Addison, Andrea
Adika, V (Mr)
Affleck, M A (Mrs)
Age Concern Cambridgeshire
Age Concern Carers' Support Centre, Swansea
Age Concern Cornwall
Age Concern Cymru
Age Concern Edinburgh and Leith
Age Concern England
Age Concern Falmouth
Age Concern Hampshire
Age Concern – Institute of Gerontology
Age Concern North Wales Central
Age Concern Northern Ireland
Age Concern Rushden
Age Concern Scotland
Age Concern Surrey
AgeNet
Agespan
AGILE/The Chartered Society of Physiotherapy
Agudas Israel Housing Association Ltd
Aitken, David
Akers, J M
Al-Hasaniya Women's Centre
Alder, Joan
Alex Constant Consultancy
Alford, R S
Allamby, Les
Allden, Richard
Allison, Roy (The Rev)
Almshouse Association, The
Alston, W C
Alzheimer Scotland – Action on Dementia

Alzheimer Scotland/Scottish Borders Dementia Carers' Panel
Alzheimer's Disease Society
Alzheimer's Disease Society – Mid Surrey branch
Alzheimer's Disease Society – Salisbury and District branch
Alzheimer's Disease Society – Sheffield branch
Alzheimer's Disease Society – Sunderland branch
Anchor Housing Trust
Anderson, J (Mrs)
Andrews, G (Mr)
Antsee, Derrick
Anwylfan Carers Group
Archard, Patricia (Mrs)
Armour, Maurice
Armstrong, M R
Arthor, S R (Mrs)
Arthritis Care
Ashby, Margaret (The Rev)
Association for Residential Care
Association of Bexhill Citizens, The
Association of British Insurers
Association of Charity Officers, The
Association of Consulting Actuaries, The
Association of Directors of Social Services, The
Association of Directors of Social Work (Scotland)
Association of Greater London Older Women
Association of Hospice and Specialist Palliative Care Social Workers
Association of Retirement Housing Managers, The
Athey, E R A (Mr)
Atkins, F L (Mr)
Atkins, Jillian K A (Mrs)
Atkins, M R, Moss, G E and Stout, I H (Drs)
Atkinson, David (MP)
Atkinson, Marion E (Mrs)
Atwill, Shirley K (Mrs)
Austin, Frances

Bacon & Woodrow (Actuaries and Consultants)

Bailey, B (Mr)

Bailey, R

Baker, Chris

Baker, Eva (Mrs)

Baker, P G (Mr)

Baldock, Martin (Canon)

Baldwin, R J (Mrs)

Balfour and Manson (Solicitors0

Balsom, Elizabeth M

Banbury, Marjorie (Miss)

Barber, S G (Dr)

Barclay, Betty M L (Mrs)

Barker, K J

Barker, P F (Mr)

Barker, Phillip

Barman, D (Mrs)

Barnes, C (Mr)

Barnes, Wyn

Barnet Community Health Council

Barnett, Elizabeth (Dr)

Barnstaple and District Trades Council

Barraclough S (Mr)

Barron, David L

Bartholomey, Annette

Bartley, A C (Miss)

Barton, M J (Mr)

Bates, P J

Battams, G F (Mr)

Bawden, R C (Mr)

Bayley, B A (Mrs)

Beasley, Ronald

Beattie, D C (Mr and Mrs)

Beaumont, Judy (Mrs)

Beck, Florence I (Miss)

Beck, Pamela C (Miss)

Becker, Marilyn (Mrs)

Beeton, C MBE (Cllr Major)

Begbie, Gilbert G

Behrman, C M (Mrs)

Bell, Alison L

Bell, C R (Mr)

Bell, Eleanor (Mrs)

Bell, Leonore (Mrs)

Bell, Martin J

Bell, Stephen W (Dr)

Bellis, John

BEN (Motor and Allied Trades Benevolent
  Fund)

Benbow, S (Dr)

Benger-Stevenson, I

Bennett, Colin B

Bennett, Grace (Mrs)

Bennett, I M (Miss)

Bennett, Maggie (Miss)

Beringer, T R O (Dr)

Berkeley, K G C

Berry, A W (Mr)

Berwick, John

Beth Johnson Foundation, The

Bett, Marion M (Ms)

Bevan, Anna RGN (Ms)

Beveridge, G (Mr)

Bevington, J C (Prof)

Beyleveld, Janet (Ms)

Bicknell E (Miss)

Bidgood, Reginald

Bills, George

Birch, Chris

Birch, Phyl (Miss)

Birch, Teresa M (Ms)

Bird, Pat (Mrs)

Birstall Methodist Church

Biscoe, Peter

Black Country Family Practice, The

Black Country Housing Association

Black, Robert

Blackburn, B R

Blackman Group, The

Blair Lodge Nursing Homes Ltd

Blake, Lynda E (Mrs)

Blamies, A C (Mrs)

Bloont, T (Mr)

Blyth, Pam

Board of Deputies of British Jews, The

Bolton, D (Mr)

Bolton Joint Strategy Team

Bolton, W (Mr)

Bond, John (Prof)

Booth, John S

Bourne, S J (Mr)

Bowden and Newtown Parish Churches

Bowden, Phyllis M (Mrs)

Bowen-Bravery, B M (Mrs)

Bower, Alan

Bowers, H M (Miss)

Bowles, Joan (Mrs)

Bowman, Clive E (Dr)

Bowman, George

Bowman, M L (Mr)

Bowman, Michael P (Dr)

Bracknell and District Mental Health Carers
  Group

Bradbury, P (Mrs)

Bradford and Northern Housing Association

Bradford Metropolitan District Council

Bradley, J P (Mr)

Bradley, K (Mr)

Bradshaw, Ann (Dr)

Brady, S (Mrs)

Bramham, John (Mr)

Brandon, David (Prof)

Brandon, Michael

Bratchell, G E

Breeds, Jon

Bregar, Olive (Mrs)

Brendoncare Foundation, The

Brent & Harrow Health Authority

Brettell, K (Mrs)

Briant, David (Mr)

Bridgeman, John H

Briggs, J L (Mr)

Brighton & Hove Council, Social Services

Brighton & Hove National Care Homes
    Association

British Association of Social Workers

British Bankers Association

British Dietetic Association Nutrition Advisory
    Group for Elderly People, The

British Geriatrics Society for Health in Old Age

British Medical Association

British Medical Association, Scottish Office

Broadbent, B M (Mrs)

Brockman, V (Mr)

Brockwell, H E (Mr)

Bromley Community Health Council

Brook, Simon S (Dr)

Brooker, Judith

Brookes, E (Dr)

Brooks, R W S (Dr)

Brooks, Richard and Shirley (Mr and Mrs)

Brooks, Stephanie (Mrs)

Broughton, David

Broughton House Home for Disabled Ex-
    Servicemen

Brown, Derek

Brown, H (Mr)

Brown, Olive (Mrs)

Brown, P E

Brown, R (Mr)

Browning, Judith (Miss)

Brownsell, Simon

Brun, Richard S (Mr)

Brunelcare

Buchan, Margaret M (Mrs)

Buckland, Lavender (Mrs)

Bullock, Michael W T (Mr)

Bunning, M (Mr)

BUPA

Burcher, M (Mrs)

Burden, G E (Mr and Mrs)

Burley, Robin

Burnett, Helen B (Mrs)

Burns, Marion

Burton, John

Butcher, C V (Mr)

Caan, Wood (Dr)

Cadman, Jean (Mrs)

Caffry, R A (Mr)

Cairns, J C and M P (Mr and Mrs)

Cairns, Margaret

Caithness Community Care Forum

Cambridge Royal Albert Benevolent Society

Camden and Islington Community Health
    Service

Cameron, Isabel (Ms)

Cardiff Community Healthcare NHS Trust

Care and Repair England

Care Forum Wales

Carers Information and Support Services

Carers National Association

Carers National Association – Belfast Central
    branch

Carers National Association – Brecon and
    District branch

Carers National Association – New Milton
    branch

Carers National Association – Newcastle branch

Carers National Association – Reading,
    Wokingham and West Berkshire branch

Carers National Association – Richmond branch

Carers Support Service in Mid Downs

Carers' Support Group Meeting at Reardon
    Court

Carewatch Care Services Ltd

Caring, Catering and Shopping Service

Caring Times

Carran, Elaine (Ms)

Carrick and Kerrier Carers Forum/Restormel
    Carers Forum

Carson, George (Dr)

Carter, Derek and Elizabeth (Mr and Mrs)

Carter, E J (Mrs)

Carter, Tom OBE (Mr)

Casey, Donal (Mr)

Cassidy, Raymond

Casson, Anna

Catholic Agency for Social Concern

Catholic Bishops' Conference of England and
    Wales Committee for Social Welfare

Cavanagh, Ron

Centre for Analysis of Social Exclusion, London

Centre for Public Services, Sheffield

Centre for Social Policy Research and
    Development, Bangor

Chamberlen, J D

Chamney, Shirley (Mrs)

Champney, Betty OBE (Miss)

Chan, Peter

Chaplin, E C (Mrs)

Chapman, E (Mr)

Chapman, E (Mrs)

Chapman, John B

Chapman, V (Mrs)

Charles, J M (Mr)

Charles, Jack

Charlwood, A J (Mr)

Cheadle and District Home Link scheme

Cheshire Alliance of Disabled People, The

Cheshire, J E (Mr)

Chesters, M Susan (Dr)

Chesterton Plc

Chivers, John C

Chivers, R and C M (Mr and Mrs)

Chorlton, M D (Mrs)

Christian Council on Ageing

Christie, Laurence

Church Army Home for Older People

Church of Scotland Board of Social
    Responsibility, The

Church of Scotland Guild, The

Citizens' Rights for Older People

City Care Homes Association

City of Edinburgh Council, The

City of Edinburgh Council, The – NW
    Edinburgh District Office

City of Sunderland Social Services
    Department

Civil Service Pensioners' Alliance

Civil Service Pensioners' Alliance – Scotland,
    The

Clarey, G A (Mr)

Clark, H W

Clark, Heather (Dr)

Clark, J (Mrs)

Clark, Janette M RGN (Mrs)

Clarke, Charles (MP)

Clarke, John D (Mr)

Clarke, P A (Mrs)

Clarkson, Duncan RGN

Clay, R M (Dr) and Clay, S A M (Mrs)

Clayphan, D W (Mr)

Clayton, Rowland

Cleaver, Jean (Mrs)

Clement, B E P (Mr)

Clifton-Brown, Geoffrey MP

Clough, Roger (Prof)

Clowes, A R

Coates, David

Coburn, Monica R (Ms)

Cockburn, Dorothy (Mrs)

Coe, Kathleen R (Mrs)

Cogill, Daphne (Mrs)

Coia, J (Mrs)

Colbeck, K

Cole, G F (Mr)

Cole, G H (Mr)

Cole, June RGN

Cole, Maureen (Mrs)

Coles, J A (Dr)

College of Occupational Therapists

Colman, Tony (MP)

Comhairle Nan Eilean Siar

Commercial Union Assurance Company plc

Community Health Sheffield Older Adults
    Clinical Advisory Group

Community Services Pharmacists Group, The

Compton, Steve A

Compton, Val (Mrs)

Condliffe, A J

Connelly, Peter J (Dr)

Connolly, C C (Mr)

ConsultAge

Continence Foundation, The

Continuing Care Conference

Cook, A J (Mr)

Cook, Harold

Cook, K H L (Mr)

Cook, Laurie

Cook, Ronald J

Cooke, D (Mr)

Cooke, J (Mr)

Coolson, Norah (Mrs)

Cooper, Colin

Cooper, John T

Cooper, Margaret J OBE (Miss)

Cormack, W M

Cornford, R M (Mr)

Cornwall Care for the Elderly

Corp, Rosina A (Mrs)

Corser, A (Mrs)

COSLA (Convention of Scottish Local
   Authorities)
Cottingham (Mrs)
Cottman, Stella (Miss)
Cottrell, Alec
Cottrell, Bill
Council of Relatives to Assist in the Care of
   Dementia, The
Counsel and Care
County Councils Network
Coverage Care (Shropshire) Ltd
Cox, Greta (Mrs)
Coxbench Hall Residential Home
Coxhill, I (Mr)
Cozens, S (Mr)
Crabtree, David W RMN
Craegmoor Healthcare
Craig, E P S (Mrs)
Crawford J (Mr)
Crawford-Young, James
Cresswell, Janet (Miss)
Cresswell, Kenneth
Crisis in Community Care Consortium
Crockett, Julia (Ms)
Croft, Mary
Crompton, Margaret E (Mrs)
Cross, L (Miss)
Crossley Mackenzie – Independent Financial
   Advisers
Crossroads Care – Derbyshire
Crossroads Caring for Carers – Penarth and The
   Vale branch
Crowley, K
Crowley, S
Crowther, Frank (The Rev)
Cruse, June
Culpin, Christine (Mrs)
Cumming, Mary (Miss)
Cummings, Peter
Cummings, Vincent
Cunningham, J (Mr)
Cunningham, Lorraine (Miss)
Cupar Elderly Forum
Currie, G E
Currie, George
Currie, James (Mr)
Curry, Dick
Curtis, Frances
Cuthbertson, James G
Cuzner, Mary
Cyngor Henoed Ceredigion
Cypriot Elderly and Disabled Group

Daish, O (Mr and Mrs)
Dale, Brenda and Eric (Mr and Mrs)
Danes, J
Daniels, C (Mr)
Darlington and Teesdale Community Health
   Council
Darwent, Joan (Mrs)
David, Christine (Ms)
Davidson, John
Davies, Eric
Davies, G M (Mrs)
Davies, H (Mr)
Davies, H C (Ms)
Davies, H S (Mr)
Davies, L (Mr)
Davies, Malcolm
Davies, Trevor
Davis, Ann E (Mrs)
Davis, Iris (Mrs)
Davis, Maureen
Davis, Peter
Davison, Chris
Dawson, Eleanor (Mrs)
Dean, Beryl
Dean, C A (Mr)
Del Greco, Winifrede
Dellor, M C (Miss)
Dellow, Marion (Mrs)
Dementia Care Trust
Dementia Relief Trust, The
Dementia Voice
Dennis, Frederick E
Derbyshire Care Homes Association
Derbyshire, Pauline (Mrs)
Deva House
Dick, Jean (Mrs)
Dickins, Mike
Dicks, J W (Mr)
Dickson, A C
Dickson, E M (Miss)
Diggle, Priscilla (Ms)
Dight, J F (Mr)
Dingley, Brian (Mr)
Dinnis, Christine G (Miss)
Diocese of Exeter
Disablement Income Group, The
Divila, Barbara (Ms)
Dix, E E (Mr)
Dixon, E A H (Mrs)
Dixon, Mary
Dod, J L (Dr)
Dodds, Jean (Dr)

Doeser, W J (Mr)

Donisthorpe Hall

Donnell, N V (Mr)

Donnelly, G (Mr)

Dorrington House (Dereham) Nursing Home for
the Elderly

Douglas, J (Mr)

Dowland, K F S (Mr)

Dowling, Monica (Dr)

Downie, Jean E

Draper, W (Mr)

Drew, Sylvia (Mrs)

Druce, Gerald

Dryden, Jean (Mrs)

Duchy Health Charity Ltd

Dudley, Derek and Elaine (Mr and Mrs)

Dudley Long Term Forum

Dukeries Third Age Group, The

Dumbreck, M (Mrs)

Dumfries and Galloway Elderly Forum

Dumfries and Galloway Health Council

Dunard Nursing Home

Duncan, Joan (Mrs)

Dundee City Council

Dunn, James

Dunn, Marjorie A

Dunne, A G (Commander, Royal Navy)

Durham, M K (Mrs)

Durling, H G (Mr)

Dustbusters Domestic Cleaning Agency

Duthie, Jennifer (Ms)

Earl, M (Mrs)

East and Midlothian NHS Trust, Medicine for
the Elderly Department

East Ayrshire Council

East Suffolk Local Health Services NHS Trust

East Sussex, Brighton and Hove Health
Authority

Eastaugh, Maureen

Eastbourne, Seaford and Wealden Community
Health Council

Eastern Health and Social Services Board,
Northern Ireland

Eastern, Northern, Southern and Western
Health and Social Services Council, Northern
Ireland

Eastleigh Housing Association

Easton, Norman

Eastview Nursing Home

Eccles, John (Mr)

Economic Beliefs and Behaviour

Edinvar

Edmunds, D M (Mrs)

Edwards, Dilys (Mrs)

Edwards, Grahame E F

Eighth Age International, The

Elizabeth Rest Home

Elkeles, Robert S (Dr)

Ellesborough House

Ellin, Libby

Elliot, Clare (Ms)

Elliott, G (Mr)

Ellis, P R (Mr)

Ellison, P A D (Miss)

Else, David M

Ely, Geoffrey

Emerging Role of the Warden, The

Eminson, L

Emmerson, Sylvia (Mrs)

Emsden, G P (Mr)

ENABLE

Entwistle, D A H S (Mrs)

Equal Arts

Essex County Council Social Services

Evans, Anne (Miss)

Evans, Anthony

Evans, D W (Mr)

Evans, G L (Mr)

Evans, John R

Evans, Robert H

Evans, W S (Mr)

Evershed, Susan (Mrs)

Everycare

Exercise Association, The

Extra Care Charitable Trust, The

Fabb, G N (Mr)

Faculty of Actuaries/Institute of Actuaries

Faculty of Old Age Psychiatry

Faculty of Public Health Medicine

Fair Havens Christian Home

Fairbairn, Andrew (Dr)

Fairhead, K (Mr)

Farr, E M (Mrs)

Farrow, J S C

Faulkner, Mary (Miss)

Fear, E S (Mr)

Fearn, Thomas J

Federation of Small Businesses

Fenn, Paul

Fennell, John N

Ferfoot Limited, Residential and Nursing Care
Homes

Fidler, Yvonne (Mrs)

Fielding, I and J L (Mr and Mrs)

Fife Elderly Forum Executive

Figg, D (Mr)

Figg, J H and Maureen (Mr and Mrs)

Financial Services Authority

Finchett, G (Mr)

Findlay, Anna

Findlay, R P (Mr)

Finlayson, K SRN (Mrs)

Firth, M D P

Firth, R (Ms)

Firth, T Howard

Fitch, Alan J

Flaxman, J L M (Mr)

Fleming, Elspeth M (Mrs)

Fletcher, G R

Flimwell Residential Home

Flynn, Shirley (Mrs)

Fold Housing Association

Ford, Malcolm

Forrest, Muriel (Mrs)

Forster, B C (Mrs)

Forsyth, Joan (Dr)

Forth Valley Local Health Council

Forway, Donald J (The Rev)

Fowler, Anne (Mrs)

Fox, Oonagh

Foy, D C

Frain-Bell, Anne H (Mrs)

Fraley, L (Mrs)

Frampton, R

Franklin, T (Mr)

Fraser, Pamela E (Mrs)

Fray, Margaret T (Mrs)

Frazer, J L (Mr)

Freeman, Dorothy K J (Mrs)

French C L (Mr and Mrs)

Friend, Alyce B (Miss)

Friend, John

Friends of Invereck Group

Friends of the Elderly

Fry, John

Fulford, June (Mrs)

Fullwell Cross Medical Centre

Furby, Michael A M (Mr)

Gage, Trevor (Mr)

Gajewski, S Janislawa (Mrs)

Gale, G E (Mr)

Galt, Grace B (Mrs)

Game, Martin

Garland, Janet E SRN (Ms)

Garnes, Eleanor (Miss)

Garnett, D M P (Miss)

Garrard, L L (Mr)

Garrioch, Ian M

Gateshead and South of Tyne Health Authority
    Continuing Care Review Panel

Gateshead Personal Assistance Pilot Project

Gay and Lesbian Humanist Association

Geddes, Henry OBE (Mr)

Geeves, Marion (Mrs)

Gelson, June (Mrs)

General and Cologne RE

George, D (Mr)

George, Leslie

George, Peter J

Gerrard Jones, Peter

Gibbs, M C F

Gibbs, M C F (Mr)

Gibbs, P N (Mr)

Gilchrist, Ruth (Mrs)

Gilfillan, R J A (Mr)

Gillan, Marjorie (Mrs)

Gillbrooke Care Centre, Fivemiletown, Northern
    Ireland

Gillingham, D (Mr)

Girlings Retirement Options

Given, Philip J

Glen, G Hilda (Mrs)

Gleneagles Group, The

Glengan, Christine

Gloin, David B

Gloucestershire Care Forum

Gloucestershire Pensioners Forum

Glover, N M (Mr)

Goad, Rita (Mrs)

Godber, Colin

Godfrey, Kenn

Goldie, A J

Golding, Anne

Goodacre, D C (Mr)

Gooding, Yvonne (Mrs)

Goodman, John G

Goodman, Pauline

Goodrick, Ian (Dr)

Gorring, D D (Miss)

Gorry, D A (Mr)

Gosden, R M (Mr)

Gould, Gerald M (Dr)

Grace and Compassion Benedictines

Grace Consulting

Graham, J (Mr)

Grand Lodge of Scotland, The

Gravatt, B R (Mr)

Gray, V R (Mr)

Greater London Forum for the Elderly

Greater Manchester Socialist Health Association

Greathead, D (Miss)

Green, David

Green, Penelope (Ms)

Green, Stanley

Greene, E (Mrs)

Greenock Medical Aid Society

Greenwich Community Health Council

Greer, Winifred (Mrs)

Gregg, P

Grey, Mona SRN OBE (Miss)

Griffith, R D (Mrs)

Grimwade, Leslie (The Rev)

Grogan, John (MP)

Guideposts Trust

Gunther, H N C (Dr)

Gwalia Neighbourhood Housing Association Ltd

Gwent Community Health NHS Trust

Gwent Federation of Women's Institutes

Hadley, A R (Mr)

Hague, J M (Miss)

Hain, P (Mrs)

Hainsworth, Margaret (Ms)

Hall, J E (Mr)

Hall, K J (Mr)

Hallifax, Lesley A (Mrs)

Hamlin, A G and M (Mr and Mrs)

Hamling, E M M (Mrs)

Hampshire Care Home Association

Hampstead Garden Suburb Fellowship

Hancock (Mrs)

Hands Off Greenwich NHS

Hanger, P J (Mr)

Hannabuss, Richard

Hannah, Margaret (Dr)

Hanover Housing Association

Hanson, D L (Mr)

Hanson, Jack OBE

Hanson, R

Harbert, W B OBE (Mr)

Harden, Eileen M (Mrs)

Harding, B (Mrs)

Harding, Michael

Harding, R J (Mr)

Hardwick, L J

Hardy, S T (Dr)

Harewarren Consultancy, The

Harman, Arthur

Harper, B A (Mr)

Harper, Glen (Dr)

Harper, K (Dr)

Harris, J P (Miss)

Harris, Jean (Mrs)

Harris, Peter M

Harris-Burland, David

Harrison, Ian

Harrison, K (Mrs)

Harrison, M M SRN (Mrs)

Harrison, Margaret/Green, Barbara

Harrison, Roy

Harry, N

Hart, Joan (Mrs)

Harvey, Frank

Harvey, Norman

Harvey, R (Mrs)

Harvey, Trevor

Hasek, P (Mrs)

Hawes, Kenneth

Hawker, Maurice O

Hawkins, Alan A (Mr)

Hawkins, Catherine CBE

Hawkins, S

Hawkins, Sally T JP

Hawksbury House

Hawthorn, Margaret S E (Mrs)

Haxton, Valerie (Mrs)

Hay Muir, Jean (Mrs)

Haysom, E M (Mrs)

Hayter, Ernest T

Health and Social Services Councils

Hearn, H P (Lieutenant Colonel)

Heathlands Village, The

Heaton, Jack and Pat (Mr and Mrs)

Heaton, Phil

Heavney, Elizabeth (Mrs)

Help the Aged

Help the Aged (Northern Ireland)

Helping Hands Home Care Service

Hemingway, John

Hemsley, John

Henderson, Patricia A

Henley, Jane (Mrs)

Hermiston, W R (Mr)

Hetherington, Elizabeth (Mrs)

Hettiaratchy, Pearl D J (Dr)

Hewer, Janet (Mrs)

Hewett, C (Mr)

Hewson, Anthony

Hewson, Muriel (Mrs)

Heywood Pensioners' Association
Hibbs, Pam CBE (Ms)
Hicks, J (Mrs)
Higgison, E (Mrs)
Highland Community Care Forum
Hildreth, D B (Mr)
Hill, C (Mrs)
Hill, E (Mrs)
Hill, Gwendolen M (Miss)
Hill, J A (Mr)
Hills (Mrs)
Hills, Barbara M (Mrs)
Hirst, Barbara (Mrs)
Hobman, David CBE
Hockey, Lisbeth (Dr)
Hocking, Barbara (Mrs)
Hodge, Eileen (Mrs)
Hodges (Mr and Mrs)
Hodges, Mary (Miss)
Hodgkinson, Maud (Mrs)
Hogg, Derek M
Hogg, Suzanne (Mrs)
Holdaway, Doug
Holdaway, M (Mrs)
Holdaway, W (Mr)
Holden, C J (Mr)
Holden, M G (Mrs)
Hollingbery, Richard
Holloway, Mary (Mrs)
Holmes, D W (Mr)
Holmested, F (Mr)
Holt, Anne
Holtham, P
Holton, A R (Dr)
Hook, Frances RGN (Mrs)
Hopkins, L E (Mr)
Hopper, B J (Mrs)
Horner, Philip R
Hornsey Housing Trust
Horsfield, T
Hosking, J (Mr)
Hotel Bristowe Mini Homes
Houlden, J L (The Rev Prof)
Housing 21
Housing Corporation, The
Howard, J A (Mr)
Howard, Michael (The Rt Hon)
Howe, Ray
Howes, A (Mrs)
Howes, John
Howie, Mary F (Mrs)
Hubrer, M M (Mrs)

Huby, Aubrey
Hudson, J P
Hughes, Alan
Hughes, Annie (Mrs)
Hughes, J B
Hughes, W K (Mrs)
Hughes, Win
Huish, Albert
Hull, Norman G
Human Genetics Advisory Commission
Humphrey, R (Mr)
Humphreys, Elsie (Mrs)
Hunt, A G (Mr)
Hunt and Almshouse Charity of the Skinners'
    Company, The
Hunt, Joan SRN RGN (Ms)
Hunter, A H D (Dr)
Hunter, G (Mr)
Hunter, Harold E
Hunter Watson, W (Mr)
Hunters Lodge Rest Home
Hurt, William
Hutton, Paul
Huxtable, George
Hyde Housing Association Ltd

IFA Association
IFACare Ltd
Ifield Park Housing Society Ltd
Ilsley, Loo (Ms)
Impaired Life Services Ltd
Impallomeni, M (Dr)
Independent Healthcare Association
Ingham, K (Mrs)
Inglis, Irvine
Inglis, James
Inkerman Housing Association
Institution of Professionals, Managers and
    Specialists
International Consumer Policy Bureau
Invalid Services Ltd/Nursing and Home Care
    Agency
Inverkeithing Medical Group
Investment and Life Assurance Group
Ipswich Hospital NHS Trust, The – Elderly
    Services Directorate
Irons, R J B (Mr)
Irving, J P (Mr)
Irwin, Jessie (Mrs)
Islington Carers Forum
Islington Chinese Association
Ittrish, R L D (Mr)

Jackson, E (Mrs)

Jackson, Eileen (Mrs)

Jackson, M H (Mr and Mrs)

Jackson, Peter G

Jackson, Philip

Jackson, Robert (MP)

Jacob, B M (Miss)

Jalie, Deidre (Mrs)

James, B J (Mr)

James Butcher Housing Association

Japhet, Jackie (Mrs)

Jardine, Colin

Jay, J B

Jeffcock, John R

Jeffery, Dorothy (Mrs)

Jeffry, Muriel L (Mrs)

Jenkin-Dann, M (Mrs)

Jenkinson, M L (Dr)

Jewish Care

John, Marion

Johns, Vera (Mrs)

Johnson, Brian (Dr)

Johnson, J C MBE

Johnson, Michael

Johnson, Moira J (Mrs)

Johnson, R D (Mr)

Johnston, Ann (Ms)

Johnston, W (Mrs)

Jones, B B (Mr)

Jones, Clare (Mrs)

Jones, E S (Mr)

Jones, Irene

Jones, Kathleen (Mrs)

Jones, Kathleen (Prof)

Jones, Lynne (MP, Dr)

Jones, Margaret

Jones, Martyn (MP)

Jones, Molly (Mrs)

Jones, Sheila (Miss)

Joseph Rowntree Foundation

Joyce, C M (Mrs)

Jukes, David

Karagianis, Pamela (Ms)

Kay, Christopher

Keane, J M

Kedward, E (Mrs)

Keeble, Sally (MP)

Keep, David (The Rev Dr)

Keighley, Brian D (Dr)

Kelly, Cecilia (Mrs)

Kelly, Sylvia (Mrs)

Kemp, E J

Kendrick, Brian H

Kent Active Retirement Associations

Kerr, Jack

Kestenbaum, Ann

Kierney, Catherine M (Mrs)

Kilvington, C T (Mrs)

Kime, G T (Mr)

King, C W (Mr)

King, Margaret (Miss)

King's College, London – Community Care
    Development Centre

King's Fund Organisational Audit

Kinghorn, P M (Miss)

Kingwood Trust, The

Kiniver Private Nursing Home

Kinmylies Parish Church

Kirk Care Housing

Kirk, R C (Mr)

Kirk Session of Milton of Campsie Parish
    Church

Kirk Session of the Church of Scotland
    Cumlodden, Lochfyneside and Lochgair,
    Argyll

Kirkham, D (Mr)

Kirkman, M J (Mrs)

Kirkmuirhill Church of Scotland

Kitch, Betty (Mrs)

Kitching, E (Miss)

Knight, Joyce (Mrs)

Knight, Lesley

Knight, S (Mr)

Knights, W J (Mr)

Knowles, George A (Mr)

Kolb, Mary

Lacayo, A G (Mr)

Lacy, G M K (Miss)

Lacy, P J H (Mr)

Laflin, J (Mr)

Lagan, Francis

Laing, Margaret (Mrs)

Lamagna, Michelle (Mrs)

Lamb, A (Ms)

Lamb, D C (Mrs)

Lamb, Douglas

Lambhill Court Ltd

Lane, A (Mr)

Lansley, Thomas S OBE

Larmour, John

LasseDonald, Eileen H (Miss)

Laurence, Sheila (Mrs)

Laver (Mr and Mrs)

Lavis, S (Mr)

Law, Jean

Law Society, The

Law, T W (Mr)

Law-Kwang, Elise

Lawless, M (Miss)

Laws, Elaine (Miss)

Lawson, E M (Mrs)

League of Friends of St Mary Abbot's
    Community Care for the Elderly

League of Jewish Women

Leahy, Brian M

Leaman, P

Ledger, J W (Mr)

Leeds City Council Dept of Social Service

Leeds Community Health Council

Leeds Metropolitan University

Leeds Older People's Community Care Forum

Legal and General

Leggatt, H D (Dr)

LeGrand, Julian/Titmus, Richard

Leigh, J (Mrs)

Leitch, Sara (Mrs)

Lennel House, Northern Ltd

Lettington, D (Mrs)

Levitt, Judith

Lewis, Barnet

Lewis, Beverley (Mrs)

Lewis, R D P (Mr)

Lewis, R P (Mr)

Lewisham Pensioners Forum

Liberal Democrat Party

Licensed Victuallers' National Homes

Lightfoot, Brenda (Mrs)

Lilly, J (Mrs)

Lindley, Eric

Lindley, J G

Lindlow, R A

Lingham, Peter

Links Unit (Continuing Care Facility)

Linton Kirk Session

Linton, Lettie (Miss)

Lion House Residential Home

Lipman (Mrs)

Lisden Nursing Home

Littleborough Pensioners Association

Liverpool Personal Social Service Society

Livesey, Brian (Mr)

Livesley, Brian (Prof)

Livock, Brenda (Mrs)

Llewellyn, J N (Mr)

Lloyd-Jones, G (Mrs)

Local Government Association

Local Government Management Board, The

Lock, T C and B M (Mr and Mrs)

London Borough of Harrow Social Services Dept

Long Term Care Team, Poulton House

Lord, K F (Mr)

Lothian Area Pharmaceutical Committee

Loud, N (Mrs)

Lovett, W A L (Mr)

Lowden, Joyce

Lowe, Edward S

Lucas, Margaret E

Lukaszewicz, Alan

Lungley, Constance (Mrs)

Lutterworth and District Carers' Support Group

Luxton, D (Dr)

Lynch, Veronica (Mrs)

Lyth, Margaret M (Miss)

Macdonald, Angus S

MacDougall, Irene (Mrs)

Macdowall, Malcolm (Mr)

MacGregor, John P

MacIntyre, Duncan

MacKenzie, M L (Mr)

Mackinlay, Elspeth

Mackintosh, I (Ms)

Maclachlan, Penelope

Macmillan Cancer Relief

Macmillan, W G (Mr)

Macpherson (Mr and Mrs)

MacPhie, Angus

Magill, John McN B (Mr)

Maitland, Patricia M (Mrs)

Malein, J F D (Mrs)

Maling, R G

Manchester Alliance for Community Care

Mann, D C

Mann, Jessie (Mrs)

Manor Care Home Group, The

Manor Rest Home

Mansfield, Pamela (Mrs)

Manufacturing, Science and Finance Union –
    Retired Members Sub-Committee

Marriott, I V (Mr)

Marsh, F

Marshall, Alan

Marshall, Fay

Marshall, J T (Mr)

Martin, A I (Mr)

Martin, Margaret

Marvin, J A (Mr)

Mason, Philip

Masters, A J and V E (Mr and Mrs)

Matthew, Anne (Miss)

Matthews, G E (Mr)

Matthews, S R (Miss)

Maxwell, Patricia

McAllion, Sue (Dr)

McCall, Alastair

McCarthy, Jane (Mrs)

McClymont, M E/Davies, J

McCordick, Marie (Ms)

McCormack, Angus

McCormack, Jane

McEwan, T R (Mr)

McFatridge, J M (Mr)

McGeachie, S (Miss)

McGough, Edward P

McGraw, Janie

McIntosh, R A G (Mr)

McKee, Tom

McKellican, J F (Dr)

McKibbin, E K RGN (Mrs)

McLaren, Irene (Mrs)

McLeish, Jean

McLeod, Alexander R

McLeod, Eileen (Mrs)

McMeekin, Hilda (Mrs)

McNeill, Peter G B

McQuade, Irene

Mead, Roger

Meakins R (Mr and Mrs)

Meares, Patrick (Prof Emeritus)

Mearns, James T

Medical Research Council

Medway Council

MENCAP (Royal Society for Mentally
   Handicapped Children and Adults)

MENCAP, Bristol

MENCAP in Northern Ireland

MENCAP, Winchester

MEND Homes for the Mentally Dependent

Mental Health Commission for Northern
   Ireland

Mental Health Commission for Scotland

Mercier G (Mr and Mrs)

Meredith, E T

Merry, Joan (Mrs)

Merry, Kenneth

Metcalfe, M (Miss)

Meteau, Gerald

Methodist Homes for the Aged

Micell, Dorothy (Ms)

Mickleburgh, Colin S JP (Mr)

Middleditch, M G (Mrs)

Millard, Christine P

Millard, Peter H (Prof)/Peel, Eleanor

Millett, T V (Mr)

Millner, Sandra (Mrs)

Mills, Susan A (Mrs)

Milne, J S (Dr)

MIND (National Association for Mental Health)

MIND, Croydon

Mitchell, B G (Prof)

Mitchell, D

Mitchell, D J (Mr)

Mitchell, L S (Mr)

Mitchell, M (Miss)

Mole, Margaret (Mrs)

Molloy, Gary

Molyneux P (Mr and Mrs)

Monk, L G (Mr and Mrs)

Monks, C H (Mr)

Montgomery, Anne M (Mrs)

Moody, E (Mrs)

Moon, Roger (Sir)

Moore, A I (Mr)

Moore, R J (Mr)

Moray Council

Moray Health Services

Moray Social Services

Morgan, D

Morgan, Margaret E

Morgan, Marjorie D (Mrs)

Morgan, P G (Mr)

Morgan, Sonia (Ms)

Morgannwg Association of Registered Care
   Homes

Morley, A (Mr)

Morris, Alan J

Morris, G P D (Mr)

Morris, N (Prof)

Morrison, N J B (Mr)

Morton, M G (Mr)

Mountfield, Peter

Muggeridge, John

Munich Reassurance Company

Munro, Alison (Dame)

Murphy, M (Mrs)

Murray, A

Murray, Janet (Mrs)

Murray, Joe

Murray, Thomas D

Mutton, Joan M (Mrs)

Nash, Joan (Mrs)

Nat West Bank Plc

National Association of Adult Placement
  Services

National Association of Citizens Advice Bureaux

National Association of Laryngectomee Clubs,
  The

National Association of Pension Funds Limited

National Association of Retired Police Officers

National Autistic Club, The

National Care Homes Association

National Centre for Independent Living
  (BCODP – British Council of Organisations of
  Disabled People)

National Centre for Volunteering, The

National Centre for Women of Great Britain,
  The

National Commission for Social Care – Catholic
  Church at Scotland

National Community Care Alliance c/o National
  Institute for Social Work

National Consumer Council

National Council for Hospice and Specialist
  Palliative Care Services

National Federation of Post Office and British
  Telecom Pensioners

National Federation of Women's Institutes

National Housing Federation

National Organisation for Adult Learning, The

National Pensioners Convention

National Pensioners Convention's Council, The

National Pharmaceutical Association, The

National Register of Carers, The

National Schizophrenia Fellowship, Midlands

National Secular Society

Nazareth House

Neilson, Bob

Neilson, M (Mrs)

Nesbitt, P E (Mr)

Network Housing Association

Neurological Alliance, The

Neve, J E (Ms)

Neville, Christine (Mrs)

Newcastle West Primary Care Group/Newcastle
  Elderly Resource Team

Newdick, Christopher

Newell, Alan F (Prof)

Newington Day Centre

Newman, Ralph

Newman, Yvonne (Ms)

Newson, B W (Mr)

NHS Confederation, The

NHS Retirement Fellowship

NHS Retirement Fellowship – Derby branch

NHS Retirement Fellowship – Nottinghamshire
  branch

Nicholls, M J (Mrs)

Nicholls, Peter

Nicholson, D S (Mr)

Nicoll, William J

Nightingale House

Nisbet, Andrew BEM

Nisbet, Cecily (Mrs)

Noble, Alex

Noden, N J

Norfolk and Norwich Pensioners Association

Norfolk County Council

Norman, Douglas J

Norris, Carol and Maguire, Pamela (Drs)

North Cheshire Health

North County Labour Group

North Devon Pensioners Convention

North East Amalgamated Pensioners
  Associations

North East Edinburgh Carers' Forum

North Staffordshire Pensioners Convention

North Tyneside Community Health Council

North Wales Health Authority
  (Registration/Inspection)

North West Norfolk Pensioners Association

North Yorkshire County Council

North Yorkshire Health Authority

Northallerton Probus Club

Northern Ireland Housing Executive

Norton, Emily (Mrs)

Norwich and District Community Health
  Council

Norwich Union

Norwood Ravenswood

NSF Northern

Nuffield Community Care Studies Unit

Nuffield Council on Bioethics

Nuffield Institute for Health

Nugent Care Society, The

Numast

Nurse, J E

Nursing Home Fees Agency

Nursing Homes in Shropshire

O'Hare, Colum RMN

O'Keefe, Ita

O'Kelly, Elizabeth MBE (Miss)

O'Neill, J (Mrs)

Oak, D J (Mrs)

Oakley, Edward S
Oglesby, A I (Dr)
Oglesby, E B (Mr)
Oliver, F (Dr)
Oliver, M J (Dr)
Oliver, S M (Dr)
Olson, Sue SRN
Open University School of Health and Social
  Welfare, The
Optimum Health Services
Orr, Peter
Overton, P (Mr)
Oxford Health and Social Services, Joint Elderly
  Commissioning
Oxfordshire Pensioners Action Group
Packham, C F
Paddock, E M (Mrs)
Padfield, M V (Mrs)
Page, R H (Mr)
Pakenham-Walsh, Mabel (Miss)
Palmer, R (Mr)
Pantlin, Michael
Panton, C (Mrs)
Parent
Pargeter, Mark
Parke, S (Miss)
Parkes, D M (Mr and Mrs)
Parkes, Dorothy I (Miss)
Parkhouse, W G (Mr)
Parrim, J R (Mr)
Parry, Jeffrey
Parsons, Alice
Patel, Chai (Dr)
Patel (Mrs)
Patel, R S
Paterson, Norman
Patients Association, The
Pawson, M
Payne, B (Mr)
Payne, Brian V (Dr)
Peake, C C (The Rev)
Pearce, Eileen (Mr)
Pearman, Guy
Pearson, E (Mrs)
Peart, Elizabeth (Mrs)
Peart, Phyllis (Miss)
Peck, Carole (Mrs)
Pengelly, R A (Mr)
Penley, Katharine (Mrs)
Pennington, John
Pension Annuity Friendly Society Ltd, The
Pensioners' Convention (Solihull)

Pensioners' Voice
Pensioners' Voice – Abington and Kingsley
  branch
Pensions Management Institute, The
Pensions Trust, The
Percy, Donald W
Perry, B (Mrs)
Perry, M (Mr)
Personal Investment Authority
Perth and Kinross Care Home Association
Perth and Kinross Healthcare NHS Trust
Pfaff, E J (Mr)
Phair, Lynne
Phillips, P E (Mr)
Phillips, Peter (Dr)
Philp, Ian (Prof)
Pick, G (Mr)
Pick, J M (Miss)
Pickerin, A E (Mr)
Pierce, A (Mr)
Pierce, Roger
Pilbeam, T (Mr)
Pilgrim Care
Pilgrim Homes
Piller, Gordon OBE (Dr)
Pilmeny Development Project
Pirnie, Mavis
Pitt, Sydney and Hilda (Mrs)
Place, J W
Plaid Cymru
Plantation Conservatives
Polari Housing
Police Pensioners Housing Association Ltd
Pollock, Allyson (Prof)
Pollock, William
Pond, Chris (MP)
Pool Cottage
Poole Local Agenda 21 Health and Social Group
Porter, A E (Dr)
Porter, K P (Mrs)
Portsmouth and South East Hampshire Health
  Authority
Poulton House Assessment and Rehabilitation
  Centre
Powell, Zoe
Powrie Neil I C JP (Cllr)
PPP Healthcare
Prama Care
Premier Care Homes Ltd
Presbyterian Residential Trust, The
Prestatyn Town Council
Price, Belinda

Price, H B (Mr)

Price, K M R (Mr)

Price, M (Mr)

Price, P Glyn

Primrose, William R (Dr)

Princess Royal Trust for Carers Centre Working in Bristol and South Gloucestershire, The

Princess Royal Trust for Carers, The – Walsall Carers Centre

Princess Royal Trust for Carers, The – South Ayrshire Carers Centre

Princess Royal Trust for Carers, The

Princess Royal Trust for Carers, The – Nottinghamshire Carers Centre

Princess Royal Trust for Carers, The – Sunderland Carers Centre

Printers' Charitable Corporation

Prior, Pauline (Dr)

Proctor, Cliff H (Mr)

Public Concern at Work

Public Service Pensioners' Council

Pye, M (Ms)

Quality Carers Ltd

Queen's House Residential Home

Queensferry Parish Church Guild

Quick, A J (Mrs)

RADAR (Roya Association for Disability and Rehabilitation)

Radice, Jennifer (Mrs)

Rafferty, L (Mrs)

Rainbow House

Rainsford, W and Mary (Mr and Mrs)

Rarkin, F (Mrs)

Rasheed, E (Mr)

Rathfelder, Martin

Ravensmount Residential Care Home

Rayner, G E

Reading Borough Council

Reardon, Tozer, White and Suntharalingham (Drs)

Reboul, Antoinette

Redbridge and Waltham Forest Retirement Fellowship

Redfarn, Phyllis M (Miss)

Redmount Nursing and Residential Home

Redruth Nursing Home

Reed, Patricia

Reed, R S (Mr)

Reed, S (Mr)

Reeve, Mary

Reeves, K C G (Dr)

Registered Nursing Home Association

Registered Nursing Home Association – Glasgow branch

Registered Nursing Home Association – West Sussex branch

Reid, Samuel

Relatives Association Scotland, The

Relatives Association, The

Rengert, Sheilah RGN (Mrs)

Residential Care Home, Exeter

Residential home in the Derbyshire area

Residential Forum

Retirement Security Ltd

Rhondda Valley NHS Trust

Richard, Ioan M (Cllr)

Richards, F (Mr)

Rickards, M (Mrs)

Rickayzen, B D (Mr)

Ridgway, M

Ridler-Rowe, Daphne (Mrs)

Rights in Community Care Group

Riverside Housing Association

Roberts, Beryl E (Mrs)

Roberts, Frank

Roberts, Jill (JP, Mrs)

Roberts, Lorna (Miss)

Robertson, Edward N

Robertson, Keith (Cllr)

Robertson, M C (Mrs)

Robertson, M E (Mrs)

Robinson, Marilyn

Robinson, Moira C

Robinson, Stella (Mrs)

Robinson, Zelda

Robson, Morag (Miss)

Rodwell, Robert O

Rogers, A (Mrs)

Rogers, Joy W (Mrs)

Rogers, Richard

Rolfe, Jan

Rolin, J M (Mrs)

Ross, A M (Mr)

Ross, Alison J (Mrs)

Rossmore Nursing Home

Rotherham Pensioners Action Group

Rothwell, Katherine (Mrs)

Rouse, T M (Mr)

Rowbotham, C (Mrs)

Rowe, Emma

Rowe, F (Mr)

Rowland, V R (Mr)

Rowley, Donald

Royal Air Forces Association, The – Fraserburgh branch

Royal British Legion, The

Royal College of General Practitioners

Royal College of Nursing

Royal College of Physicians

Royal Institute of Public Health and Hygiene/Society of Public Health

Royal Masonic Benevolent Institution

Royal National Institute for the Blind

Royal Pharmaceutical Society of Great Britain

Rudge, M R (Mr)

Ruglys, Eileen A

RUKBA (Royal United Kingdom Beneficient Association)

Russell, B M (Mrs)

Rutherford, Jane (Mrs)

Ryan, Mick

Sadler, Shirley

SAGA Services Ltd

Sait, M (Miss)

Sale, Richard

Salter, Heather RGN

Saltwell, R J (Mr and Mrs)

Salvation Army, The

Sampson, S W

Sanderson, E

Saunders, Marcia

Savage, Gerald A (Mr)

SCOTCH

Scott, Philip

Scott, Sheila

Scottish Amicable

Scottish Association of Care Home Owners

Scottish Association of Health Councils

Scottish Ex Servicemen's Charitable Organisation

Scottish Old Age Pensioners' Association

Scottish Provident

Scottish Widows

Scrivener, D S (Mrs)

Scurfield, M (Ms)

Sear, Brian

Sedgwick Noble Lowndes

Segal Quince Wickstead Ltd

Select a Home

Senior, William

SENSE, The National Deafblind and Rubella Association

SERVE

Seymour, George M

Shah, Dipak

Shared Care Scotland

Sharp, A R

Sharp, Clifford

Shater, P (Mrs)

Shaw, David

Shaw, J (Mrs)

Shaw, J R (Mr)

Shea, George

Sheard, C

Shearing, T G (Mr)

Sheddon, Rhea M O L (Dr)

Sheldon Grange

Shell, J H H (Mr)

Shelmerdine, N A (Mr)

Shephard, Allan Charles

Shephard, D J (Mr)

Shepherd, Michael

Shepherd, Moira (Mrs)

Shepherd, Richard (MP)

Shepperdson, Billie

Shipley, Debra (MP)

Shotter, Marjorie

Shuker, D (Mr)

Shutt, Christine (Mrs)

Sibbons, A J

Sidmouth Voluntary Services

Signpost Housing Association

Simmans, A F G (Mr)

Simmonds, Bill and Greta (Mr and Mrs)

Simms, E (Mrs)

Simpson, Beryl F (Mrs)

Simpson, Kay (Mrs)

Simpson, Thomas J (The Very Rev)

Sims, M J (Miss)

Simsova, S (Mrs)

Sinclair-Webb, S W (Mrs)

Skelton, Marybelle

Skene Group, The

Slater, Patrick

Slator, C W (Mr)

Sleath, Ken and Doreen (Mr and Mrs)

Smallwood, Herbert

Smart, Brian

Smart, Norah

Smith, Anne (Mrs)

Smith, B (Mr)

Smith, Bryan G

Smith, C E (Mrs)

Smith, D G (Mr)

Smith, Douglas and Margaret (Mr and Mrs)

Smith, E (Mrs)

Smith, Joan (Mrs)

Smith, John M

Smith, K W (Mr)

Smith, M J (Mr)

Smith, P J (Mr and Mrs)

Smith, Patricia

Smith, R (Mr)

Smith, Sidney F

Smith, Sovati (Ms)

Snaith, H L (Mr)

Snee, Tom OBE

Social and Economic Group – Hereford and
    Worcester Local Agenda 21, The

Society of Chiropodists and Podiatrists, The

Solomon, John

Soroptimist International of Scotland South

Soroptimist International of Torquay and
    District

Soroptimist International of Wolverhampton

South and East Belfast Trust

South East Essex Advocacy for Older People

South East Staffordshire Community Health
    Council

South Pembrokeshire Home and Day Care
    Consortium

Southdown Housing Association

Southin, P (Mrs)

Southworth, H D (Mr)

Sparkes, P A (Mrs)

Speck, Elma (Mrs)

Spencer, G L (Mr)

Spooner, E H (Miss)

Sporie, Ann (Miss)

Sri Sathya Sai Centre Central London

SSAFA Forces Help

St Andrews Management Institute

St Columba's Parish Church Guild, Largs

St Francis Nursing Home

St John Ambulance

St Joseph's Convent

St Peter and St James Charitable Trust, The

Stagg, P J (Mrs)

Stainton, D L G (Mr)

Stamoulakatos, Nicholas

Standing Conference of Women's Organisations

Stanford, Andrea (Mrs)

Stanley, M J

Staples, C

Starkey, Geraldine (Mrs)

Stattam, C M (Mrs)

Stebles, Malcolm R D (Dr)

Steeds, Paul and Hilary (Mr and Mrs)

Steele, R E (Mr)

Steer, E A BEM (Mr)

Stephens, Ralph (Mr)

Stephens, W J (Mr)

Stephenson Cyril

Steven, C (Mrs)

Stevens, B M

Stevens, E J (Mr)

Stevens, Jean M (Mrs)

Stevenson, L

Stewart, D F

Stewart, Ian M

Stewart, J (Mr)

Stone, M M (Mrs)

Stonewall Housing Association

Strand, Brian

Strathclyde Forum

Streeting, Christine (Ms)

Stroke Association, The

Sturgeon, Pamela and Eddie (Mr and Mrs)

Sturn, H A (Mr)

Suffolk Carers

Suffolk County Council

Suffolk Health

Suffolk Pensioners Association – Folkestone
    branch

Sullivan, M and V

Sumpton, John

Supple, Barry

Sussex Housing Association for the Aged

Swailes, Thelma E (Mrs)

Swain (Mr and Mrs)

Swan, Nancie R (Mrs)

Swanson, Norna

Swenney, Wilma

Swift, Dinah (Mrs)

Swift-Hook (Mrs)

Swindon Borough Council

Swinton, Alan

Swiss Re Life and Health

Talbot, Celia (Ms)

Talbot, Marjorie

Talman, F (Mr)

Tamworth Mental Health Development Group

Tanner, John

Tarnowski, C (Mrs)

Tate House Support Group

Tatham, Michael

Tattersfield, A J (Mr)

Taylor, D C (Mr)

Taylor, E (Mr)

Taylor, Janet RCN/RMN (Mrs)

Taylor, John

Taylor, K (Mrs)

Taylor, L (Mrs)

Taylor, Margaret (Mrs)

Team of local authority care managers

Tedman, Cyril

Tewson, Michael B

Thacker, S (Dr)

Theaker, E (Mrs)

Third Age Trust, The

Thomas, E B J (Miss)

Thomas, J M (Mr)

Thomas, Ron

Thomas, Stanley J

Thompson, Francis

Thompson, Patricia M (Mrs)

Thompson, Peter

Thompson, R E (Mrs)

Thompson, R G (Mr)

Thompson, W G (Mr)

Thorpe (Mrs)

Tickner, Molly

Tierney, Dell

Timothy, G S (Mr)

Todd, Mark (MP)

Todd, Veronica L (Mrs)

Topham, Pauline B (Dr)

Towell House

Tower Hamlets Healthcare NHS Trust

Townend, E H (Mr and Mrs)

Towns, Robin P

Townswomen's Guilds

Trades Union Congress

Tragheim, J R (Mrs)

Transport and General Workers Union – retired
   members' association (SW region)

Troon and District Elderly Forum

Tuck, P (Mrs)

Tucker, Eric H

Tully, Isabel (Mrs)

Tunbridge Wells Equitable

Tunstall Group PLC

Turley, L F (Mr)

Turnbull, Maurice G

Turner, Betty E (Mrs)

Turner, E (Mrs)

Turner, George (Dr)

Turner, Gill (Dr)

Turner, Margaret

Tuthill, Paul

Tuttle, P M (Mr)

Tyler, Nick

Tyler, Paul CBE (MP)

Tyrrell, Norman

UKCC

Underwood, R E

Unilever

UNISON

UNISON – Herefordshire Branch Retired
   Members Section

UNISON – Retired Members Section, West
   Glamorgan

United Care Associations

United Kingdom Home Care Association Ltd

Universal Health Consultants, Consulting
   Actuaries

University College London

University of Bradford – Policy Research
   Institute on Ageing – Ethnicity

University of Essex – Department of Computer
   Science

University of Keele – Centre for Planning and
   Management

University of Northumbria at Newcastle

University of Plymouth Faculty of Human
   Sciences

Unsworth, Paul

Unthank, C W (Mr)

Urquhart, John

Uttley, Edith (Mrs)

University of the Third Age, Bath branch

Van Langenberg, J (Mrs)

Van-Cauter, D A (Mrs)

Vasey, Frank

Viewpoint Housing Association Limited

Vincent, John

VOICES/DGAA Homelife

Voller, S (Mr)

Voluntary Organisations Disability Group

Wachenje, Vivienne (Mrs)

Waddicor, P E E (Mrs)

Wade, Peter

Waite, S E (Mrs)

Wakefield, N D (Mr and Mrs)

Waldron, Michael

Wales Pensioners, Penyblanc branch

Walkden, Mona (Mrs)

Wallace, Bridget M/Whittle, Peter M

Wallam, Gordon

Waller, Hermione (Mrs)

Walley, Joan (MP)

Walmsley, G L (Dr)

Walton, Ann RGN (Mrs)

Wandsworth Pensioners' Forum

Wareham, Peter

Warren, H J (Mr)

Warren, P (Mrs)

Warwickshire Care Services Ltd

Waters, Dorothy (Miss)

Watkinson, John H

Watson, D A (Mr and Mrs)

Watson, G G (Mr)

Watson, Geoff (Mr and Mrs)

Watson, Harry

Watson, Patricia B (Mrs)

Watson, Philip J

Watson, R A (Mrs)

Watson, William G

Waverley Nursing Home

Weacon, Gladys (Mrs)

Weatherhead, A E (Mrs)

Weaver, P (Mrs)

Webber, R (Mr)

Webber, W J

Webster, S G P (Dr)

Weight, Pauline (Mrs)

Welch, Hilary

Weldon, John

Welfare Benefits Unit

Welland Practice, The

Wells, D H (Mr)

Wells, Keith

Wells, Mary D (Miss)

Wells, W M

Welsh Carers Alliance

Welsh Institute for Health and Social Care

Welsh, John

Welwyn Hatfield Council

Wentworth Grange Nursing and Residential
   Homes

West Church Guild, Haddington, East Lothian

West Cumbria Carers

West Dunbartonshire Council

West, Jayne (Ms)

Westbrook, J H (Mrs)

Western Health and Social Services Area Board
   HQ, Northern Ireland

Wevill, Peggy (Mrs)

Whales, Joyce

Wheatley, D E (Mr)

Whichers Insurance Brokers

Whipp, David (Mr)

Whitaker P (Mrs)

White, Dorothy OBE

White, Elsie M (Mrs)

White, H (Mrs)

White, K L (Mrs)

Whitehead, P (Mr)

Whitfield, G J (Mr)

Whitmore, Glynis (Mrs)

Whitmore, Glynis RGN (Mrs)

Whitmore, Kathleen (Mrs)

Wholey, J C (Miss)

Whyte, Penny (Mrs)

Wiggins, Margaret

Wilding, M (Mr)

Wilkinson, B (Mrs)

Wilkinson, Rosemary

Wilks, A (Mrs)

Willetts, G P (Mrs)

Williams, Alma

Williams, Brenda (Mrs)

Williams, Cyril

Williams, F R (Mr)

Williams, H D (Mrs)

Williams, J CBE (Prof)

Williams, John

Williams, R (Mr)

Williams, Vina

Williamson, J (Prof)

Williamson, J H

Willis, Mary Elizabeth SRN (Mrs)

Wilson, Charlotte M (Ms)

Wilson, F J (Mrs)

Wilson, Irvine and Glennis (Mr and Mrs)

Wilson, M P

Wilson, Marjorie

Wilson, Sue SRN (Ms)

Wilson, Thomas L H

Wilson, Vera (Mrs)

Wilton, W J (Mr)

Wiltshire Health Care NHS Trust

Winchester and Eastleigh Healthcare NHS Trust

Winchester, Peter

Windlesham Community Home

Winfield, June M (The Rev)

Winkworth, Lesley (Mrs)

Wise, Stanley R (Mr)

Woelfel, Martin

Wolf, M J (Mr)

Wolfenden, Dorothy M (Mrs)

Wolverhampton Metropolitan Borough Council,
   Social Services Department

Wood, Eleanor (Mrs)

Wood, Frank E

Wood, Margaret (Mrs)

Wood, P C (Mrs)

Woodrow, John

Woodruff, Gillian (Ms)

Woollard, D M (Mrs)

World Medical Journal

Wren, Elizabeth (Mrs)

Wrench, J F

Wright, D P (Mr)

Wright, Diana

Wright, Denys F

Wright, Jenny

Wright, Mike

Wright, R G (Mr)

Wright, W A (Mr)

Wyatt, R A (Mr)

Wythenshawe Pensioners Association

Y Plas Residential and Nursing Home

Yorkshire Care Group

Young, Denise

Young, Kay

Young, Michael

Young, Wilfred (Mr)

Zara, A A

Zlotnick, Annie

Appendix 7

MEMBERSHIP OF THE ROYAL COMMISSION'S REFERENCE GROUP

Age Concern
Age Concern (Northern Ireland)
Age Concern, Cymru
Age Concern, Scotland
Alzheimer's Disease Society
Association of British Insurers
Association of Directors of Social
  Services
Association of Directors of Social Work
  (Scotland)

Board of Deputies of British Jews
British Association of Occupational
  Therapists (also College of Occupational
  Therapists)
British Bankers Association
British Council of Organisations of
  Disabled People
British Geriatrics Society
British Youth Council
Building Societies Association

Carers National Association
Chartered Society of Physiotherapy, The
Chinese in Britain Forum
Commission for Racial Equality
Continuing Care Conference
Convention of Scottish Local Authorities
Council of Churches for Britain and
  Ireland
Cypriot Elderly and Disabled Group

Disability Scotland
Disability Wales
Disablement Income Group, The

Help The Aged

Independent Care Organisers Network
Independent Healthcare Association
International Ministerial Council of Great
  Britain

John Belcher

Local Government Association

MENCAP (Royal Society for Mentally
  Handicapped Chidren and Adults)
MIND (National Association for Mental
  Health)

National Association of Pension Funds
National Association of Citizen's Advice
  Bureaux
National Care Homes Association
National Consumer Council
National Council of Hindu Temples
National Council for Voluntary
  Organisations
National Housing Federation
National Pensioners Convention
Network of Sikh Organisations
NHS Confederation

Peter Gatenby

RADAR (Royal Association for Disability
  and Rehabilitation)
Royal College of General Practitioners
Royal College of Physicians
Royal College of Nursing
Royal National Institute for Deaf People
Royal National Institute for the Blind

Saga Group Ltd
Scottish Association of Care Home
  Owners

UK Action Committee on Islamic Affairs
United Kingdom Home Care Association

Voluntary Organisations Disability Group

Womens National Commission

Appendix 8

CONTENTS OF RESEARCH VOLUMES 1, 2 AND 3

Volume 1: The Context of Long-Term Care Policy

Contents

Chapters:

Volume 2: Alternative Models of Care for Older People

Contents

Volume 3: Community Care and Informal Care – Part 1

Contents

Volume 3: Community Care and Informal Care – Part 2

Contents

Appendix 8

Acknowledgements

Printed in the UK for the Stationery Office Limited
on behalf of the Controller of Her Majesty's Stationery Office
Dd 5068537, 3/99. 61743, Ord J00 68989